The Concept of Ideology
and Other Essays

The
Concept of
Ideology
and Other Essays

GEORGE LICHTHEIM

Random House · New York

The author is grateful to the following publications for permission to reprint:

Archives Européennes de Sociologie for "Society and Hierarchy" (originally titled "Class and Hierarchy," V, 1964);
Commentary for "The Politics of Conservative Realism" (June 1963), "Tyrants Ancient and Modern" (originally titled "Xenophon versus Hegel," November 1963), and "Reflections on Trotsky" (January 1964);
Encounter for "An Intellectual Disaster" (May 1963) and "Rosa Luxemburg" (June 1966);
History and Theory (The Wesleyan University Press) for "Sartre, Marxism, and History" (III, 2, 1963) and "The Concept of Ideology" (IV, 2, 1965);
New Statesman for "Leviathan" (September 6, 1963), "From Pascal to Marx" (September 4, 1964), "The German Ideology" (April 23, 1965), and "Rousseau and de Maistre" (September 16, 1966);
The New York Review of Books for "Forward to Utopia" (February 20, 1964), "Metahistory" (May 28, 1964), "Philosopher in Revolt" (January 28, 1965), "Beyond the Fringe" (March 25, 1965), "The Revolution of 1848" (May 20, 1965), "Hegel" (July 15, 1965), and "The European Civil War" (February 3, 1966);
Partisan Review for "Empire and After" (originally titled "Power and Ideology," Summer 1963) and "Two Revolutions" (originally titled "Varieties of Revolutionary Experience," Summer 1964);
St. Antony's Papers for "Oriental Despotism" (originally titled "Marx and the 'Asiatic Mode of Production,'" XIV, 1963).

Library of Congress Catalog Card Number: 67-14472

Manufactured in the United States of America
by H. Wolff, New York
Designed by Jaime Davidovich

FOR JEAN FLOUD

What is rational is real and what is real is rational.

—HEGEL, Preface to *Philosophy of Right*

Contents

part four: SURVIVALS AND NEW ARRIVALS

Introduction

• This volume opens with a quotation which relates by implication to the major theme of the entire collection of writings presented, all of which, composed and published between 1962 and 1966, are reproduced with only minor textual and stylistic alterations. The common bond uniting them will, it is hoped, stand up to critical examination. Its firmness evidently cannot be measured by the author's belief in the presence of unity linking the various parts, nor can proof of its existence be offered in the form of a general thesis which the individual essays might be supposed to illustrate. The link, if there be one, is not demonstrable apart from the argument as it unfolds through writings ranging over a fairly wide variety of topics. Whatever thematic unity there is, its presence must be felt in the use made of the concept central to the entire discussion: that of ideology.

The title of the book has been taken from the introductory essay; originally published as a self-contained study, it is now turned into a curtain raiser. It seemed proper to begin in this fashion because in what follows the status of political ideology remains a permanent concern. The argument embraces three centuries of Western history—from the Puritan upheaval of the seventeenth century, by way of the French Revolution and the intellectual systematizations of the nineteenth century, to the totalitarian movements of our own age. While not arranged in chronological order, the discussion adheres to this general scheme, with occasional side-glances at such curious survivals as anarchism or such recent arrivals as the existentialist fashion in contemporary philosophy. The title essay itself, after going at some length into the history of the concept, tries to determine the role of "ideology" as a political phenomenon and then quite naturally fastens upon the greatest and most successful of the mid-nineteenth-century systematizations, that of Marx, whose sociology is the theme of the two succeeding essays. The topic here chosen, after a brief excursion into the significance of class, is one with which we have all become familiar and which has the twofold attraction of being at once historically important and politically relevant: the relationship, real or fancied, of Oriental despotism to contemporary totalitarianism. This particular paper (originally the basis of a seminar discussion in Oxford and later published in a British academic journal) may also be read as a critical commentary upon some American studies devoted to the same subject. I hasten to disclaim any knowledge of Far Eastern affairs beyond that available to the ordinary non-specialist; my purpose was merely to clarify the status of a particular concept, that of the "Asiatic mode of production." It is doubtless more than a coincidence that—as a result of the Sino-Soviet conflict—this topic, with which specialists were familiar until its discussion was banned in the USSR around 1930, has once again become respectable and even politically relevant.

With Part Two we enter if not calmer waters, at any rate depths and shallows of another sort. We are indeed still pursued by the concept of ideology, but are no longer concerned with its genesis around the time of the French Revolution and the first stirrings of socialism. Instead, we are brought up against what might be termed the ideological reflex of Atlantic Community affairs—principally the dissolution of the British Empire, the formation of an American one, and the tentative efforts to provide this imperial newcomer with an appropriate ideology: once more a materialization of our concept, though concealed this time behind the wordy quarrel between conservatives and radicals (supporters and critics, that is, of the American attempt to step into Britain's place) with a nostalgic Tory, Professor Arnold Toynbee, cast in the role of uneasy bystander. In the remainder of this section the American reader will encounter other familiar names, notably Strauss, Morgenthau, and Marcuse. By way of transition to Part Three he is also introduced

to a specimen of German metaphysics in the tradition of the
philosophy of history, and to some reflections on Hegel. This
harrowing experience should prepare him for the critical excursions of the following section, where, like Banquo's ghost,
the shadows of Rosa Luxemburg and Leon Trotsky briefly stalk
the scene while night descends upon an arena shortly to be
occupied by clashing armies—those engaged in the European
civil war between Communism and Fascism. Appropriately, this
part closes with some critical reflections upon the fate of Marxism in its East European avatar. We thus arrive at what is currently known as the post-Stalin era, an age in which philosophers
creep out once more to feel the sun and to assure their readers
that nothing of extraordinary importance has taken place in the
interval between their earlier and later publications.

With the concluding essays of Part Four we revert, by a
somewhat circuitous route it is true, to our historical and intellectual starting point: the French Revolution and its contemporary reincarnation in the rival systems of French sociology,
existentialism, and neo-Marxism, with a retrospective glance at
the seventeenth-century upheaval which in France is associated
with the name of Descartes. The reader who has followed us
until this point, and who still remembers the remarks in Part
Two devoted to Hobbesian realism and statecraft, will have no
difficulty in tracing the link between Macpherson's learned investigations and the discoveries attributed to Goldmann. The
justification of this somewhat complicated procedure lies in the
fact that one cannot approach Sartre before having dealt, at
least briefly, with the Cartesian heritage. The seventeenth century, after all, means different things to Frenchmen and Anglo-
Saxons. In Britain and American it suggests Hobbes and Locke;
in France it evokes Descartes, Pascal, and Racine. Even Sartre's
existentialized Marxism is firmly rooted in this tradition, which
is why this section concludes with a critique of his philosophy
after first dealing rather more briefly with the Tocquevillean
heritage as represented by Raymond Aron's reflections on the
upheaval of 1848. French liberalism and neo-Marxism are thus
brought together, and if the whole argument leads back to the

starting point, the resulting gain in logical coherence will not, it is hoped, be attributed solely to the external arrangement of the pieces. There is, in fact, a theme, and it has been pursued with what the author, at any rate, regards as a fair degree of consistency. "In my end is my beginning" is not a bad maxim for essayists, as well as for purveyors of plays or novels.

If the nineteenth century appears to occupy the central place in these discussions, the reason must now have become obvious: it was the time when historians, philosophers, and politically conscious writers throughout Europe were united in a common effort to understand the significance of those twin upheavals, the French Revolution and the Industrial Revolution. The effort gave birth, among others, to the new discipline of sociology, starting with the intellectual systems of Comte and Marx, and going on to the German school of thought associated with Max Weber and the "sociology of knowledge." In the process, mental boundaries were crossed, notably the border between history and science, thus encouraging the hope that it might become possible to apply to historical phenomena the generalizing procedures already firmly established in the natural sciences. This theme is pursued throughout in somewhat unmethodical fashion. The only systematization—one evident, it is hoped, to the reader who is willing to follow the argument—is that inherent in this volume's guiding principle.

This may be described by saying that a historical structure is not a mere assemblage of its constituents (in more technical language, of external relations), but rather that which holds them together and imposes their real nature upon them. Or one might say that their "nature" is the manner in which they exemplify the logic of the whole of which they form part. This approach is contrary to the assumptions habitually made by the plain man and by the empiricist philosophers who stand ready to back him up. Both assume that historical relations are external to each other; that events in history are contingent, in the sense that the reverse of what actually happened might equally well have occurred; that history, insofar as it is at all intelligible, is made by and for individuals; that these individuals can alter its course by altering course themselves; that historical events are analyzable into the motives of those who participated in them; and that the only generalizations permissible are those that can be supported by statistical evidence. Since the author happens not to believe these propositions, he can neither expect sympathy from readers accustomed to regarding them as certainties nor fall back upon common-sense arguments, for common sense is precisely what underlies the empiricist mode of perception. Empiricism is indeed more than thought adapted to the business of current affairs: it is practical common sense raised to the level of doctrine. It generalizes the notions entertained by the plain man, introduces a minimum of logical order into them, and then feeds them back to their originator as the latest word in philosophic wisdom. Anyone trying to grasp what the title of Part One describes as "historical logic" must first of all step outside this mental universe. Oddly enough, such a posture, while difficult at the first try, is by no means impossible to attain. It is not, however, brought about by a simple reversal of the common-sensible form of discourse. The obverse of the empiricist procedure is to be encountered in the existentialist mode of thought currently fashionable in France or at any rate among French writers influenced by German philosophy. As in many other domains, Britain and France here too supply the convenience of sustained polarity: what passes for conventional wisdom on one side of the Channel is dismissed as boring folly on the other. An echo of these debates (and of the antecedent conflict between Anglo-French rationalism and German romanticism) is discernible in American writings on the subject, notably in those produced by recent European immigrants. To suggest that both empiricism and existentialism are blind alleys is to fall under the suspicion of trying to advance the claims of German metaphysics. Whether this charge is well founded, readers must judge for themselves. They will not, at any rate, have to fend off the propagandist notions associated with one school or the other, nor will they be offered a choice between Sartre's existentialized Marxism and the more orthodox version associated with Lukács. What it is hoped they will encounter instead is an effort to retain the use of one's critical faculty when confronted by all or any of these rival creeds. If a general note is struck, it is rather one of skepticism in the face of doctrines whose link is with a particular national culture or with an ideologically defined political movement. In this respect at least no distinction is drawn between German romanticism, British empiricism, French existentialism, or the Russianized version of Marxism—all by now decidedly outmoded, though the author would be hard put to suggest what may be expected to take their place.

So much, or so little, for the philosophy of history. What of the conflicting claims of those embattled armies of academic scholars, the historians and the sociologists? Sociology, it has been said (by a sociologist), is history with the hard work left out, while history is sociology with the brains left out. Unsympathetic readers of this book will doubtless find occasion to verify this dictum. They are offered a further target: it is the author's belief that the urgently required integration or interpenetration of sociology and history will not come about until the practitioners on both sides have agreed on a common set of intellectual tools, and that these tools will, as in the past, be furnished not by the specialists themselves but by philosophy. The fact that we are nowhere in sight of such a consummation is no reason for dismissing its coming as improbable. In any case, it is along these lines that progress should be looked for. And with this final fling at the reigning empiricist orthodoxy, the author retires from the stage and rings up the curtain.

G. L.

London
March 1967

part one

THREE STUDIES
IN HISTORICAL LOGIC

The Concept of Ideology*

• Few concepts play a larger part in present-day discussions of historical and political topics than does that of ideology, and yet it is not always clear what meaning is applied to the term by those who employ it. Even if one confines one's attention to the utterances of sociologists and historians, leaving out of account the terminological misuse seemingly inseparable from ordinary political discourse, it is apparent that different and conflicting meanings are intended by writers who casually refer to the "ideology" of this or that political movement.

From the vulgar misunderstanding inherent in the familiar phrase "we need a better ideology to fight the enemy," to the refinements of academic dispute over "the ideology of science," one encounters a terminological vagueness which appears to reflect some deeper uncertainty about the status of ideas in the genesis of historical movements.

It is here intended to clarify the theme by examining the different significations attached to the term "ideology," and the shifting status of the phenomenon itself, granted that a propensity so widespread as the duplication and distortion of reality in thought lends itself to the historical approach. If this initial assumption is allowed to pass as a working hypothesis, it is hoped that the term "ideology" will be shown to possess both a definite meaning and a particular historical status: the history of the concept serving as a guide to the actual interplay of "real" and "ideal" factors whose dialectic is obscurely intended in the formulation of the concept itself. The subject has recently been

* *History and Theory*, IV, 2 (1965).

dealt with by, among others, Mr. Ben Halpern.[1] In what follows
it is not proposed to take issue with his analysis, but to pursue a
line of thought suggested by the present author's concern with
the manner in which the ideology concept relates to what is
usually known as the "philosophy of history," notably in its Hegelian form.

The Revolutionary Heritage

Historically, the term "ideology" made its first appearance at the
time of the French Revolution, its author, Antoine Destutt de
Tracy, being one of the group of *savants* whom the Convention
in 1795 entrusted with the management of the newly founded
Institut de France.[2] During the brief period of its predomi-
nance—until Napoleon in 1801 made his peace with the
Church, and concurrently turned against the liberal intellectuals
who had helped him into the saddle—the Institute was associated in the public mind with an outlook which indeed pre-
dated the Revolution, but was now made official and brought
into relation with the practice of the new regime. In 1794, at the
height of the Terror, the guiding ideas of the faith had been
given their final expression, under the most dramatic circumstances possible, by Condorcet in his *Tableau historique des
progrès de l'esprit humain;* but it was under the Directory, with
moderate liberalism briefly in the saddle, that the "idéologues"
of the Institute placed the official seal on his doctrine.[3] Their
prestige flattered the vanity of Bonaparte, who in 1797 became
an honorary member of the Institute. How much the distinction
meant to him appears from the fact that during the Egyptian
campaign of 1798-1799 he signed his proclamations to the Army
as "Général en chef, Membre de l'Institut." It was a justified

1 " 'Myth' and 'Ideology' in Modern Usage," *History and Theory*, I, 2
(1961), 129-149.
2 Georges Lefebvre, *La révolution française* (Paris, 1957), p. 443. The
creation of the Institute was part of an attempt to provide France with
a nationwide system of higher learning committed to the philosophy of
the Enlightenment.
3 *Ibid.*, p. 578: "Destutt de Tracy se proposait de déterminer par l'observation comment se forment les idées: de là le nom de l'école."

appreciation of their influence over the educated middle class
that in 1799, at the time of the coup d'état de Brumaire, in-
duced him to seek the support of the "idéologues," who in turn
helped to promote his accession to power.[4] It was likewise fear
of their hold over public opinion which in January 1803 led him
to cap his growing personal despotism (and his Concordat with
Rome) by the virtual destruction of the Institute's core, the
classe des sciences morales et politiques, from which liberal and
republican ideas radiated throughout the educational "establishment." The story of Bonaparte's degeneration can be written in
terms of his relations with the "idéologues": down to the day in
December 1812 when—returned to Paris from the disaster in
Russia—he blamed them, in an address to the Conseil d'Etat,
for the catastrophe into which his own despotism had plunged
the country.[5]

The "ideologists" of the Institute were liberals who regarded
freedom of thought and expression as the principal conquest of
the Revolution. Their attitude was "ideological" in the twofold
sense of being concerned with ideas, and of placing the satisfaction of *"ideal"* aims (their own) ahead of the "material" interests on which the post-revolutionary society rested. They could
put up, at least temporarily, with an enlightened dictatorship
which safeguarded the major gains of the Revolution, but not
with a regime which visibly steered back towards an absolutism
supported by established religion. Napoleon ignored them,
though he defended the social foundations of the new order and
in 1815, after his return from Elba, made a last attempt to win

---

[4] *Ibid.*, p. 534: "Arrivé à Paris . . . il montrait une discrétion toute ré-
publicaine et fréquentait l'Institut, où il fraternisait avec les idéologues."
Cf. A. Aulard, *Histoire politique de la révolution française* (Paris, 1926),
p. 694, for the illusions of the liberal intellectuals, who firmly expected
Bonaparte to inaugurate the enlightened commonwealth of their dreams.

[5] "C'est à l'idéologie, à cette ténébreuse métaphysique qui, en cherchant
avec subtilité les causes premières, veut sur ces bases fonder la législation
des peuples, au lieu d'approprier les lois à la connaissance du coeur humain
et aux leçons de l'histoire, qu'il faut attribuer toutes les malheurs de notre
belle France." Cited in Hans Barth, *Wahrheit und Ideologie* (Zürich,
1945), p. 30; cf. Taine, *Origines de la France contemporaine* (Paris,
1898, II, pp. 219-220). On other occasions he put it more briefly, e.g.,
"Cannon killed feudalism. Ink will kill modern society." (Napoléon, *Pensées* [Paris, 1913], p. 43).

their support. Under the Bourbon Restoration they headed the liberal opposition. In 1830 the July Revolution, by introducing parliamentary government, at long last realized one of their chief aims, though in a somewhat prosaic form. Marx, from a different standpoint, shared Napoleon's disdain for them. In 1845, remarking upon the manner in which the bourgeois character of the Revolution had gradually disclosed itself, he commented ironically upon their illusions, having previously noted that "Robespierre, Saint Just, and their party fell because they confused the realistic democratic commonwealth of antiquity, which rested on the basis of real slavery, with the modern spiritualist-democratic representative state based on the emancipated slavery of bourgeois society." [6] Yet the ideologists, whatever their political fancies, had another and tougher side to them: they were the forerunners of positivism. The Institute under their direction became a center of experimental studies. While Destutt de Tracy turned his attention to the history of ideas, Cabanis pioneered experimental psychology, Pinel placed the treatment of mental illness on a new foundation, Dupuis (in his *Origine de tous les cultes*) treated the natural history of religion in an empirical manner; others extended the new viewpoint to the history of literature and art. This intellectual explosion was the counterpart of the better known and perhaps even more brilliant achievements of Lagrange, Laplace, Monge, Berthollet, Cuvier, Saint-Hilaire, and Lamarck in the natural sciences, which between 1790 and 1830 raised France's contribution in this field to a pinnacle of achievement never equaled before or since. When Comte around 1830 synthesized the new world-view (in the light of what he had learned from the far more

[6] *Die Heilige Familie* (1845 [reprinted Berlin, 1953]), p. 191; cf. *The Holy Family* (London, 1957), p. 164. "It was not the revolutionary movement as such that became Napoleon's prey on the 18th Brumaire . . . it was the *liberal bourgeoisie*. . . . Napoleon was the last stand of revolutionary terrorism against the bourgeois society which had likewise been proclaimed by the Revolution. . . . If he despotically suppressed the liberalism of bourgeois society—the political idealism of its daily practice— he showed no more concern for its essential material interests . . . whenever they conflicted with his political interests. His contempt for the industrial *hommes d'affaires* was the counterpart of his scorn for the ideologues" (*ibid.*, translated from the 1953 German edition, pp. 193-194).

original Saint-Simon), he was drawing upon the work of a generation of scholars who had already transformed the inherited eighteenth-century view by introducing the historical approach. If the ideologists continued the rationalist tradition, they also began the process of modifying it, though—unlike the German Romantics—they did not abandon its basic principles.[7]

The twofold character of the liberal "ideology," as a system of normative ideas and as an incipient critique of the very notion of absolute norms, makes its appearance already in the work of Destutt de Tracy from which the school derived its name. His *Eléments d'Idéologie* (1801-1815) presents a "Science des idées" for which he cites the authority of Locke and Condillac.[8] They are praised for having inaugurated the "natural history of ideas"—that is, the scientific description of the human mind—though Condillac had qualified his naturalism by retaining the traditional religious emphasis upon the substantive reality of man's soul and the uniqueness of man compared with the animal creation.[9] For Destutt, who superimposed the materialism of Cabanis upon the Lockean sensationalism of Condillac, the study of "ideology" is part of zoölogy. What he means is that human psychology should be analyzed in biological terms; that is, without paying attention to religion. Moral problems are relegated to metaphysics, described as a realm of illusory fancies "destinés à nous satisfaire et non à nous instruire." [10] The true foundation of the sciences is rather to be found in a "Science des idées" which will describe the natural history of the mind, that is, the manner in which our thoughts are formed. There is no supersensible reality behind the individuals and their several "ideas" (sensations and notions).

Il est seulement à remarquer qu'il n'existe réellement que des individus et que nos idées ne sont point des êtres réels existant

---

[7] Lefebvre, *op. cit.*, p. 578, includes Madame de Staël's *La littérature considérée dans ses rapports avec les institutions sociales* (1800) among the notable productions of the school.
[8] A. Destutt de Tracy, *Eléments d'Idéologie* (2nd ed., Brussels, 1826), I, p. 3; cf. Barth, *op. cit.*, pp. 16 ff.
[9] Condillac, *Oeuvres complètes* (Paris, 1798), III, p. 592.
[10] Destutt de Tracy, *op. cit.*, p. xiv.

hors de nous, mais de pures créations de notre esprit, des manières de classer nos idées des individus.[11]

But this "materialist" theme is crossed by a normative purpose: the "Science des idées" is to yield true knowledge of human nature, and therewith the means of defining the general laws of sociability. The reduction of individual "ideas" to generally held notions is intended to lay bare the common ground of human needs and aspirations, thus providing the lawgiver with the means of furthering the common good. What is "natural" is also "social." Once human nature is properly understood, society will at last be able to arrange itself in a harmonious fashion. Reason is the guarantor of order and liberty.[12] As with Condorcet, Destutt's aim is pedagogical: it is to lay bare the guiding principles of republican citizenship. His theorizing has a practical, normative, purpose. The freeing of the human mind from ignorance and superstition is not undertaken for its own sake, but because only a mind delivered from error can perceive those universal laws which make it plain "que la nature lie par une chaîne indissoluble la vérité, le bonheur et la vertu." [13] The pathos of the Enlightenment is retained in the "Science des idées," for all its incipient naturalism. Reason progressively discloses a true picture of humanity which constitutes the foundation of civic virtue. Morality is anchored in nature. The best social order is that which corresponds to the permanent needs of man.

The antecedents of this faith are Baconian and Cartesian. To Condillac, who preceded the ideologues and the Revolution, it had already seemed plain that Bacon's criticism of the "idols" must be the starting point of that reformation of consciousness which was the principal aim of the Enlightenment.[14] Bacon's

---

[11] *Ibid.*, p. 301.

[12] "Le perfectionnement des lois, des institutions publiques, suites des progrès des sciences, n'a-t-il point pour effet d'approcher, d'identifier l'intérêt commun de chaque homme avec l'intérêt commun de tous?" Condorcet, *Tableau historique* (Paris, 1822), p. 292.

[13] *Ibid.*, p. 10.

[14] "Personne n'a mieux connu que Bacon la cause de nos erreurs, car il a vu que les idées, qui sont l'ouvrage de l'esprit, avaient été mal faites, et que par conséquent pour avancer dans la recherche de la vérité il fallait

idolum becomes Condillac's *préjugé*, a key term also in the writings of Holbach and Helvétius. The idols are "prejudices" contrary to "reason." To remove them by the relentless application of critical reasoning is to restore the "unprejudiced" understanding of nature. Holbach maintains that

> l'homme n'est malheureux que parce qu'il méconnaît la Nature
> . . . La raison guidée par l'expérience doit enfin attaquer dans
> leur source des préjugés dont le genre humain fût si longtemps la
> victime. . . . La vérité est une; elle est nécessaire à l'homme.
> . . . C'est à l'erreur que sont dues les chaînes accablantes que
> les Tyrans et les Prêtres forgent partout aux nations.[15]

Helvétius (a favorite of both Marx and Nietzsche) develops this notion in the direction of a rudimentary sociology of knowledge: "Our ideas are the necessary consequence of the societies in which we live." [16] Skepticism is held in check by the rationalist faith inherited from Descartes: reason has the power of correcting its own errors.[17]

For Helvétius, the idols (*préjugés*) are the necessary fruit of social constraint and selfish interest, but he is convinced that they can be discredited by reason and removed by education. "L'éducation peut tout." [18] The cure for popular superstition is pedagogy on a national scale. This is the point where Marx later introduced his criticism of the Enlightenment.[19] Helvétius in fact never succeeded in clarifying the relationship of "interest"

---

les refaire." Condillac, *Essai sur l'origine des connaissances humaines*
(*Oeuvres*, I, p. 507); cf. the article on Bacon in the *Encyclopédie*, III,
and d'Alembert's "Discours préliminaire."

[15] Holbach, *Système de la Nature* (Paris, 1770), Preface.

[16] Helvétius *De L'Esprit*, (1758), p. 114; cited by Barth, *op. cit.*, p. 62.
For Rousseau's share in the elaboration of this attitude cf. Iring Fetscher,
Rousseaus politische Philosophie (Neuwied, 1960), *passim*.

[17] "ce qu'on nomme le bons sens ou la raison, est naturellement égale
en tous les hommes . . . la diversité de nos opinions ne vient pas de ce
que les uns sont plus raisonnables que les autres, mais seulement de ce que
nous conduisons nos pensées par diverses voies" (Descartes, *Discours de la
méthode*, cf. *Oeuvres* [Pléiade, 1952], p. 126.)

[18] Helvétius, *De l'Homme* (1773), II, p. 332.

[19] Cf. *Theses on Feuerbach*: "The materialist doctrine that men are
products of circumstances and upbringing . . . forgets that it is men who
change circumstances and that the educator himself needs to be educated.
Hence this doctrine necessarily divides society into two parts, of which one
is superior to the other. . . ."

to "education." Wandering off into cynicism, he anticipated Nietzsche by arguing that the sole motor of human action is self-love and the will to power.

> Chacun veut commander parce que chacun veut accroître sa félicité. . . . L'amour du pouvoir fondé sur celui du bonheur est donc l'objet commun de tous nos désirs . . . toutes les passions factices ne sont-elles en nous que l'amour du pouvoir déguisé sous ces noms différents. . . .[20]

A suggestion which greatly pleased Nietzsche when he came across it.[21]

The confusion in which Helvétius landed himself was inherent in a "materialism" which treated the mind as the passive receptacle of sense impressions. At the same time he retained enough of the rationalist faith to remain confident that "prejudices" could be shown up as such, and that interest psychology could be subordinated to an objective understanding of the real needs of society. The "justesse de l'esprit" displays itself in the discovery of general laws whose truth is demonstrable. Their application to social life is a political problem, that is, a problem of power. Philosophy and politics have their common ground in education, whereby inherited prejudices (mainly religious) are overcome and replaced by insight into the true nature of man and his environment. The place of religion is taken by a secular morality, inherently social because man is a social being.

By and large—and allowing for disputes between deists, materialists, and agnostics—this was the faith which the "ideologues" of the Institute inherited from their pre-revolutionary ancestors and which eventually became the official doctrine of French democracy and indeed of the French Republic. The point here is that, for all the inherent skepticism with respect to shared beliefs, the power of rational thought was not seriously called in question. Almost a century later, Comte's positivism, notwithstanding its authoritarian features, was still rooted in the same confidence. His complacent certainty that the "philosophie positive" represented the "véritable état définitif de l'intelligence

---

[20] Helvétius, op. cit., I, pp. 238-239.
[21] Cf. Barth, op. cit., p. 316.

humaine" [22] may today strike one as humorous, bearing in mind the paucity of discoveries attributable to the new method; but there is no mistaking the rationalist pathos which rings through his pseudo-religious rigmarole. Compared with the older generation, the change lies in the hierarchical straitjacket imposed upon the social order by a theorist in whom the generous optimism of the Enlightenment had congealed into a worried concern with social stability.[23] For Comte the "development of the human mind" issues in the recognition that all historical phenomena are subject to "invariable natural laws," [24] but this chilling thought somehow sustains reason's faith in itself. To anticipate Engels' later formulation (itself an amalgam of Comtean and Hegelian determinism), freedom is anchored in the recognition of necessity. *Science* enables us to bind these extremes together. The dogmatism of Comte does not subvert the conviction that the study of society yields the discovery of universal rational principles.

The Hegelian Tradition

Although Comte on some points anticipates Marx (or at any rate the version of Marxism subsequently canonized by Engels and his successors), his critique of the "ideologists" cannot be regarded as the forerunner of Marx's onslaught on the "German ideology," which latter had evolved quite independently of the French variant. The two lines of development must not be confused just because Marx affected to believe that Feuerbach and the Young Hegelians were the legitimate heirs of the *idéologues* (whence the title of his bulky tract which was not published in full until 1932).[25] The officially sanctioned "German ideology"

[22] Charles Le Verrier, ed., *Cours de philosophie positive* (Paris, Garnier), I, p. 23.
[23] For this aspect of Comte cf. Herbert Marcuse, *Reason and Revolution* (London, 1955), pp. 342 ff.
[24] Comte, *op. cit.*, p. 26.
[25] For the following cf. *Die deutsche Ideologie: Kritik der neuesten deutschen Philosophie in ihren Repräsentanten, Feuerbach, B. Bauer und Stirner, und des deutschen Sozialismus in seinen verschiedenen Propheten, Marx-Engels Gesamtausgabe* (hereafter MEGA), V (1932); and the various translations.

of the 1840s had come into being as a reaction against the theory and practice of the French Revolution. Its true originator was Hegel, who from his youthful Jacobinism[26] had gradually moved to an almost Burkean worship of continuity, without ever quite renouncing his faith in universal reason and the rule of law.[27] His radical critics retained the historical approach he had introduced, and at the same time restored the moral iconoclasm he had abandoned. Their target was the conservative "Christian-German" ideology then invested with a quasi-official function by the pre-1848 regime. In assailing it, Feuerbach, Bruno Bauer, and the left-wing Hegelians in general inevitably went back to the ultimate source of their own faith: the French Enlightenment and its naturalist critique of theology and metaphysics.[28] A few years later Marx was to claim that their criticism of the official ideology was itself ideological. The precise significance he gave to this charge needs to be understood in the light of the philosophical situation then prevailing.

The belief that general concepts, though held by particular individuals, are of universal application, is common to all thinkers who can be described as rationalists. It was retained by Hegel, notwithstanding his disillusionment with the outcome of the French Revolution, in which he had originally seen the practical working of Reason. Kantian philosophy had already synthesized Cartesian rationalism and Lockean empiricism in a procedure which restored the primacy of mind over matter: general concepts, though rooted in experience, were held to be independent of experience, inasmuch as they organized the sense

26 Cf. *Briefe von und an Hegel* (Leipzig, 1887); *Hegels theologische Jugendschriften* (Tübingen, 1907), *passim*.

27 Cf. *Philosophy of Right* (1821): "It is part of education, of thinking as the consciousness of the single in the form of universality, that the ego comes to be apprehended as a universal person in which all are identical. A man counts as a man in virtue of his manhood alone, not because he is a Jew, Catholic, Protestant, German, Italian, etc. This is an assertion which thinking ratifies, and to be conscious of it is of infinite importance" (Tr. T. M. Knox, Oxford, 1942, ¶ 209, p. 134).

28 Cf. Bruno Bauer, *Das entdeckte Christentum. Eine Erinnerung an das achtzehnte Jahrhundert und ein Beitrag zur Kritik des neunzehnten* (1843). For the influence of Holbach, Helvétius, and the *Science des idées*, on Feuerbach, Bauer, and Marx, cf. Barth, *op. cit.*, pp. 73 ff.

data into intelligible wholes. The imposition of order upon the chaos of sense impressions was the work of the mind, which was in possession of the true and universal forms of understanding, the categories. The dependence of the individual mind upon the material presented by the senses—that hobby-horse of empiricism, from Locke to Hume—was not disputed, but treated as a state of affairs which occupies merely the foreground of reasoning. The "given" experience present to the individual is not an assemblage of brute "facts," but an ordered whole. In extending this Kantian approach from the realm of nature to history, Hegel affirmed the governing principle of the idealist faith: matter is organized by mind. Experience—the shibboleth of the British school—ceased to be a final datum. The way to the attainment of universality lay in grasping the principles which held the sensible world together.

Seen from Hegel's standpoint, Kant had remained in a halfway position between empiricism and true universalism. The latter required the assumption that the mind recognizes a world independent of the subject, whereas the Kantian categories were merely the necessary forms of any singular subject's possible experience. They constituted a phenomenal world, one and the same for all experients, yet Kant never took the decisive step of acknowledging that the world can be common to all experients only if all finite minds are differentiations of a universal mind: he did not, that is, conceive Mind as a "concrete universal." Reason for him is not indeed passive, but the individual consciousness is not seen as transcending itself, and its activity is not viewed as the immanence of a universal reason working through finite minds. If Kant in consequence has "no philosophy of Nature, only a philosophy of natural science," [29] Hegel on the contrary has a philosophy of History precisely because for him Reason is at once general and particular: a concrete universal which differentiates itself into particular thinking minds. On this view, the problem for the individual thinker is to apprehend the movement of Reason, of which his own thinking is a reflex. What manifests itself to philosophic thought is the history of

[29] G.R.G. Mure, *An Introduction to Hegel* (Oxford, 1940), p. 105.

Mind—veiled by its embodiment in Matter, but still plainly discernible as the motive force of the universal process. When "stood on its feet" by materialism, this philosophy yields the conviction that the logic of history is decipherable through an understanding of man's capacity to "produce" his own world. Beyond the recorded facts there lies the totality of history which men have made, and are therefore able to understand. It is worth stressing this continuity, so often obscured by emphasis upon the naturalist inversion effected by Feuerbach and Marx. Feuerbach indeed "saw through" Hegel's terminology to the theology of Spirit lying behind it, but his return to the naturalism of the French Enlightenment did not imply acceptance of the empiricist mode of reasoning. Nature is a universal for Feuerbach, as history is for Marx. This is not to say that either of them was uncritical of Hegel's manner of treating logical concepts. (It was left for Marx's less intelligent followers to personify History into an independent entity: a misunderstanding against which he had protested in advance.) [30]

We are here concerned with the concept of ideology, not with the truth of Hegel's philosophy. What needs to be retained is that on Hegel's assumption the problem of overcoming the particularity of thinking is not insoluble; nor does it follow that because philosophers—or for that matter ordinary men—are born and raised under particular circumstances, they cannot rise above them. Man is essentially a thinking being, and as such able to apprehend the concrete universality which is history. Our historical concepts possess true generality because they relate to a universal agent that unfolds through the histories of particular peoples and civilizations. This agent for Hegel is Mind, for Marx it is human activity, *praxis*: the practice of men struggling to subdue nature and to develop their own latent powers. The determinant in each case is conscious activity, though Marx protests that for Hegel the historical process tends

[30] "History, like truth, becomes a person apart, a metaphysical subject, of which the real individuals are merely the bearers," *Die Heilige Familie*, p. 116.

to become an independent entity superior to the individuals who compose it.[31]

The problem of ideology (in the sense of "false consciousness" or "imperfect consciousness") arises for Hegel because in his view individuals, and even entire nations, are instruments of history, executors of a process whose meaning is concealed from them, and which becomes self-conscious only *post festum* in the philosopher who sums up the sense of the epoch.[32] Hegel was aware that history is set in motion by men's interests and passions. He did not question its rationality just because men commonly behaved in an irrational manner: the process had its own logic, which was not that of the individuals. The "cunning of reason" [33] could be observed in the manner in which the Idea (the rationality of the whole) triumphed at the expense of its own agents. The individual's fate was swallowed up in the dialectic of the process. The youthful Marx rebelled against this worldview, which struck him as theological; he lived to see it reinstated (with his own silent acquiescence) by Engels, though it was only gradually that the wheel came full circle, with the determinist emphasis upon "general laws" governing the course of history: laws apparently general enough to conform to Hegel's "cunning of reason," and scientific enough to be acceptable to a generation raised on positivism.[34]

[31] "Hegel's conception of history presupposes an abstract or absolute spirit which develops in such a way that humanity is nothing but a mass which more or less consciously bears it along. Within the framework of empirical exoteric history, Hegel introduces the operation of a speculative esoteric history. The history of humanity becomes the history of the abstract spirit of humanity, a spirit beyond the real man. Concurrently with this Hegelian doctrine, there developed in France the theory of the doctrinaires, who proclaimed the sovereignty of reason in opposition to the sovereignty of the people. . . ." *Ibid.*, p. 57; cf. MEGA, 1/3, p. 257; *The Holy Family*, p. 115.

[32] *Vorlesungen über die Geschichte der Philosophie*, ed. Lasson (Leipzig, 1930), I, pp. 9 ff., 25 ff., 78 ff.; cf. C. J. Friedrich, ed., *The Philosophy of History* (New York, 1956), Introduction and *passim*; Marcuse, *op. cit.*, pp. 224 ff.

[33] *Ibid.*, I, p. 83; cf. *The Philosophy of History*, p. 33.

[34] Engels, *Ludwig Feuerbach and the Close of Classical German Philosophy, passim*. Cf. Engels to Mehring, July 14, 1893 (in Marx-Engels *Selected Correspondence* [Moscow, 1956], p. 541): "Ideology is a process

For Hegel the problem had been to justify the ways of God to man. He did not doubt that these ways could be understood, at any rate retrospectively. This understanding is the work of philosophy, which in every age makes its appearance when a particular phase of Spirit has come to a close. Philosophy does not change the world: it interprets it and thus reconciles the world to itself. Yet Hegel's own philosophy was to change the world—if only because, even on its most conservative interpretation, it was subversive of revealed religion.[35] On the other hand, his system—more particularly his teachings on Right and the State—appeared to his radical critics as the "ideology" of the political status quo: its intellectual projection and justification. From here it was only a step to the notion that speculative philosophy as such barred the way to that reconstruction of the world which was required to realize the aims of philosophy: liberty and rationality. This step was taken by Marx, with the help of Feuerbach who had taught him to regard speculative thinking as the ultimate barrier to the understanding of man's role in the world.

The Marxian concept of ideology thus fuses two different principles: Hegel's insight into the transitory character of the successive manifestations of spirit, and Feuerbach's materialist inversion of Hegel, with its stress on the this-worldly character of natural existence. Separated from each other these concepts remained speculative; joined together they yielded an explosive mixture. The explosion, however, did not depend for its effect on the kind of skepticism which follows from the alleged discovery that abstract thinking does not yield access to universal truths. The despairing conclusions drawn by Kierkegaard from this conviction do not form part of the intellectual revolution underlying the new philosophy of history: they belong—with Nietzsche's kindred writings—to the attack on rationalism

accomplished by the so-called thinker consciously, it is true, but with a false consciousness. The real motive forces impelling him remain unknown to him; else it simply would not be an ideological process."
[35] Barth, op. cit., pp. 78 ff. To Hegel's followers the matter presented itself in a somewhat different light: since his philosophy was the fulfillment of speculative thinking in general, its appearance plainly marked the end of European history; cf. K. Löwith, Von Hegel zu Nietzsche (Stuttgart, 1950), pp. 44 ff. This may well have been Hegel's own view.

which in our own age has given rise to the existentialist analysis of the lonely individual. Nietzsche and Kierkegaard—just because they are concerned with the individual's role in a world whose functioning is indifferently taken for granted—have nothing to say about the manner in which history operates. Their revolt against rationalist metaphysics issues in subjectivism. Among the first universals to be cast overboard by these influential critics of rationalism was the concept of humanity.[36]

From Hegel to Marx

What Marx meant by "ideology" appears plainly enough from the *Theses on Feuerbach*, where the latter is blamed for not having carried through to the end his inversion of Hegel's system. He says, for example:

> Feuerbach sets out from the fact of religious self-alienation, the duplication of the world into a religious and a secular one. His work consists in resolving the religious world into its secular basis. But the fact that the secular basis deserts its own sphere and establishes an independent realm in the clouds, can only be explained by the cleavage and self-contradiction within the secular basis.[37]

[36] Kierkegaard still tried to find logical flaws in Hegel's system. With Schopenhauer's disciple Nietzsche, subjectivism and aestheticism have already reached the point where logic is consciously discarded. One cannot take seriously Nietzsche's so-called critique of traditional thought. When he says (*Jenseits von Gut und Böse*, in *Werke*, ed. K. Schlechta [Munich, 1960], II, p. 571), "It has gradually emerged that every great philosophy has hitherto been the confession of its author and a kind of unintended and unnoticed *mémoires*," he is being trivial in the Voltairean manner, which is caricatured throughout this overrated essay; cf., his similar observations (in *Ibid.*, p. I, 448) on the "hereditary fault of philosophy": "All philosophers share the fault of proceeding from the currently existing man [*vom gegenwärtigen Menschen*] and expecting to reach the goal through analyzing him. Insensibly they have an image of 'Man' as an *aeterna veritas* . . . as a sure measure of all things. Yet everything said by the philosopher about Man at bottom only applies to the men of a very limited period. Lack of historical sense is the hereditary fault of all philosophers. . . ." That this kind of thing should have been taken seriously *after* Hegel testifies to a state of affairs perhaps best described as the collapse of responsible thinking.

[37] Bottomore and Rubel, eds., *Karl Marx: Selected Writings in Sociology and Social Philosophy* (London, 1956), p. 68.

This radicalization of Feuerbach's naturalist starting point (itself a continuation of a tradition rooted in antiquity) left intact the rationalist principle which Marx shared with Hegel: namely, the belief that cognition gives access to universal truths not present in immediate experience. The Marxian conception of world history as a process of human self-alienation draws on Feuerbach's impassioned protest against the sacrifice of nature and of real, living, human beings, whose activities and whose sufferings Hegel had obscured. But Marx retains the Hegelian conviction that in the final analysis "history makes sense." The historical process vindicates Reason because it can be understood. To this extent Marx always remained a Hegelian, for all the emphasis upon "the real history of real people" which occupies so prominent a place in his polemics against his former associates.[38]

Marx's conception of ideology as "false consciousness" leads back to the problem of establishing the true consciousness which will enable men to understand their role. There is only one truth about history, and only one criterion for judging the discrepancy between what men are and what they might become: this criterion is supplied by philosophy, specifically by its understanding of man as a rational being. Thus philosophy, as the norm of reality, entails an implicit critique of this reality. Yet Marx also held that the philosophy of every age is the "ideological reflex" of determinate social conditions. How then could it function as the source of normative judgments pointing beyond the existing state of affairs? The problem did not arise if human self-alienation was conceived in the manner of Fichte and Hegel, as a mere misfortune which could be rectified by opposing a true consciousness to a false one. This had been Marx's standpoint in 1843, when he was already a revolutionary, but not yet a materialist.[39]

[38] *Deutsche Ideologie*, pp. 28 ff. and *passim*. In 1844-1845 Marx (then resident in Paris) had partly excerpted Destutt de Tracy's *Eléments d'Idéologie*, and his use of the term "ideology" reflects a clear awareness of the devaluation it had meanwhile undergone.
[39] Cf. *Ein Briefwechsel von 1843*, in *Der historische Materialismus*, S. Landshut and J. P. Mayer eds. (Leipzig, 1932), p. 226. "The reform of

It might seem that on the materialist assumptions Marx accepted as part of his conversion to socialism in 1844-1845, he was bound to arrive at a radical historicism and relativism. But although in many places the language of the *Holy Family* and the *German Ideology* (not to mention the *Communist Manifesto*) seems to support this conclusion, he did not in fact do so. He took over from his French predecessors the critical demolition of traditional metaphysics, yet he also went on ascribing a rational content to history. The rationality was a hidden one and had to be discerned in the logic of the "material" process itself, not in the "ideological" reflex it left in the minds of the participants. Like Hegel, he distinguished between Reality and Appearance. The reality of the historical process for Hegel was alienated Mind coming to terms with itself; for Marx it was alienated human labor reflecting itself in an ideological cloud-cuckooland. What he was later (in *Das Kapital*) to describe as the "fetishism of commodities," appears in his early writings as human self-alienation, whereby man's creations acquire a status independent of their creator.

The Marxian concept of ideology takes shape in this context, and from the start has a meaning different from that which it had for his eighteenth-century predecessors. Interest psychology is replaced by a metaphysic of human nature whose outline Hegel had developed in the *Phenomenology of Mind*. Alienated social activity is to Marx what alienated mental activity is to Hegel. For both, the distinction between Reality and Appearance is involved in the manner in which *real* processes are transformed into *apparently* fixed and stable characters. Reality is process, appearance has the form of isolated objects. The task of critical thinking is to grasp the relations which constitute these apparent objects.

---

consciousness consists only in this, that one enables the world to become aware of its own consciousness, that one awakens it from its dream, that one *explains* its own actions to it. Our entire purpose, as with Feuerbach's critique of religion, can only consist in transforming the religious and political questions into the self-conscious human form. . . . It will then appear that the world has long possessed the dream of something of which it need only possess the consciousness in order to have it in reality."

This approach still left unsolved the problem of relating the social content of ideology to the rational meaning of the process, as it differentiates itself through its various concrete manifestations. The historical character of the Marxian dialectic, and with it the problem of ideology in the modern sense, is a consequence of the discovery that there is not—as Feuerbach had thought—a single universal human standpoint from which to judge the alienations imposed by history; there are only particular human standpoints, corresponding to forms of society which arise from the interplay of material conditions and (more or less) conscious attempts to organize the "productive forces." The dialectic of being and consciousness is worked out in history; not, as Hegel had implied, as a shadow-play reflecting a metaphysical process, but as the "real" play. The "actors" are individuals and groups whose changing circumstances are mirrored in varying modes of thought. These modes are "ideological" in that the participants fail to comprehend the situation in which they are involved. But even the most thorough clarification of their actual historical role cannot, it would seem, enable them to transcend the particularity of their standpoint, since this is bound up with the concrete needs of their time and place. The only difference between "objective" and "ideological" thinking appears to lie in the capacity of the critical intellect to comprehend the particular determinations which condition each successive phase of human activity.

The principle that "social being . . . determines consciousness" [40] appears to imply that every social order (however defined) has forms of consciousness peculiar to it. Yet Marx also asserts that "mankind always sets itself only such tasks as it can solve," [41] thus placing a statement about the whole process within the framework of a doctrine intended to supersede the "pre-scientific" viewpoint. To invoke "mankind" is to make an assertion about the totality of history, however empirical and non-metaphysical the writer's intention. There is not in Marx

[40] Marx, A Contribution to the Critique of Political Economy, preface; Selected Works (Moscow, 1951), I, p. 363.
[41] Ibid.

a clear distinction between sociological statements relative to particular situations, and philosophical generalizations pertaining to history as a whole. How is the dilemma to be met?

The principle that social being determines consciousness must be understood as itself an historical one: it refers to a state of affairs which has characterized history from the very beginning, but which is due to disappear when a rational order has been created. For the attainment of such an order implies the conscious direction of social life, hence the emancipation of consciousness from blind, uncomprehended, necessity. Consciousness is ideological because it is powerless. When it becomes the determining factor, it sheds its blinkers along with its dependence on material circumstances. *A rational order is one in which thinking determines being.* Men will be free when they are able to *produce* their own circumstances. Historical materialism is valid only until it has brought about its own dialectical negation. When this state has been reached, it will no longer be possible to speak of historical "laws," for history is subject to "laws" only insofar as it is unconscious, that is, insofar as it is *not*, properly speaking, human history at all. The mature consciousness which in retrospect comprehends the necessity of this lengthy process of "prehistory" will not be an ideological one: it will be shared by all men, and will mark mankind's understanding of its own past.

Marx preserved the original motive of his thinking (together with the conception of history he had inherited from Hegel) by refusing to recognize the dilemma inherent in the principle that modes of thought are to be understood as "expressions" of changing social circumstances. He took it for granted that, though consciousness is conditioned by existence, it can also rise above existence and become a means of transcending the alienation which sets the historical process in motion. The *truth* about man is one and the same for all stages of history, even though every stage produces its own *illusions*. This truth is likewise the criterion for the practical activity which seeks to overcome man's alienation from his "true" being. The concept of ideology

illumines the historical circumstance that men are not in possession of the true consciousness which—if they had it—would enable them to understand the totality of the world and their own
place in it. Marx regarded his theory as a step towards the attainment of such a consciousness. The unity of mankind, and
the universality of truth, were as real to him as they were to
Hegel, and it was left to his disciples to destroy the coherence of
this thought by abandoning its unspoken assumptions and
transforming his doctrine into a variant of positivism.

From Metaphysics to Positivism

The second half of the nineteenth century witnessed the dissolution of rationalist metaphysics and the rise of positivism,
which from a particular school of thought in France transformed itself into the general method of the natural and social
sciences. In this atmosphere, sociology took shape as the application of positivist principles—themselves rooted in the world-
view of the eighteenth-century Enlightenment—to the study of
institutions. Comte's *philosophie positive* in part still reflected
its founder's link with the early socialist critique of society.[42]
With Herbert Spencer this antagonism turned into its opposite,
though the original motive broke through again in Spencer's rebellious ex-pupils who renounced his individualist approach and
developed the Fabian amalgam of Benthamite utilitarianism
and socialism.[43] With the Fabian school indeed, British sociology, after a lengthy interval of liberal individualism, returned to
its positivist and quasi-socialist origins. In France a parallel development is associated with the name of Durkheim. In both
cases the "objective" study of social institutions gradually transcended the individualist framework. If Comte (who had derived his basic ideas from Saint-Simon) converted socialism into

[42] D. G. Charlton, *Positivist Thought in France During the Second
Empire 1852-1870* (Oxford, 1959), *passim*.
[43] Cf. Beatrice Webb, *My Apprenticeship* (London and New York,
1926), pp. 112 ff., 123 ff. The study of Fabian origins in recent years has
done much to clarify the manner in which the Comtean impulse reached
these late-Victorian intellectuals by way of J. S. Mill and the novels of
George Eliot.

sociology, his French and British pupils reverted to the "ideology" he had spurned. They then discovered in piecemeal fashion that the "laws" of history left room for conscious activity
which, to be effective, had to be grounded in the study of institutions. The "religion of humanity," which for them increasingly took the place of the official religion, required active participation. This activism did not contradict the scientific credo, for
it was held that society's growing complexity demanded public
intervention. Such action, then, was justified not simply on humanitarian grounds—though crass poverty and misery furnished
an adequate motive—but on the grounds of rational obligation.

Comte's positivism did indeed raise the problem of "value
judgments," for science merely described the facts, leaving it to
the individual to judge them in accordance with his moral
standards. But precisely because "value judgments" were excluded from science, they were free. Comte's moral neutrality
left the field open for action guided by the desire for improve-
ment of a social order judged imperfect in terms of inherited
(secular or religious) morality. It even contained a normative
element in the idea of a universal order transcending national
differences. His evolutionary doctrine, however determinist in
retrospect (or in prospect), had room for the kind of humanitarian impulse that transformed itself into a critique of the established order when it encountered concrete social problems
such as poverty or unemployment. British evolutionary socialism
was able to merge with empirical sociology because both shared
the conviction that the study of "objective facts" would enable
society to overcome the latent irrationalities embedded in the
established order. The problem of "ideology" was not experienced as such, since it was taken for granted that all reasonable
people were agreed on fundamentals. Similarly the phenomenon
of class was not seen as a theoretical problem, but rather as a
practical obstacle to the attainment of a moral consensus.
Classes were undesirable because they barred the way to a community in which personal values could be genuinely shared. In
this respect the working class had no advantage: it too possessed
no more than a limited perspective which stood in need of being

transcended. While society was split into classes—whether mutually antagonistic or merely indifferent to each other—it lacked that unity which would enable individuals to meet on a common human footing. Hence classes were immoral, as well as being historically outmoded, since their existence was no longer justifiable on grounds of necessity. Any sectional standpoint was in principle as undesirable as any other, though the working class might temporarily benefit from a favorable prejudice, on the grounds of having in the past been made to carry a burden which ought in future to be equitably shared. Insofar as there was a problem of "false consciousness," it arose from these historic limitations, which were shared by all. Scientific insight into this state of affairs was also the means of transcending it: to begin with in thought, and increasingly—through moral and political action—in practice.[44]

These attitudes ultimately went back to the Enlightenment view of human progress as intellectual progress. This had been the standpoint of the *idéologues* and their successors, notably the Saint-Simonians. If Comte had removed the socialist component from sociology, he had retained the notion that the growth of positive knowledge was beneficial because it enabled men to understand the "laws" of social evolution. From there it was a short step to the conclusion that knowledge of the laws would make it possible to refashion society in accordance with moral values. In France this step was taken by Durkheim, whose public posture could be regarded as an uneasy balance between the positivism of Comte and the socialism of Marx.[45] But what was the source of the moral values? According to Durkheim they

---

[44] For the above cf. above all the writings of the Fabian school. The counterpart of this evolutionary socialism was an economic doctrine which —unlike the labor theory of value—proceeded from the marginal utility stress on the contribution made by each individual to the sum total of social wealth and well-being. Socialism is here defined as a state of affairs where—economic inequality having been eliminated—everyone will be recompensed in accordance with his freely chosen performance: in technical language, wages and prices will correspond to marginal utilities. Cf. Henry Smith, *The Economics of Socialism Reconsidered* (Oxford, 1962), *passim*.

[45] Emile Durkheim, *Socialism and Saint-Simon*, ed. Alvin W. Gouldner (London, 1959), pp. x ff., 90 ff.: cf. also Morris Ginsberg, *Essays in Sociology and Social Philosophy* (London, 1956), I, pp. 41 ff.

came to the individual from society: not a mere natural totality, but the concrete embodiment of ideal norms. Then how had the norms become embodied in social conduct? If the question was an historical one, it led to an examination of the manner in which different societies had organized themselves at different times around certain regulative principles. But no investigation of this kind could get beyond the factual statement that particular obligations had at one time or another been accepted as binding. If a crisis arose because the moral consensus broke down, the individuals forming society were faced with the need to establish a new consensus, but it was not explained on what grounds they were to make a choice. Durkheim was no relativist, but he got out of the difficulty only by hypostatizing "society" into an entity superior to its members. When confronted with the resulting difficulties he fell back on the notion of conscience. At this point he might have had to overstep the boundary of science and acknowledge the existence of a problem of moral conduct, which in turn involved the problem of philosophy in general. This, however, would have entailed an explicit recognition that the whole train of thought led beyond the area mapped out by the *philosophie positive*. In practice Durkheim was obliged to treat his own values as moral absolutes, though the paradoxality of this procedure seems to have worried him. The same may be said of Max Weber.[46]

The Romantic Revolt

Mention of Weber raises the question why positivism encountered so much more resistance in late-nineteenth-century Germany than in the West. Although this is properly an historical

---

[46] Cf. Karl Löwith, "Max Weber und Karl Marx," in *Gesammelte Abhandlungen* (Stuttgart, 1960), especially pp. 30 ff; so far as Weber ever clarified his standpoint he may be said to have done so in his "Der Sinn der Wertfreiheit," and "Wissenschaft als Beruf," both in *Gesammelte Aufsätze zur Wissenschaftslehre* (2nd ed., Tübingen, 1951), pp. 475 ff., 566 ff. Cf. also H. H. Gerth and C. W. Mills, eds., *From Max Weber: Essays in Sociology* (London, 1947), *passim*. For a more recent discussion see W. G. Runciman, "Karl Marx and Max Weber," in his *Social Science and Political Theory* (Cambridge, 1963).

topic, it leads back to philosophy, for what stood in the way of a more rapid assimilation of positivist concepts was the German metaphysical tradition. Since this had been given its final formulation by Hegel, it might have been supposed that the traditional philosophical standpoint would be championed by the Marxists, inasmuch as they considered themselves to be in the Hegelian succession. Marxism, however, had itself been given a positivist interpretation by Engels. In consequence there was no real confrontation at all. What happened rather was that— idealist metaphysics having been discarded—the heritage of classical philosophy was shared out between positivism and vitalism, with the Marxists *de facto* ranged on the positivist side. The romantic opposition, as in France, took up the cudgels against rationalism in general, though in the German setting a writer like Nietzsche exercised an influence to which there was no parallel in France. In principle the resulting cleavage was a general European phenomenon, but only in Germany was the anti-rational trend strong enough to impose itself temporarily as the dominant one; in the end it even succeeded in promoting a political upheaval.[47]

It would be misleading to treat this situation in terms of a straight conflict between rationalism and irrationalism. The classical rationalist position had in fact been abandoned by the Marxists as much as by everyone else. Even for the academically influential neo-Kantians, philosophy figured merely as the "beyond" of science. What remained after this intellectual debacle was the clash between positivism and vitalism, and since philosophy no longer supplied any guiding ideas, the debate took place at the level of sociological, or psychological, deflation of general concepts. Nietzsche's vulgarization of Schopenhauer (who can-

[47] H. Stuart Hughes, *Consciousness and Society* (New York, 1958), *passim*. For Gerth and Mills (*op. cit.*, pp. 61 ff.) Weber represents a synthesis of the Marxian and the Nietzschean approach to the problem of ideology, *i.e.*, the problem of relating ideas back to their (social or psychological) roots. This seems to credit Nietzsche with rather more intellectual penetration than he actually possessed. In any event the popularly effective counterpoint to his position was furnished by Engels and his successors. In political terms this corresponded to the polarization of German intellectual life into Social Democratic and National Socialist versions of post-liberal thinking.

not be described as an irrationalist) had its parallel in Engels' popularization of Hegel. Both were writing for the general public, but Nietzsche had the advantage of addressing himself to readers already predisposed by a century of literary romanticism to come down on the irrationalist side. In the struggle for influence over the educated public, which opened in the 1890s and came to a momentous climax in the 1930s, the Nietzscheans gained ground at the expense of the *soi-disant* Marxists in the degree to which they were able to pose as heirs and defenders of a peculiarly German tradition. Yet the extremes met over the issue of replacing religion by "religious atheism": both Engels and Nietzsche believed in "eternal recurrence." (For that matter, Engels had enough affection for the world of the Edda to satisfy the tastes of a whole army of Nordic enthusiasts.[48])

If one abstracts from the not very successful neo-Kantian revival, which remained an academic affair, the situation briefly sketched here remained unchanged until the first faint stirrings of the neo-Hegelian renaissance on the eve of 1914. Around 1880 it really must have seemed to educated Germans that philosophy was dead. Not surprisingly this was the moment when the debunking of universal concepts attained its peak. So far as Nietzsche was concerned, this was largely a matter of radicalizing the thinking of Schopenhauer, who for all his skepticism

[48] Nietzsche's elaboration of the concept of eternal recurrence is too well known to require citation. For Engels' surprisingly similar (though quite independently developed) attitude, see the Introduction to his *Dialektik der Natur, MEGA*; cf. Marx-Engels *Selected Works* (Moscow, 1951), II, pp. 57 ff. especially pp. 72-73: "It is an eternal cycle in which matter moves, a cycle that certainly only completes its orbit in periods of time for which our terrestrial year is no adequate measure, a cycle in which the time of highest development, the time of organic life, and still more that of the life of beings conscious of themselves and of nature, is just as scantily meted out as the space in which life and self-consciousness come into operation; a cycle in which every finite mode of existence of matter . . . is equally transient, and wherein nothing is eternal but eternally changing, eternally moving matter. . . . But however often, and however relentlessly, this cycle is completed in time and space, however many millions of suns and earths may come into being and go out of being . . . we have the certainty that matter remains eternally the same in all its transformations, that none of its attributes can ever be lost, and . . . that with the same iron necessity with which it will again exterminate on the earth its highest creation, the thinking mind, it must somewhere else and at another time once more engender it."

about the role of the intellect had still left unchallenged the principle that true cognition of the world is possible. Schopenhauer retained the distinction between objective (that is, disinterested) and erroneous (because interested and subjective) thinking. His target was intellectual corruption, not the intellect as such. When he said that people's judgments were "mostly corrupt and merely an expression in favor of their party or class," [49] he was being cynical about his contemporaries, without therefore giving way to despair about the capacity of the mind to reach valid conclusions. This step was taken by Nietzsche who debased Schopenhauer's skeptical pessimism into a destructive nihilism. The essential coarseness of Nietzsche's mind is concealed by a style modeled on that of his master, and by a declamatory pathos that employs the phraseology of the Enlightenment for the purpose of wrecking the already shaken belief in reason.

> We live only through illusions. . . . The foundations of everything great and alive rest upon illusion. The pathos of truth leads to destruction.[50]

From this irrationalism it was only a short step to the biological vitalism of the Third Reich and its ideologists. Nietzsche's critique of religion—ostensibly a revival of the eighteenth-century tradition—issues in a subjectivism no less anthropocentric than theology itself. The characterization of the world as "senseless" merely inverts the theological claim that the universe exists for the purpose of manifesting a providential concern for man. Since Nietzsche has "seen through" this illusion, he appeals for a faith centered upon the "will to power"—a biological metaphor. The critique of ideology is reduced to the destruction of religious idols (and the fabrication of new ones). The residual link with the eighteenth-century tradition is retained only in externals such as the French title of Nietzsche's *Götzendämmerung*: a work originally translated (at the sugges-

---

[49] *Sämtliche Werke*, ed. Hübscher (Leipzig, 1937-1941), V, p. 479; cf. Barth, *op. cit.*, p. 199.
[50] *Gesammelte Werke* (Munich, 1923-1929), VI, pp. 17, 74.

tion of its author) as *Crépuscule des idoles*.[51] In all essential respects he turned his back on the rationalist tradition. The principal "idol" he set out to smash was the belief in reason.

If there can be no valid perception of universals it is pointless to inquire into the meaning of history. What remains is "the eternal flux of all things," "perpetual change": the trivial notion that everything has its moment in time. "There are no eternal facts, just as there are no absolute truths." [52] Here too Nietzsche encounters Engels.[53] The chief difference is that his tone is hysterical, whereas that of Engels is complacent—a distant foreshadowing of political cleavages yet to come. Neither man was able to salvage the classical heritage invoked in their respective writings.

The critique of ideology, when delivered from such a standpoint, reduces itself to what is called *unmasking*. Nietzsche is tireless in stripping the "mask" from respectability, from bourgeois morality, from idealist metaphysics, and of course from Christianity. History for him is a masquerade: not in the Hegelian sense that its logic reveals itself through transitory events and personalities, but in the sense that men drape their "real" biological drives and goals in idealist costumes. All thought is ideological; its unconscious function is to serve the life process. In contrast to this cynicism, Engels—who unlike Nietzsche retained the rationalist vocabulary, along with a proper respect for the classical tradition (whose meaning he had forgotten)— holds that *almost* all thinking is ideological; he takes a cheerful

[51] *Friedrich Nietzsches Briefwechsel mit Franz Overbeck*, Oehler and Bernoulli, eds. (Leipzig, 1916), p. 453.
[52] *Werke*, XI, p. 154.
[53] Cf. *Ludwig Feuerbach*, in *Selected Works* (Moscow, 1951), II, p. 351: "The great basic thought that the world is not to be comprehended as a complex of ready-made things, but as a complex of processes . . . this . . . thought has . . . so thoroughly permeated ordinary consciousness that . . . it is now scarcely ever contradicted . . . If . . . investigation always proceeds from this standpoint, the demand for final solutions and eternal truth ceases once for all . . . one no longer permits oneself to be imposed upon by the antitheses . . . between true and false, good and bad . . . necessary and accidental. One knows that these antitheses have only a relative validity." (This, however, does not prevent Engels from asserting in the very same passage that throughout all these relative processes "a progressive development asserts itself in the end.")

view of the matter, in as much as historical causality can be understood and guided.

> Men make their own history, whatever its outcome may be, in that each person follows his own consciously desired end, and it is precisely the resultant of these many wills operating in different directions . . . that constitutes history. . . . The will is determined by passion or deliberation, but the levers which immediately determine passion or deliberation are of very different kinds.

> . . . the philosophy of history, particularly as represented by Hegel, recognizes that the ostensible and also the really operating motives of men who act in history are by no means the ultimate causes of historical events; that behind these motives there are other motive powers which have to be discovered. But it does not seek these powers in history itself, it imports them rather from outside, from philosophical ideology, into history.[54]

Behind the historical shadow-play there is a realm of "real" causation which can be understood. It is thus possible to grasp the logic of the process, but since it rolls on endlessly, one cannot assign any ultimate meaning to it. Matter being eternal, and its endless motion the only "law" of which we can be certain, history is reduced to the status of a singularity within the domain of nature. "Dialectical materialism" and romantic vitalism concur in the belief that Reality is Process, though the former retains a hankering for the rationality which was once the principal theme of philosophy. This at least provides a criterion for distinguishing between "objective" and "ideological" thinking. For Nietzsche the distinction is meaningless: all thought is a species of poetry, and the real Being of the world remains irreducible to discursive reasoning.

The Logic of Science

At this level a serious analysis of the problem of ideology was not possible. Its restatement around 1900 was due to Max Weber, who had benefited from the neo-Kantian revival. For Weber, who had assimilated the historical relativism of Dilthey,

[54] *Ibid.*, II, pp. 354-355.

science was both autonomous and morally neutral. At the same time the implications of this standpoint were no longer veiled by metaphysical remnants. In particular it was not possible for Weber to be complacent about the over-all progressive direction of history. As he saw it, there was no guarantee that the rationalization of existence would promote the aims traditionally enshrined in philosophy. Matters were, if anything, getting worse —at any rate from the standpoint of one who valued personal freedom. This pessimistic outlook made it possible for Weber to divorce normative judgments from factual statements in a more radical fashion than Dilthey had done. Positivism acquired a Stoical cast: it underpinned the "freely chosen" standpoint of a thinker who saw himself defending a lost cause.[55]

Weber is important for our theme because his approach involved a sharpened distinction between the two meanings of "ideology." The term—as has been shown—can signify both the consciousness of an epoch and the "false consciousness" of men unaware of their true role. What a culture thinks about itself may be "ideological" in one sense without being so in the other; thus for example if the Middle Ages developed thought-forms which "reflected" the feudal-hierarchical structure of society, the official ideology might nonetheless serve as an accurate guide to that particular reality, just because it was mirrored in the categories. This is the sense in which the term is commonly employed both by Marx (though not by the epigoni) and by Weber. Plainly on this assumption there need be no question of "unmasking" anyone or anything. On the other hand, thinking may be "ideological" in the narrower sense of distorting, rather than reflecting, the reality it describes. Thus for Marx economics was either "scientific" or "ideological," depending on whether or not it gave an objective account of the socio-economic process. Ricardo in his eyes was none the less scientific for being bour-

---

[55] Löwith, *op. cit., passim* develops this theme through an analysis of Weber's relationship both to the historical Marx and to the "vulgar Marxism" of the epigoni; cf. also Runciman, *op. cit.*, pp. 43 ff. The subsequent development of Weber's critique of modern society and its ideologies is linked with the name of Schumpeter: cf. in particular the latter's *Capitalism, Socialism and Democracy* (London and New York, 1950).

geois. Marx, however, also retained the notion that thought-forms impose their own limitations, so that, for example, Ricardo (or any other economist employing his concepts) was limited by his inability to transcend the mental framework proper to the bourgeois epoch: social categories cannot be transcended in thought until they have (in principle at least) been questioned in practice. In tacitly retaining this approach, Weber fell heir to the problem of accounting for the role of "ideology": not as the conscious or unconscious distortion of reality in the interest of some group, but as the intellectual reflex of determinate social processes. Unlike Marx, for whom history as a whole exemplified a hidden rationality, he relativized sociology by severing it from philosophy: every culture has its own norms and values which enter into the perception of what is called "reality." Its norms are binding only upon those who accept them, though this does not invalidate them, since it is their fate to be "objective" and "subjective" at the same time. There is no way of transcending this situation, for the growth of rationality leads only to an awareness that it is not possible to ground value judgments in a universally accepted doctrine of human nature.

At this point the critique of ideology—originally a philosophical theme—turns into relativism. History and sociology combine to make it appear that consciousness cannot transcend its time horizon, since the concepts imposed upon the raw material of experience are themselves historical. Something like this had been suggested by Hegel, and following him by Marx, but they were saved from relativism by the belief that both the nature of man and the logic of history could still be grasped in an act of intellectual intuition. With Dilthey and Weber, the subjectivism already inherent in the neo-Kantian interpretation of the categories as empty forms imposed upon an unknown and unknowable material leads away from the notion of truth as universal. Now that reason has lost its status as a concrete universal, history is no longer seen as an intelligible totality held together in the last resort by the fact that it is one and the same for all men. What remains when this faith has been discarded is the subjective freedom of each individual to act according to reason,

his reason; a freedom necessarily limited by the right of all others
to do the same. Men act from freely chosen standpoints which
are ultimately incompatible, on the basis of convictions which in
the final analysis cannot be rationally justified. In this perspective the "ideological" character of thinking ceases to be a problem. It is accepted as an aspect of a situation which—since it
cannot be altered or transcended—must be stoically endured.

The Sociology of Knowledge

The preceding section was concerned with the manner in which
the ideology problem was formulated between, roughly speaking, 1860 and 1920. The dates are not chosen at random, just as
it is not a matter of accident that the earlier debate had run
from the French Revolution to the 1848 upheaval.[56] In both
cases we are dealing with a social transformation which found its
intellectual counterpart in a distinctive manner of conceiving
the role of ideas. This would probably be agreed even by critics
of "historicism," and for the rest it may be suggested that a
statement such as the foregoing does not commit one to anything beyond the bare assertion that there must be *some* correspondence between the collective experience of a culture and
the way in which this experience is generalized in thought. It
does not follow that either Marxism or positivism are to be understood as the "ideological reflex" of their age, though on the
trivialized interpretation of "historical materialism" which we
owe to its orthodox-exponents such a conclusion might seem to
impose itself. From the standpoint here chosen the matter appears somewhat differently.

It has already been suggested that Weber did not really "turn
Marx upside down" (*e.g.*, in asserting that Protestantism was a
key factor in the rise of capitalism), but rather developed a
"bourgeois" counterpart to the Marxian theory of history. It is

[56] Marx's *Zur Kritik der politischen Ökonomie*, with the well-known
Preface stating the "materialist conception of history," appeared in 1859;
Weber's lecture on "Wissenschaft als Beruf" was delivered in 1919: a
date which may be regarded as the effective end of the historical epoch
that had given rise to both positivism and "orthodox Marxism."

true that in one important respect he went beyond Marx, in that his sociology concerned "industrial society" as such; it thus became relevant, during the following generation, for capitalism and socialism alike. But while this topic is of the first importance for contemporary sociologists, it is somewhat tangential to our problem. In any case it is possible to share Weber's pessimism about the future of freedom in an increasingly rationalized and bureaucratized world, without therefore accepting the neo-Kantian divorce between factual and value judgments as an ultimate datum for the reflective consciousness. The same applies to his notion that all possible standpoints are relative, not merely to the position of their holder (hardly a shattering revelation), but to the rationale of the process (if it can be discovered) which has transformed the naïve hopes and aspirations of the eighteenth-century Enlightenment into our current disenchantment. Talk of "process" involves the assumption that history does have a discernible logic, but since this was not denied by Weber we are not moving outside his frame of reference in asking how far the "sociology of knowledge" is able to clarify the ideology problem.

Although the step from *Wissenschaftslehre* to *Wissenssoziologie* was taken by Karl Mannheim, one is, I think, justified in treating Mannheim's work as an epilogue to that of Weber. It is no longer a secret that an important link between them was provided by George Lukács, notably in *History and Class-Consciousness*: a work which for many years led an underground existence before being recognized as the influence it was. Here both Mannheim's derivation from Weber, and his dependence on the early Lukács, are taken for granted, and the question is asked how far the concept of ideology was clarified by this belated fusion of the Marxist and the positivist standpoint.[57]

[57] For the following, cf. Georg Lukács, *Geschichte und Klassenbewusstsein: Studien über marxistische Dialektik* (Berlin, 1923); Karl Mannheim, *Ideology and Utopia* (London, 1936; 2nd ed. 1960); and *Essays on Sociology and Social Psychology*, ed. Kecskemeti (London, 1953); Karl R. Popper, *The Poverty of Historicism* (Boston, 1957). The last-mentioned work is virtually a critique of Mannheim, who appears in it as the incarnation of "holistic" thinking and "historicism," and it is questionable how far its generalizations are appropriate to other targets.

If Weber could be described as a "bourgeois Marx," Mannheim appeared to the cognoscenti (that is, to those aware of his background, and of the somewhat tenuous link between his circle and the Budapest Marxists who staffed the brief Soviet experiment in 1919) as a "bourgeois Lukács"—not perhaps quite fairly, since he regarded himself as a Socialist, and in his later writings even made something of a fetish of economic planning.[58] None of this concerns us here; our topic is furnished by the manner in which he and Lukács—starting from a parallel awareness of the dilemma raised by the radical historicism of Dilthey and the resigned relativism of Weber—conceived the problem of ideology. Mannheim's exposition of the subject in *Ideology and Utopia* (first published in 1929) may be taken as read. The same cannot be said of Lukács, notwithstanding his later prominence as a purveyor of more or less orthodox Marxism-Leninism.[59] In 1923, when *Geschichte und Klassenbewusstsein* appeared—to be promptly disowned by its author when it encountered the inevitable critical barrage from Moscow—it was rightly regarded as a challenge to "orthodox Marxism" and positivism alike. Lukács in fact had revived the Hegelian conception of history and fused it with Lenin's revolutionary activism into an explosive mixture—far more explosive than the authorized version to which Communism was already committed, for Lukács really went through with the notion that the proletariat was the "identical subject-object of the socio-historical process." [60] Not only was it the class destined to make an end of bourgeois society: its coming triumph signaled the *practical* resolution of *theoretical* problems insoluble from a bourgeois standpoint, including the Kantian problem.[61] And this conclusion was developed not in the usual philistine manner, which virtually negated the very existence of philosophy, but through

[58] Cf. his *Mensch und Gesellschaft im Zeitalter des Umbaus* (Leiden, 1935); *Diagnosis of Our Time* (London, 1943).

[59] No reference is intended here to Lukács' writings on art, notably the two massive volumes on aesthetics (*Die Eigenart des Aesthetischen* [Neuwied, 1963]) recently published as part of the *Collected Works* now being edited in West Germany.

[60] *Op. cit.*, pp. 80 ff.

[61] *Ibid.*, pp. 134 ff.

an analysis of logical and epistemological concepts which sought to establish their essentially historical character. Lukács in 1923 not merely revived the Hegelian dialectic: in his own fashion he did what Hegel had done in the *Phenomenology* when he treated the categories as manifestations of Spirit.[62] With this intellectual *tour de force*—a unique achievement, whose level was never remotely recovered by its own author: in his later years a pedestrian exponent of Marxist-Leninist scholasticism—the "heritage of classical German philosophy," vainly invoked by Engels in his platitudinous essay on Feuerbach, seemed in fact to have been secured for the Marxist school.

Lukács and Mannheim

From our present standpoint it is plain enough that this was a mirage, and not only because history refused to follow the road mapped out by the theorist. Writing almost a decade before the rediscovery of Marx's *"Paris Manuscripts,"* Lukács had intuitively fixed upon the alienation and restitution of man as the pivotal point in the Marxian world-view.[63] This gave him the metahistorical standpoint he needed to gain a critical view of the whole process. But while he thus eluded the relativism inherent in the orthodox approach, he involved himself in a different dilemma: a standpoint outside empirical history is a metaphysical standpoint, and while this is no criticism of Hegelian (or any other) philosophy, it becomes problematic for a Marxist. Thus when confronted with orthodox indignation, Lukács was unable to maintain his position. To do so he would have had to acknowledge that the category of "totality," which played the key role in his thinking, transcended not merely the artificially foreshortened positivist world-view, but any conceivable standpoint compatible with what is called science. Lukács had seen

[62] Unfortunately this cannot be demonstrated in detail. For the rest it must suffice to mention the evident influence of Lukács on the work of Herbert Marcuse.

[63] Cf. the lengthy essay "Die Verdinglichung und das Bewusstsein des Proletariats" (*op. cit.*, pp. 94 ff.) which presents a critique of idealist philosophy in conceptual terms derived from Hegel (and incidentally dismisses Engels' criticism of Kant as the absurdity it is).

well enough that empiricism can never attain to an intellectual grasp of the "concrete totality" of history. What he failed to see —or shrank from admitting to himself when it was suggested to him—was that the empiricism of science is the only possible standpoint for a thinker who is determined to get on without the help of metaphysics. His own "wager" on the revolution— though in the circumstances of the day not an irrational one— contained an element of romantic subjectivism which he refused to acknowledge. From a purely theoretical viewpoint there was no particular reason why the proletariat—rather than the intelligentsia or some other group—should have been seen as the "identical subject-object" of history. In fact, if it was a question of establishing a standpoint transcending the class struggle (not that Lukács had any such intention) the intelligentsia had a better claim.

This, as we know, was Mannheim's solution, but before coming to it, let us see how the role of consciousness is to be understood on Lukács' assumptions. As he is the only Marxist to have written an entire book on the subject, it may be as well to consider what he has to say. Starting from the Hegelian-Marxian view of history as a concrete totality of seemingly unrelated circumstances, he begins by criticizing the manner in which empiricism has made a fetish of science as the correct description of those frozen structures that confront the individual as "social reality." [64] The dialectical method, which restores the intelligibility of the process, also discloses the ideological character of those pseudo-empirical and "scientific" forms of thought which present the typical antinomies of declining late-bourgeois culture—*e.g.*, the conflict between the individual and society—as though they necessarily pertained to every stage of history. The Marxian dialectic is able to perform this role because (unlike Hegel's idealist dialectic, with its retrospective attention fixed upon the past) it transcends both the status quo and the catego-

---

[64] *Op. cit.*, pp. 22 ff. In addition to the sociological method oriented on Comte and Spencer, Lukács also condemns those Marxists who had gone back to Kant. For in doing so they had ignored the fact that "Marx's critique of Hegel is . . . the direct continuation and development of Hegel's own critique of Kant and Fichte" (p. 31).

ries which are its intellectual counterpart. These categories reflect a particular reality whose meaning is concealed from the individual by the bourgeois mode of thought, the latter finding its apotheosis in the cult of positive science. All the typical dilemmas of modern life—the cleavage between theory and practice, form and content, science and metaphysics, and so forth—arise from this situation. The sharpest conflict is that between the progressive rationalization of particular aspects of existence and the mounting irrationality of the whole. The overcoming of this split—not merely in theory but in practice—is the task of *consciousness:* specifically the consciousness that transcends the bourgeois era, namely Marxism. With history moving toward a climax involving the fate of mankind,[65] the growing antagonism between the ruling class and the proletariat (which latter is compelled, for the sake of self-preservation, to fight for the attainment of ends not necessarily present *as such* to each of its individual members) assumes the aspect of a race between "blind" necessity and conscious purpose. For the automatism of the historical process, on which "vulgar Marxism" before 1914 had relied for the attainment of its ends, is quite capable of promoting a universal catastrophe.[66] The transition from the "realm of necessity" to the "realm of freedom" is not itself a necessary step. On the contrary, it is precisely during this critical transitional period that the blind automatism of the existing reified structures takes on the character of a fateful drift which can only be stemmed by the revolt of the exploited class. The latter, for all its empirical shortcomings, is the historical incorporation of mankind's will to escape from self-destruction. Its consciousness, which transcends the fixed categories of a society in process of dissolution, coincides with the "true" consciousness of mankind. This self-awareness is not a scientific one, for *science is itself an illusion*—the last and greatest of bourgeois illusions, and one which, if not overcome, must unfailingly promote the catastrophe of humanity. The conflict between bourgeoisie and proletariat thus involves the fate of mankind. But

65 *Op. cit.*, p. 82.
66 *Ibid.*

the empirical proletariat is itself subjected to the ideological confusions and crises typical of bourgeois society in the era of its decomposition, and therefore—here Lukács takes leave of classical Marxism and adopts the Leninist standpoint—it requires the leadership of a revolutionary *party* which incarnates the consciousness of the epoch.[67] In the end, therefore, the consciousness on which literally everything depends is once more that of a group of individuals, for of course the party itself has to be *led*. In his later years Lukács showed himself ready to face the implications of this dialectic: if Reason could be located in a group, it could also find its temporary embodiment in an individual who had substituted himself for the group.

What made this analysis seem both convincing and overwhelmingly urgent was the author's intellectual distinction. In the early twenties, prophets of doom abounded in Central Europe; one more or less would have made no difference. What distinguished Lukács was the firmness with which he placed his message within the context of classical German philosophy. His analysis of Kantian and neo-Kantian thinking—lengthily developed[68] in the intricately allusive style he had adopted from his prewar teachers in Heidelberg—employed the Hegelian-Marxist vocabulary with telling effect, to the end of demonstrating that the crisis of contemporary thought heralded the imminent catastrophe of the society which had given birth to this very philosophy. He had indeed guessed correctly, though he erred in supposing that "the revolution" would prove him right. What actually happened was that the European crisis gave rise to the rival totalitarianisms of Communism and Fascism. His own side, moreover, repudiated him, and this although he had worked out the appropriate philosophical rationale of Leninism. The apocalyptic vision of a crisis in which the fate of mankind was in the balance had its effect upon the intellectual elite of European Marxism; but it appalled the new Muscovite orthodoxy, already committed to its own brand of scientism, and it was useless as a means of promoting revolutionary optimism

[67] *Op. cit.*, pp. 261 ff., 276 ff., 298 ff.
[68] *Ibid.*, pp. 122 ff.

among the masses. It therefore remained an underground doctrine, and its author a licensed heretic who in the end repudiated his own insights in favor of a refurbished "dialectical materialism." This necessarily entailed a commonplace transcript theory of perception, in the place of the dialectical theory of cognition put forward in the 1923 work. With this return to orthodoxy, the problem of ideology once more assumed subordinate status: there was a true consciousness (that of the working class, or rather of "its" party) and a false one (that of the "class enemy"), but *both had the same structure*. It was simply a question of replacing "bourgeois science" by "socialist science" or—even more absurdly—"bourgeois ideology" by "proletarian ideology." That "science" itself represents an "ideological" manner of thinking which of its nature cannot yield an adequate report of the world—this truly startling and genuinely "revolutionary" notion, which Lukács had extracted from Hegel, disappeared from view. Its own author came to renounce it. It was after all a good deal easier to stick to the time-honored notion that science tells us all we need to know, provided it is not distorted by "reactionary" class interests. This had been the message of orthodox Marxism, as formulated by Engels, Plekhanov, Kautsky, and Lenin himself (though Lenin's *practice* was wildly at variance with it and demanded a wholly different theory of cognition). In returning to this tradition. Lukács was not merely playing safe, but in all probability also satisfying a deep-seated psychological craving for spiritual certainty: the heretic had found peace in the haven of a new secular church.[69]

In the light of the foregoing, Mannheim's work appears as, so to speak, the dialectical counterpart to Lukács' abortive breakout. *Ideology and Utopia* (1929) was the positivist's rejoinder to *History and Class-Consciousness* (1923). Mannheim (who in 1919 had steered clear of Lukács' political commitments) adapted what he could use for his own purpose, which was

[69] Though in his quasi-philosophical writings he never quite managed to shake off his youthful concern with the role of the mind and the irreducible character of spiritual experience. Unfortunately this topic, which is of importance for an appreciation of Lukács' work on aesthetics, cannot be developed here.

frankly "theoretical" in the contemplative sense condemned by
Lukács, for whom theory was meaningless if not joined to a particular practice. *Ideology and Utopia* is full of passages which
reflect its author's awareness of the issues Lukács had stirred up
a few years earlier. In particular, Mannheim's analysis of the
manner in which ideological notions are formed rests upon the
philosophy of consciousness developed by Hegel and his successors.[70] Thus for him too consciousness does not simply "reflect"
the world of experience, but on the contrary helps to shape it.[71]
The notion of "false consciousness" (ideology in the precise or
narrow sense) is linked to the discussion of Kant and Hegel.
The traditional Marxist standpoint is dismissed as untenable, in
that it tries to exempt itself from the verdict inherent in its own
approach: socialism too must be treated as an ideology.

> With the emergence of the general formulation of the total con-
> ception of ideology, the simple theory of ideology develops into
> the sociology of knowledge. What was once the intellectual arma-
> ment of a party is transformed into a method of research in social
> and intellectual history generally.[72]

As with Comte a century earlier, socialism turns into sociology, but this time the problem of relativism is frankly faced.

> Once we recognize that all historical knowledge is relational
> knowledge, and can only be formulated with reference to the po-
> sition of the observer, we are faced once more with the task of
> discriminating between what is true and what is false. . . . The
> question then arises: which social standpoint *vis-à-vis* of history
> offers the best chance for reaching an optimum of truth? [73]

We are back with Max Weber. In fact Mannheim's position
can be defined very precisely as an amalgam (doubtless he regarded it as a synthesis) of Weber and Lukács. What was new
and original was the answer he gave to his own question: the

[70] *Op. cit.*, pp. 57 ff.
[71] "This does not imply that the subject merely reflects the structural
pattern of the external world, but rather that, in the course of his experience with the world, he spontaneously evolves the principles of organization that enable him to understand it."
[72] *Ibid.*, p. 69.
[73] *Ibid.*, p. 71.

THE CONCEPT OF IDEOLOGY

optimal standpoint is that occupied by the social group which specializes in forming general concepts—the intelligentsia.

By linking the sociology of knowledge to the position of a definite stratum in society, Mannheim had anchored the exercise of freedom in the group interest of the intellectuals.[74] This was a step beyond Weber, for whom the problem of cognition was bound up with the role of the lonely thinker confronting the world. Mannheim's concern with group thinking does not, however, meet the objection that only a particular "historic" class at a particular moment of time can reshape the historical situation. The world of the individual is always a "given" one, in that it is experienced as a totality which the critical intellect cannot significantly alter. A group is still made up of individuals whose minds are engaged with various aspects of experience and whose differing standpoints will probably cancel out. This play of opinion and mutual cancellation of "prejudices" is in fact regarded by Mannheim as essential to the emergence of an adequate scientific standpoint.

> The task of a study of ideology which tries to be free from value-judgments is to understand the narrowness of each individual point of view and the interplay between these distinctive attitudes in the total social process.[75]

Yet the reference to the "total social process" seems to presuppose a different and more philosophical viewpoint. On the assumptions made by Mannheim *qua* sociologist, there is no good reason why he should casually invoke the totality of history

[74] *Op. cit.*, p. 143: ". . . the intellectuals are still able to arrive at a total orientation even when they have joined a party. Should the capacity to acquire a broader point of view be considered merely as a liability? Does it not rather present a mission? Only he who really has the choice has an interest in seeing the whole of the social and political structure. Only in that period of time and that stage of investigation which is dedicated to deliberation is the sociological and logical locus of the development of a synthetic perspective to be sought. . . . We owe the possibility of mutual interpenetration and understanding of existing currents of thought to the presence of such a relatively unattached middle stratum. . . ."
[75] *Op. cit.*, p. 72. Cf. also further on: "The prevailing philosophic view which cautiously admits that the content of conduct has been historically determined, but which at the same time insists upon the retention of eternal forms of value . . . is no longer tenable."

when it suits him. In fact when he does so he is employing language which makes sense only on the (Hegelian) supposition that the Whole determines its parts, and that the logic of history must be understood before one can proceed to the business of empirical investigation.[76]

The Problem of Consciousness

The problem of history is the problem of consciousness. It was Hegel who first pointed this out, and his successors—including Marx, who inverted his logic but did not replace it by a radically different manner of thought—continued to pose the question he had raised: how could the rationality of history be perceived by the intellect, given the fact that men are both inside and outside the historical process? The subsidiary problem of "false consciousness" arose from the awareness that the various possible standpoints were inadequate as well as incompatible. Meantime the analysis of cognition had led to the search for the "identical subject-object" of history: a universal whose activity was synonymous with the disclosure of history's peculiar logic. The pursuit of this aim over the past two centuries is not simply to be understood as a dispassionate search for objective truth, though belief in a *ratio* common to all men was inherent in the attempt to discern an historical logic. The intellectual effort was itself a factor in that theoretical and practical unification of the world which is now proceeding under our eyes. The mounting concern over the phenomenon of "false consciousness" was an index to the awareness that the future of civilization—if not the existence of mankind—may come to depend on the attainment of a "true consciousness" in which indi-

[76] *Op. cit.*, p. 83. "The study of intellectual history can and must be pursued in a manner which will see in the sequence and coexistence of phenomena more than mere accidental relationships, and will seek to discover in the totality of the historical complex the role, significance, and meaning of each component element." The inconsistency inherent in such utterances (for which Mannheim might indeed have invoked the authority of Dilthey and Troeltsch) exposed their author to the charge that, for all his skeptical airs, he was really an historicist at heart; cf. Popper, *op. cit.*, p. 80.

viduals and groups belonging to the most varied societies and cultures can share. From the standpoint here chosen it may thus be suggested that the attempt to discern a logic of history was more than an idle play with concepts: it responded to a practical purpose which in our own age has become more urgent as the globe shrinks, and historically divergent and disparate cultures press against one another. Because these pressures are experienced as ideological conflicts among people holding different and incompatible aims in view, it remains the task of the critical intellect to evolve modes of thought which will enable men to recognize the common purpose underlying their divergencies.

In this perspective, the transformation undergone by the concept of ideology appears as an index to the tension between the actual historical process and a critical consciousness nourished by the traditions of classical rationalism. In its original eighteenth-century form, the concept represented an implicit critique of society from the standpoint of early liberalism: a standpoint which was itself "historical" in that it took for granted (and therefore treated as "natural") the social relations proper to a particular phase of European history.[77] This naïve certainty disappeared during and after the French Revolution. The latter marked a turning point in that the critique of existing (traditional but decaying, hence plainly irrational) institutions could no longer be delivered in the name of apparently self-evident principles. For the new institutions, which claimed to be in accordance with reason, turned out to be rational only in terms of the particular historical purpose they served: the emancipation of the "third estate" could not forever be equated with the attainment of a natural order conceived as the embodiment of absolute reason. Hence the fleeting balance attained around 1800 gave way to a deepening skepticism about the very "ideol-

[77] Jürgen Habermas, *Theorie und Praxis: Sozialphilosophische Studien* (Neuwied, 1963), *passim*. For a recent defense of the positivist standpoint, cf. Arnold Gehlen, *Studien zur Anthropologie und Soziologie* (Neuwied, 1963), *passim*. For a critique of positivism from a neo-Hegelian viewpoint, cf. Herbert Marcuse, *One-Dimensional Man* (Boston, 1964), *passim*. For a critical view of the neo-Marxist position, cf. Morris Watnick, "Relativism and Class Consciousness: George Lukács," in *Revisionism: Essays on the History of Marxist Ideas* (London and New York, 1962), pp. 142 ff.

ogy" whose original proponents had set out to trace the natural history of ideas. In Hegel's philosophy, which arose directly from the urge to comprehend the meaning of the Revolution, there already appears in germ the notion that forms of consciousness are relative to changing historical situations. The universality of the whole has to be reconstructed, as it were, from the entire sequence of historical fossils—the latter comprising *inter alia* the conscious (subjective) aims of the individuals who occupy the foreground. These aims now appear as unconscious means of realizing a hidden purpose; they have become "ideological" in a sense not intended by the original *idéologues*.

This is the concept of ideology which Marx inherited from Hegel. It served him as a means of discrediting the universal claims of the liberal ideology he encountered in his passage from philosophy to politics. At the same time he retained the rationalist faith in an objective logic of the historical process—now understood as the process of man's self-creation. To Marx, as to any Hegelian, the actual world of empirical perception was only an imperfect realization—at times indeed a caricature—of the real or rational world, in which man's essential nature (his rationality) will have overcome the reified existence he leads while the surrounding object-world is not perceived as the product of his own creativity. The attainment of this liberated state is the work of history, whose dialectic is not disclosed by empirical perception, but by critical (philosophical) reflection upon the totality of the process. An understanding fixed upon isolated aspects of this totality necessarily falls short of the goal of philosophical reason. It is *ideological* at a second remove, in that it mistakes the reified structures of immediate experience for permanent constituents of reality. It treats phenomena such as war, poverty, class conflict, etc., and so on as permanent features of history, instead of viewing them as temporary objectivations of mankind's gradual and painfully slow emergence from the realm of nature. So understood the concept of ideology recovers its ancient pathos: it is now employed to demonstrate the transitoriness of those arrangements which—irrational in themselves—nonetheless serve the rationality of the whole.

It is only with the loss of this dimension that "ideology" ceases to denote *false consciousness*. It now becomes synonymous with any kind of consciousness that can relate itself to the ongoing activity of a class or group effective enough to make some sort of practical difference. This is the ideology concept of contemporary positivism. Its limited practical relevance ought not to veil its incompatibility with the intellectual tradition (ultimately rooted in classical thought) that is intended when one speaks of the philosophy of history. This philosophy arose from a complex of theoretical and practical problems, of which the original *idéologues*, and their eighteenth-century forerunners, took note in sketching a rudimentary model of world history. Essentially what concerned them was the growth of rationality and the imposition of conscious control upon "natural" chaos. The pragmatic character of this enterprise was never wholly obscured by its theoretical language. It was from the first an attempt to impose an ideal order upon the world, by making an appeal to man's "nature." Its success or failure was and is bound up with the power of Reason to see through the veil of illusions to the enduring realities of human existence. An understanding of what is involved in the concept of ideology is thus at the same time an exercise in that historical imagination which enables us to see our predecessors as men engaged in an enterprise whose outcome still concerns us. In Hegelian language we may say that—the final category retaining and preserving within itself the content of all the previous ones—the unification and pacification of the world (if it can be achieved) will demonstrate that history is indeed a concrete universal. For it is only at this level that what is called world history becomes synonymous with mankind's collective emergence from the state of nature. Whatever their residual differences, this is a perspective which liberalism and Marxism have in common.

Society and Hierarchy*

I

• Intellectual life in Poland has run a checkered course since 1945. A semi-liberal phase, during which something like "ideological coexistence" prevailed, was brought to an end in 1949 when the Stalinist ice cap spread to the satellites. The consequent mental freeze-up lasted until about 1955, to be succeeded first by a gentle thaw, and then by what in Poland is referred to as the "spring in October" of 1956. Since then there have been climatic variations which on the whole have left the major gains of 1956 intact. The process has recently been analyzed at length in Mr. Z. A. Jordan's important study *Philosophy and Ideology*,[1] a volume in the *Sovietica* series published by Fribourg University (Switzerland). This heavily documented work has the special merit of clarifying the relationship of Polish sociology to the country's pre-1939 intellectual tradition. It makes the point *inter alia* that there was a Marxist trend in pre-war Poland which did not depend on Leninism, and to which sociologists could turn after 1956, when the Soviet monopoly had been broken.

The dominant school before the Second World War was, however, that of Florian Znaniecki (1882-1958) whom no one could describe as a Marxist. He was in fact an empiricist who owed something to Durkheim and much to his own prolonged residence in the United States. Under his influence, Polish sociology acquired an orientation familiar to Western students of the subject and quite unacceptable to the doctrinaire Marxist-Leninists who took command in 1945-1949. It was a major tri-

---

* *European Journal of Sociology*, V (1964).
[1] (Dordrecht, 1963.)

umph for them when Znaniecki's best-known pupil, Josef Chalasinski (b. 1904), suddenly went over to them: primarily, it seems, from a conviction that liberalism was exhausted and had nothing further to contribute to either science or society. There were, however, alternative ways of looking at this situation, and after 1956 it became possible for a veteran empiricist such as Professor Ossowski to suggest a *via media* which steered clear of liberal individualism, without for that reason swallowing whole the Marxist-Leninist doctrine to which his distinguished colleague had become a temporary convert. The subsequent changes in the intellectual climate are illustrated by the fact that in 1959 Chalasinski once more reverted to an independent position and was duly penalized by losing his chairmanship of the Academy of Science, while by 1965 he had swung back so far to Marxist-Leninist orthodoxy as to be severely critical of Adam Schaff's discreet moves towards a "humanist" interpretation of Marx.

These circumstances are not irrelevant to a consideration of the late Professor Ossowski's important work *Class Structure in the Social Consciousness*, now at last available in an English translation.[2] Its publication in 1957 (as the author indicated in his preface to the 1963 English-language edition) was a direct sequel to the political events of the preceding year which at last made it possible to scrutinize the theoretical claims of the Leninist school. By now it has once more become questionable whether anything quite so outspoken would pass the censorship, for the pendulum has swung back some distance. This is not to suggest that Ossowski's approach is of the kind which appeals to the more uncritical exponents of liberal individualism in the United States—they can hardly fail to be shocked by his suggestion that the American Creed is a barrier to sociological realism: "As in other capitalistic countries, here too the propaganda disseminated by the ruling class is opposed to sharp divisions in the mode of perception of the social structure because it is opposed to the idea of class struggle. In the United States one must look

[2] (London, 1963); cf. *Struktura Klasowa W Spolecznej Swiadomosci* (Lodz, 1957); a West German edition (*Die Klassenstruktur im sozialen Bewusstsein*) appeared in 1962.

elsewhere for the dichotomic aspect of the social structure. One must look to the relation between the Negro and the white population. In this sphere the dichotomy has endured until the present time. . . ." (p. 36). No encouragement here for liberals. But no comfort either for Leninists in the following observations:

> When the conceptual system and problems of bourgeois sociology were being formulated, when the ideas of Marx and Engels were being developed into a great and cohesive doctrine, the social consequences of the second technical revolution . . . which were to transform the social life of the twentieth century were not yet known. . . . A social system based on the nationalization of the means of production was also unknown. No one could yet have had any experience of the kind of planning which was over a great part of the globe to embrace in a centralized system almost the entire economy, including the production of the so-called "cultural values," and to take over the direction of the labor force, the large-scale distribution of privileges and discriminations, and the conscious shaping of the social structure. . . . Faced with these new experiences, it is hard to resist the impression that the conditions in which the theories of the nineteenth century originated have handicapped the further development of the social sciences (pp. 2-3).

"After the Second World War," the author observes in his preface (dated June 1962), "Poland was an area in which the sociological concepts of Western Europe and the United States clashed with the Marxist method of interpreting phenomena according to the line laid down by the Party. This clash between various ways of thinking stimulated the raising of some special questions . . . and encouraged the search for problems of world-wide importance, despite the view expressed in official circles about the distinctness of the social problems found in the so-called 'Western world' and those of the socialist countries." For all its tactful phrasing, this observation makes it plain why the publication of a realistic inquiry into present-day problems had to await the Polish "spring in October," for between 1949 and 1956 it was not enough to employ Marxist concepts: one had to assert the uniqueness of the "socialist camp" and the radical incompatibility of "bourgeois" and "proletarian" sociology, a di-

chotomy accepted during those hectic years even by some erstwhile empiricists. It was only after the collapse of this faith that
scholars like Ossowski were allowed to get on with their work.
In doing so they discovered that the problems which mattered
to them had perforce to be discussed in terms derived from
Weber and Parsons, as well as Marx. It is the special significance
of Ossowski's work that he places before the reader a study of
class conflict in modern society which transcends the mental
barriers imposed by ideological orthodoxy on both sides of the
great divide.

I I

The problem of class is fundamental to Marxist sociology, and
not surprisingly it stands at the center of Ossowski's critique of
Marx. His conclusion may be anticipated by saying that he regards the Marxian doctrine as time-bound in the sense which
Marx himself imported into the analysis of social history: its
categories are shown to have been derived from a particular
stage in the evolution of industrial society—the bourgeois stage
—which is now closed. In Ossowski's words:

> . . . the experiences of recent years incline us to formulate the
> Marxian concept of social class in the form of a law which estab-
> lishes a functional dependence; the more closely the social system
> approximates to the idea of a free and competitive capitalist soci-
> ety, the more are the classes determined by their relation to the
> means of production, and the more are human relationships deter-
> mined by ownership of the means of production (p. 185).

Under present-day conditions this simple correlation tends to
vanish.

> In situations where changes of social structure are to a greater
> or lesser degree governed by the decision of the political authori-
> ties, we are a long way from social classes as interpreted by Marx,
> Ward, Veblen, or Weber, from classes conceived of as groups
> determined by their relations to the means of production or, as
> others would say, by their relations to the market (p. 184).

The nineteenth-century relationship of state to society having been transformed, both the liberal and the Marxian approach lose much of their relevance.

> In situations where the political authorities can overtly and effectively change the class structure; where the privileges that are most essential for social status, including that of a higher share in the national income, are conferred by a decision of the political authorities; where a large part or even the majority of the population is included in a stratification of the type to be found in a bureaucratic hierarchy—the nineteenth-century concept of class becomes more or less an anachronism, and class conflicts give way to other forms of social antagonism (*ibid.*).

These conclusions have been stressed, partly because the reviewer happens to agree with them, but also because it is in their light that one is bound to judge the conceptual analysis which takes up a good deal of the earlier chapters. Ossowski approaches his major theme, the critique of Marxism, by way of an elaborate investigation into the concept of class. The "dichotomic conception" of society as an assemblage of privileged and oppressed groups is analyzed historically, with reference to traditional revolutionary literature (not neglecting its religious roots), and then confronted with alternative models drawn from the social sciences. The Church fathers, the leaders of the English, American, French, and Russian revolutions, and the classical economists (up to and including Marx), are ransacked for evidence, and in the process the reader is given to understand that the "dichotomic picture" which underlies the *Communist Manifesto* contains important elements of poetic mythmaking. Ossowski notes, however, that Marx the sociologist (as distinct from Marx the revolutionary) operated with a more complex functional scheme, namely the three-class model derived from Adam Smith. Here the social classes—landowners, capitalists, laborers—are seen as functional groups rooted in the economic process. While substantially accepting this picture as valid for the market economy (bourgeois society), Ossowski rejects it for our present situation, east or west of the divide. Thus the Marxian method is finally turned against its originator: the

class struggle is seen to have taken the form it did during a definite historical period which has now come to an end. Setting
aside the "dichotomic scheme," which always rested on a simplified view of society as the rule of the oppressed majority by an
exploiting minority, the genuinely empirical and scientific account given in socialist literature of bourgeois society at its
nineteenth-century peak is shown to have lost its topical value
with the progressive dissolution of that society and its replacement by a differently structured one. This takes care of the conventional criticism of Marx by liberal ideologists anxious to conserve the myth of classlessness. At the same time a critical side
glance is directed at Soviet ideology, which in Ossowski's view is
beginning to resemble its American counterpart in its insistence
that Soviet society, though not (yet) completely classless, is
nonetheless socially harmonious and free of major antagonisms.
There is more than a touch of irony in the observations he devotes to the theme that "classless" does not necessarily mean
"equal":

> Marx's view of the future communist society is associated so
> closely with the term "classless society," and this term has been so
> colored by the striving for universal equality, that the phrase used
> above ("a classless and egalitarian society") might seem redun-
> dant. *But experience has shown* [reviewer's italics] that the term
> "classless society" has acquired another meaning than that in-
> volved in the Marxian ideal type. The abolition of the class sys-
> tem can be understood as the wiping-out of only those inequali-
> ties which result from class divisions. In this sense the abolition of
> social classes does not necessarily mean the abolition of the status-
> hierarchy or of economic inequalities. The liquidation of levels in
> the social structure does not necessarily involve the destruction of
> the social ladder. The abolition of the system of class privileges
> does not entail the abolition of all the privileges whereby individ-
> uals differ from one another. The point is—which of these privi-
> leges are regarded as not being associated with the class-system (p.
> 97).

This is plain enough, and by itself sufficient to indicate the
difference between the mental climate of Warsaw and Moscow.
For the rest, Ossowski follows Marx in treating the concept of

class as the legitimate successor to that of rank or estate, at any rate since the time when the combined impact of the industrial revolution and the democratic revolution destroyed the privileged estates. Some polite irony is expended on the familiar notion that there are no classes in the United States because there is no caste hierarchy in that country (leaving aside the Negro problem). Ossowski has little difficulty in showing that classes (in the Marxian sense) are nowhere more important than under conditions where capitalism has done away with all, or most, non-economic forms of dependence. To the extent that "class" is currently beginning to matter a little less in advanced industrial countries, this is not because these countries are democratic and "socially mobile," but *because market relations are losing their former pre-eminence.*

This last point needs to be dwelt upon, not merely for its evident topical importance, but because it is central to Ossowski's manner of approaching the subject. His purpose is to get away from rival forms of apologetic, and this necessitates a critical attitude towards certain tendencies predominant in American sociology at the present time. He does not by any means ignore stratification according to income, ethnic descent, or social status as experienced by individuals, but treats these features as subsidiary to social analysis according to objective (economic) criteria. "Synthetic gradation," which takes account of the prevailing value systems, is seen as a complication of "economic gradation"—at least so long as market relationships are paramount. "Descent as a determinant of social status is a relic of an estate or caste system. But descent from a wealthy family has continued to play a part in determining social status in bourgeois democracies. Style of life, which is one of the criteria in modern class hierarchies, is in certain respects a legacy of the estate system. The estate tradition of social distance between the various strata has also survived" (p. 51). What he terms "synthetic gradation," "a gradation which we encounter in the social consciousness of various social milieux in the world of yesterday and today," cuts across "simple gradation" according to measurable economic criteria. It also cuts across the functional relationship established under early capitalism, notably the three-class model suggested (or discovered?) by Smith. Ossowski notes (p. 61) that in the United States "class structure is . . . most frequently conceived in terms of a scheme of gradation, but we do in certain instances encounter a functional scheme. Adam Smith's traditional triad here assumes the form of the 'three major functional groups in American society.' These are the farmers, 'labor,' and 'business.'" It is not entirely clear whether Ossowski regards the employment of one or the other model as primarily a matter of convenience. This would of course run counter to the traditional Marxian approach, which treats functional relations as basic, and social gradations as secondary. One has the impression that he is occasionally puzzled by the difficulty which arises when different "models" are viewed as alternative ways of interpreting an infinitely complex reality. "When social status is determined by a synthetic ranking scale," he says (p. 56), "studies of social stratification will be concerned with social consciousness"; while earlier he remarks that "objective relations can be justifiably presented only in terms of a simple gradation," *i.e.*, in accordance with economic criteria.

This leads to a distinction between "economic class" and "social class" which (in the reviewer's opinion) does little to clarify the matters. Are we to understand that social classes are encountered "in the social consciousness," whereas economic classes subsist in themselves? By comparison with such a puzzling notion, even Marx's well-known Hegelian distinction between the "Klasse an sich" and the "Klasse für sich" is a model of simplicity. At least it reduces the whole problem to one of class-consciousness, whereas the choice beween "simple gradation" and "synthetic gradation" suggests the alarming possibility that the understanding of societies may depend upon changing intellectual fashions. No doubt "the concept of synthetic gradation . . . is one of the two ways of conceiving class structure that are most widespread in our time" (p. 56), but that in itself is no great recommendation. One wants to know how realistic this approach is, *i.e.*, how much it tells us about the real world.

Model-building is all very well, but not all models are equally useful. In a later chapter Ossowski remarks that "semantic differences are usually a symptom of differences which reach into the core of the matter (p. 160). The "core of the matter" cannot itself be another semantic quarrel over models, or even over "the assumptions which govern the choice from among differing conceptions of definition" (p. 161). It must have something to do with the actual structure of social reality, as perceived (or not perceived—which happens quite frequently) by the theorist. Fortunately Ossowski's work abounds in insights which would have been closed to him had he contented himself with registering the almost limitless possibilities of conceptual model-building. When he notes "Marx's belief in the immense importance of class divisions" (p. 175), the immediately following observation that "in this respect too we can contrast the Marxian conception not only with American interpretations of the structure of American society, but also with the Stalinist conception of classes in the Soviet Union" is clearly intended to signify more than the possibility of a choice between these differing views. At other times, however, a kind of conceptual relativism creeps in, *e.g.*, remarks such as "Different beliefs about reality will thus find expression in differing conceptions of social class or of the class system. For example, where Soviet ideologists see two non-antagonistic classes and a 'stratum' of intelligentsia, an American sociologist or a Russian *émigré* will perceive six or ten classes as the levels of social stratification" (p. 177). This seems to suggest that it is all a matter of viewpoint: not a very helpful approach, and possibly not Ossowski's real opinion either. Critics of a dogmatic "Establishment" may at times be compelled to take refuge in relativism as a means of undermining doctrinaire certitudes. Still, methodological skepticism, however useful as a corrective to dogma, has its own peculiar shortcomings and in the end carries its own penalties. If there is a general criticism to be made of Ossowski's work—and possibly of the philosophical school from which he stems—it is that he occasionally gives the impression of indifference to this danger.

III

A point that has to be considered in this context is where Ossowski stands in relation to Soviet theorizing on the one hand, and contemporary Western academic sociology on the other. His personal independence of both schools requires no emphasis. "Stalinism" and "bourgeois ideology" appear in his work as a pair of opposites linked by a common concern to make the study of the facts rhyme with presuppositions of a purely political kind. This is the normal socialist viewpoint, and as such certain of a ready echo in Western Europe, as well as among East European scholars no longer wedded to "dogmatism." The extent to which in the Poland of 1956-1957 the critique of institutionalized Leninist teaching could be carried, may be gathered from the following passage:

> In its official interpretation Christianity justified the discrepancy between the principles of Christ's teaching and reality, on the grounds of the corruption of human nature, which made it impossible for the kingdom of God to be realized here on earth. For its part, Marxism had at its disposal the theory of dialectical development. By appealing to this it was possible to justify processes which seemed reactionary from the viewpoint of the aims of Communism, processes in which the gap dividing reality from the postulated future was actually increasing. Using such an interpretation of the dialectical process it was possible to strive for the attainment of a social order in accordance with the postulate of equality by combating egalitarian trends, even for instance by combating the feeling that emerged in periods of general shortage that the types of ration-cards issued to children should not be dependent on their parents' status. It was possible to strive to achieve a state of freedom by placing increasingly severe restrictions on it (p. 189).

This critique of Stalinism is clearly related to some earlier observations (pp. 110 ff.) in a section headed "The problem of classlessness in Soviet society," where the reader is *inter alia* told that "from the viewpoint of Marx and Lenin, 'non-antagonistic' classes constitute a *contradictio in adiecto*." In Soviet theory, the author remarks in passing (p. 113), "The idea that a new

privileged class may be created as a result of the increasing range
of income-differentials is not considered at all." Stalinist doctrine allows for economic privileges and discriminations, provided they do not impinge upon state ownership of the means
of production. That the "state" is itself the collective property
of the new privileged class is a circumstance which falls outside
the conceptual framework that sustains the official ideology. For
Ossowski this is an aspect of a wider problem: the emergence of
a new social hierarchy east and west of the great divide. At the
ideological level, the problem that confronts apologists of the
status quo lies in harmonizing the growth of inequality with
the concept of classlessness. As Ossowski puts it, "the concept of
the classless non-egalitarian society . . . is used for the characterization of one's own society in the leading countries of both
the socialist and the capitalist world" (p. 117).

It is arguable that liberalism and Marxism do not experience
the same difficulty in dealing with this phenomenon, since the
liberal creed does not place much stress upon substantial equality (as distinct from "equality of opportunity"), but this is perhaps a minor point. In principle, we may agree that the situation
is experienced in ways which are similar, save that the "open
society" of the West does not require a monolithic myth to sustain it and an infallible authority to back it up. Here perhaps
Ossowski is at fault: for all the obvious resemblances (when one
thinks of the disingenuous talk about "people's capitalism"), it
may be thought that he might have stressed the function of the
totalitarian strait-jacket in contrast to the pluralist character of
Western society and the consequent relative freedom of criticism. An intellectual position independent both of the Soviet
creed and of the conventional assumptions dominant in Western society, can accomplish one of two things: it can point beyond accepted thought patterns to a new synthesis or it can content itself with registering the inadequacies of the prevailing
modes of thought. I have already cited Ossowski's observations
on the relationship of state to society. Here he breaks new
ground, or at any rate affirms a distinctively modern standpoint,
in stressing the reversal of the nineteenth-century pattern. If the

state was ever an epiphenomenon, it has certainly ceased to be one, and to that extent the Marxian analysis (not to mention its liberal predecessor) is no longer applicable. This is true and important, and one only wishes that Ossowski had said more about it. The reviewer is less happy with the author's concern over the methodology of class analysis. Once it has been shown that the concept of class was appropriate to the epoch which began with the French Revolution and ended in our own days (p. 126), it is surely unnecessary to torture oneself with doubt over the respective usefulness of "models" representing quite different levels of abstraction (and quite different stages in the evolution of social theory):

> Do we follow Marx in placing the main emphasis on the system of privileges and discriminations, on exploitation and in general on asymmetrical relations of dependence? Or do we follow Madison or Max Weber (when he speaks of class structure) in stressing the distinctness of interests? Or again, are we at one with modern American sociologists in acknowledging class consciousness as the most socially-important fact in the domain of intergroup relations, and do we, in describing a "class" society—despite the suggestive terminology—give primacy to the characteristics which Weber links with his concept of an estate, not with the concept of class? (p. 139).

This seems needlessly confusing. Madison (hardly a systematic thinker) had barely sensed the transformation of "rank" into "class" which was only just beginning when he wrote. Weber, on the other hand, coupled his analysis with considerations proper to Wilhelminian Germany, a country in which capitalism had not (yet) completely transformed the pre-bourgeois order. At the same time he was paradoxically conscious of certain problems lying beyond the horizon of the liberal age, and to that extent he employed his successful bowdlerization of Marx (in which he was presently succeeded with even greater aplomb by Schumpeter) in a manner pointing to our current post-liberal preoccupations. As for the more fashionable "modern American sociologists," it is perhaps charitable to suppose that they are

not aware of the extent to which they draw on unexamined sup-
positions current in the milieu in which they live and move and
have their being. Can one really say that they "take class-
consciousness as a criterion of the class system" (p. 138) when
their labors seem largely devoted to the systematic blurring of
the distinction between (functional economic) groups in the
classical (Smithian and Marxian) sense, social strata arising
from the division of labor, and transient differences due to "up-
ward social mobility"? What can be the use of contrasting or
combining such diverse "models," unless it be for the purpose
of showing that even under "classical" conditions the function-
ally separated major classes of society split up into sub-groups?
But who ever doubted this? Conversely, given the fact that the
classical model has been partly rendered inoperative by the
transformation of the society to which it was proper, are we to
suppose that its place can now be taken by the so-called "psychological concept of class"?

The reviewer has the impression that Ossowski was troubled
by these questions because on his (philosophical) assumptions
it seemed probable that the desired synthesis could finally be
attained by combining as many different viewpoints as possible,
while allowing for the inevitable ideological elements in each of
them. This of course is standard procedure among adherents of
Wissenssoziologie. One is conscious of partisanship in express-
ing the opinion that their approach has a tendency to bog down
in skepticism. If every system of thought is ideological, and if
every ideology is sustained by illusions, the distinction between
genuine (though limited) insight and mere obfuscation cannot
be long maintained. On the whole it seems more sensible to
work on the principle that some systems are superior to others,
though this does not justify the Leninist nonsense about "class
standpoints." One may agree that many important scientific ad-
vances have initially depended upon metaphysical assumptions
which later had to be discarded, or upon generalizations which
subsequently had to be qualified. For the rest, the extent to
which a system of thought escapes from social or cultural "con-

ditioning" is measured by its achievements, though it has to be admitted that unanimity on this subject is difficult to establish. Nor does it seem particularly desirable that it should.

In conclusion, it may be suggested—perhaps a little unfairly—that in this part of his work Ossowski in 1956-1957 was groping for the concept of "industrial society," since then made familiar in Western sociology by the work of Dahrendorf and others. I say "groping" because it does not really carry one very far to be told about the rise of "a new middle class . . . a class of civil servants, trade union officials, local government officers, a class of technicians, white-collar workers and minor executives in the large industrial establishments" (p. 183). This is familiar stuff and does not by itself suggest that the classical model is out-moded. "Minor executives," even though swollen in number, don't make a new social order, unless the "major executives" are no longer the same people. It is perfectly true that since "the time of de Tocqueville and Marx" the new stratum has expanded to a point where "this marginal group among the classes in the Marxian scheme has so increased in size in contemporary America that it is impossible not to regard it as a class, especially when we consider general trends of development in the United States" (p. 183). And no doubt "this new class, which has a corresponding group in the 'stratum' of non-manual white-collar workers in state and local government and in party offices in the U.S.S.R. is, it would seem, even characterized by its own social attitudes and its own sub-culture" (*ibid.*). But unless it serves as the basis for a new directing stratum, this circumstance in itself has little political (or theoretical) relevance. What has changed the situation is the fact that there is a new ("techno-cratic") directing and governing stratum, which is about to take over the state, after having successfully captured the key positions within modern industrial society. Is it not precisely this development which helps to account for the circumstance (noted elsewhere by the author) that the modern state shows a quite novel capacity for refashioning society through a planned "revolution from above"?

In this context it is legitimate to ask whether we may not be able to salvage something from the Marxian analysis, even though the three-class model Marx inherited from Smith and Ricardo no longer reflects the reality of modern, post-bourgeois, industrial society. As has rightly been remarked, for Marx the concept of class led not to a static theory of social stratification, but to a dynamic theory of social change—where "change" refers not to internal modifications within a given social system, but to the total ("historical") transformation of the whole society. For the purpose of such a theory (which could dispense with photographic accuracy in picturing social trivia) the three-class model, or even the simplified two-class model (with the landowners subsumed under the general category of property owners) was adequate. Class was employed as an analytical category relative to the historical process which was expected to transform a particular society, the bourgeois one, into its own opposite. Even if one believes that Marx made the analytical mistake of identifying bourgeois with industrial society (and thus failed to see that a socialist order would not necessarily be classless), it is arguable that his general mode of approach is more fruitful than the prevailing academic fashion which dispenses with the concept of "laws of development." That a relentless application of Marx's own analysis leads to pessimistic conclusions concerning the prospects of a genuinely egalitarian form of socialism, is of course no objection at all. One has the impression that Ossowski would have assented to this conclusion. At any rate it is within these terms that his own work appears destined to take its place when an account of contemporary social thought comes to be written.

Oriental Despotism*

I

• Since the appearance in 1957 of Professor Karl A. Witt-fogel's important work on Oriental society[1] it has gradually become known in academic circles that there exists a problem in Marxist sociology which has to do with Marx's and Engels' views on Asiatic society, and with the gradual abandonment of these views in the Soviet Union, notably during the so-called Stalinist era. In what follows I propose to take for granted some awareness of the standard Soviet approach in these matters, with the obvious proviso that one cannot foretell the possible consequences in the theoretical sphere of a more thorough de-Stalinization, let alone of an open conflict between the U.S.S.R. and China. A partial return to genuine Leninism, as distinct from Stalinism, is a possibility which must be taken into account, but for reasons which cannot be elaborated in this space even this would not help much towards a restoration of the authentic Marxian approach, to say nothing of a critical interpretation of Marx's and Engels' writings on the subject of Asiatic society. The reader who is interested in Leninism, as distinct from Marxism, must be referred to Professor Wittfogel.[2]

* (Originally titled "Marx and the 'Asiatic Mode of Production,'"), *St. Antony's Papers*, XIV (Oxford-London, 1963).

[1] *Oriental Despotism: A Comparative Study of Total Power* (New Haven, and London and New York, 1957).

[2] *Ibid.*, pp. 372 ff. For a reasonably intelligent and scholarly restatement of the orthodox Leninist standpoint cf. the Introduction to the selection entitled "Marx on China 1853-1860," ed. Dona Torr (London, 1951). Anyone curious to sample a specimen of authentic Soviet writing, as distinct from what might be called Anglo-Leninism, is advised to compare this doctrinaire but scholarly piece of editing with the characteristically dishonest and imbecilic Introduction to the Marx-Engels selection on India issued by the Moscow Institute of Marxism-Leninism in 1959 under the title *The First Indian War of Independence*.

It has to be admitted at the outset that this distinction is not quite watertight, inasmuch as Lenin—at any rate down to 1917 —did operate within the Marxian concept of an "Asiatic society" and an "Asiatic mode of production." It is apparent, however, that even in those early writings of his in which he characterized the Tsarist regime as semi-Asiatic, he did not relate this concept clearly or systematically to the dominant role of the bureaucracy, but rather tended to overstress the role of the landowners, or even to describe the Tsarist government as one dominated by the landed nobility. The resulting medley of genuinely theoretical concepts and merely political slogans revolved around the question whether Russia might or might not relapse into what Lenin himself at times described as "the restoration of our old 'semi-Asiatic' order" or as "the restoration of the Asiatic mode of production." The most one can say is that he was aware of the problem, both as a theoretical issue having to do with the character of Oriental society and as a practical concern for those who wished to break with Russia's semi-Asiatic past. The matter was complicated by the factional debates in which he was involved, and which at various times led him to stress one aspect rather than another. Thus in 1905 he was quite ready to advocate a bourgeois development and even to suggest that the revolution then in progress would, if it were victorious, "for the first time really clear the ground for a widespread and rapid European, not Asiatic, development of capitalism" in Russia;[3] whereas from 1906 onwards he showed a tendency to water down the "Asiatic" concept and to employ the ambiguous terms "medieval," "patriarchal," or "pre-capitalist." [4] In 1911, in a comment on Tolstoy's writings, he reverted once more to the theme, this time to suggest that down to the revolution of 1905 Russia had been a country where "the Oriental, the Asiatic order" predominated. By this he evidently meant more than that Russia had until then been governed autocratically, since that would

[3] Cf. *Two Tactics* in *Selected Works* (London, 1947), I, p. 375.

[4] Wittfogel, *op. cit.*, p. 394. In a pamphlet written in 1907 he even used the term "state feudalism," which had apparently been coined by one of his Menshevik opponents a year earlier to designate the peculiar character of Russian medievalism.

also have been true of Bourbon France, or of Prussia before 1848; but what exactly he did mean is not quite clear, though he went on to say that the upheaval of 1905 was "the beginning of the end of 'Oriental' quiescence," which rather suggests that he was thinking along lines familiar to Marxists at that time.

The opposite of "quiescence" is "movement" and most Socialists—following Marx—were then in the habit of giving qualified approval to the capitalist form of progress, though without idealizing it and while stressing its catastrophic impact on backward countries and exploited classes. The roots of this attitude are clearly traceable to the *Communist Manifesto*, where it is observed that capitalism "batters down all Chinese walls" and "compels all nations on pain of extinction to adopt the bourgeois mode of production." [5] The reference to Chinese walls is scarcely accidental: when Marx drafted the *Manifesto* the first Opium War had recently been fought, and there is a characteristic remark in the same passage on "the barbarians' intensely obstinate hatred of foreigners," which "the bourgeoisie" has to overcome in its relentless march to world domination: the process whereby it "draws all, even the most barbarian, nations into civilization." Whatever he thought of the means whereby this result had been accomplished, the distinction between Eastern barbarism (or "stagnation") and Western progress ("civilization") was one that Marx in 1848 was not disposed to question.

II

When we turn to the writings composed by Marx—with some assistance from Engels—in the early 1850s, we encounter the same ambivalent attitude towards "progress" that had already characterized the *Manifesto*, plus a special undertone arising from the fact that both men were then settled in England and commenting upon British colonial affairs in a leading American newspaper.[6] Though one would not gather as much from the

[5] Cf. Marx-Engels, *Selected Works* (Moscow, 1958), I, p. 38.
[6] Cf. *Marx on China*; there is still no adequate English-language edition of the mass of articles contributed by Marx and Engels to the *New York*

Soviet editors of their works, their strictures upon British rule in India, or the British government's behavior towards China, were substantially in tune with the "bourgeois" radicalism of the period, and in some respects anticipated the standard anti-colonialism of later American writing. Marx's caustic comments on British colonial policy clearly went down well with his American readers for reasons which had little to do with his own theoretical approach. In some respects indeed he took a more tolerant view of British rule than they did, since he tended to regard the impact of capitalism upon Oriental society as beneficial in the long run, whereas the *Tribune*'s line reflected an anti-industrial bias which he did not share. Thus on June 14, 1853, one finds him writing to Engels:

> The *Tribune* of course trumpets Carey's book with all its might. Both indeed have this in common that under the guise of Sismondian-philanthropic-socialistic anti-industrialism they represent the protectionist, i.e., the industrial bourgeoisie of America. This also explains the secret why the *Tribune*, despite its "isms" and its socialistic humbug, can be the "leading journal" in the United States. . . . I have continued this camouflaged warfare in a first article on India, in which the destruction of the native industry by England is described as *revolutionary*. This will be very shocking to them.[7]

The reference is to an article entitled "British Rule in India" which appeared in the *Tribune* on June 25, 1853,[8] and in which Marx for the first time expressed a considered opinion about the nature of Oriental society. It is amusing to find that one of the key ideas of this important article had been suggested by an im-

---

Daily Tribune (hereafter *NYDT*) between 1852 and 1862. The two-volume edition arranged by D. Ryazanov (*Gesammelte Schriften von Karl Marx und Friedrich Engels 1852-62* [Stuttgart, 1920]) covers only the first four years of that period; the official East German *Gesammelte Werke* presents the complete text, but laboriously translated into German, instead of the original English-language version, and must therefore be treated with caution.

[7] Marx-Engels, *Selected Correspondence* (Moscow, 1956), p. 102.

[8] Cf. "Die britische Herrschaft in Indien," *Gesammelte Werke* (Berlin, 1960), 9, pp. 127 ff.; *The First Indian War of Independence 1857-1859* (Moscow, 1959, London, 1960), pp. 14 ff.; quotations are from the latter work which presumably reproduces the original text; cf. also the photo-offprint facing p. 128 of the Berlin edition.

promptu remark dropped by Engels. On June 6, 1853, in a letter
to Marx on the general subject of Oriental history,[9] Engels had
thrown out the suggestion that "an Oriental government never
had more than three departments: finance (plunder at home),
war (plunder at home and abroad), and public works (provision
for reproduction). The British Government in India has admin-
istered Nos. 1 and 2 in a rather more philistine fashion[10] and
dropped No. 3 entirely, so that Indian agriculture is being ru-
ined." Marx incorporated these observations in his article, and
went on to outline some ideas on the genesis of Oriental society
and the "Asiatic mode of production":

> Climate and territorial conditions, especially the vast tracts of des-
> ert extending from the Sahara through Arabia, Persia, India and
> Tartary, to the most elevated Asiatic highlands, constituted artifi-
> cial irrigation by canals and waterworks the basis of Oriental agri-
> culture. . . . This prime necessity of an economical and
> common use of water, which in the Occident drove private enter-
> prise to voluntary association, as in Flanders and Italy, necessi-
> tated in the Orient, where civilization was too low [sic] and the
> territorial extent too vast to call into life voluntary association, the
> interference of the centralizing power of government. Hence an
> economical function devolved upon all Asiatic governments, the
> function of providing public works.[11]

For Marx and Engels this state of affairs ("the Hindu . . .
leaving like all Oriental peoples to the Central government the
care of the great public works . . .") was connected with a circumstance to which Marx referred in the same article, namely
the dispersion of the population "in small centres by the domes-
tic union of agricultural and manufacturing pursuits," i.e., in
self-governing villages; now these small units, "inoffensive
though they may appear, had always been the solid foundation
of Oriental despotism," their inhabitants being totally indifferent to whatever went on around them, including massacres and

---

[9] Selected Correspondence, pp. 99 ff.; cf. Marx-Engels Gesamtausgabe
(hereafter MEGA), Third Department, I, pp. 480 ff., for the full text.
[10] Cf. Selected Correspondence: "in a rather narrow-minded spirit"; this
is clearly a mistranslation due to the translator's failure to appreciate irony.
[11] Op. cit., p. 16. Cf. Henry M. Christman, ed., The American Journalism of Marx and Engels (New York, 1966), p. 96.

foreign invasions.[12] It was this passivity which had made despotism possible in the first place. But how had "this undignified, stagnatory, and vegetative life . . . this passive sort of existence" come into being? The exchange of letters hints at an answer. On June 2, 1853, Marx observes apropos of François Bernier's eighteenth-century *Travels Containing a Description of the Dominions of the Great Mogul*: "Bernier rightly considers the basis [*Grundform*] of all Oriental phenomena—he refers to Turkey, Persia, Hindustan—to be the *absence of private property in land*. This is the real key, even to the Oriental heaven." [13] Engels echoes this judgment in his answering letter of June 6: ". . . The absence of property in land is indeed the key to the entire Orient. Herein lies the political and religious history. But how does it come about that the Orientals did not arrive at landed property, even in its feudal form? I think it is mainly due to the climate, taken in connection with the nature of the soil, especially the great stretches of desert. . . . Artificial irrigation is here the first condition of agriculture, and this is a matter either for the communes, the provinces, or the central government." Follow the remarks about the character of Oriental rule which have already been quoted and which Marx reproduced in his article.

At this stage, then, Marx and Engels are agreed that (1) there is no Oriental feudalism; (2) its absence is synonymous with the non-existence of private landed property, which in turn is due to climatic conditions; (3) the centralized Oriental despotism has arisen from the need to provide artificial irrigation; (4) the forcible destruction of the system by the British, whatever its motivation, is about to introduce the preconditions of "progress" in the Western sense, albeit at immense cost. In the Hegelian manner, Marx in his article poses the historical problem philosophically ("The question is, can mankind fulfil its destiny

[12] *Ibid.*, pp. 18-20. Cf. Marx to Engels, June 14, 1853, *MEGA* III/1, p. 487; *Selected Correspondence*, pp. 103-104: "I believe one cannot imagine a more solid foundation for a stagnant Asiatic despotism. And however much the English may have Hibernicized the country, the breaking up of these stereotyped archaic forms was the *sine qua non* of Europeanization." (Tr. from German text.)

[13] Cf. *MEGA* III/1, p. 477; *Selected Correspondence* pp. 97-99.

without a fundamental revolution in the social state of Asia? If not, whatever may have been the crimes of England, she was the unconscious tool of history in bringing about that revolution"). In our context this is immaterial, except insofar as it supplies the explanation of his readiness to include the destruction of Indian handicrafts among the *faux frais* of history. The real theoretical problem lies elsewhere. When Marx, in a subsequent article on India,[14] looks forward to the time when the Indians will "reap the fruits of the new elements of society scattered among them by the British bourgeoisie," he is simply being "progressive" in a manner which today permits every Asian nationalist to applaud him, especially since he also alludes to the time when "the Hindus themselves shall have grown strong enough to throw off the English yoke." But if Marx had merely been another nineteenth-century progressive his views would not command special interest. The question is what can be made of his scattered and unsystematic notions about Oriental society and the "Asiatic mode of production."

Before turning to this theme it may be as well to round off the factual account with some quotations from Marx's references to China which date from roughly the same period, *i.e.*, the 1850s. In this connection little weight need be given to his (or Engels') humorous forecast of a time to come when the last European reactionaries, having taken refuge in Asia and finally reached that ancient bastion of conservatism, the Great Wall of China, would find inscribed upon its gates the dreadful words: "*République chinoise—Liberté, Egalité, Fraternité.*" [15] If the joke shows anything, it is that to Marx and Engels in 1850 "the revolution" signified more or less what it did to all their democratic contemporaries.[16] "Chinese socialism," they observe with a touch of condescension, "may stand in the same relation to European socialism as does Chinese philosophy to that of Hegel. But it is nonetheless an amusing circumstance [*sic*] that the oldest and most unshakable empire on earth should within eight

14 *NYDT*, August 8, 1853; cf. *Selected Works*, I, p. 356.
15 *Neue Rheinische Revue*, London, January 31, 1850 (reprinted in book form [Berlin, 1955], see p. 121); cf. also *Marx on China*, p. xvii.
16 *Ibid.*

years have been brought by the cotton-bales of the English
bourgeoisie to the eve of a social revolution which cannot fail to
have the most important consequences for civilization." [17] That
Marx and Engels regarded this prospect as "amusing" as well as
inevitable testifies not only to the sense of security and superiority which they shared with most other Europeans but also to
their intellectual descent from Hegel, who in his lectures on
world history had drawn an unflattering picture of the Celestial
Empire.[18] Marx's essential Hegelianism, whenever he has occasion to discuss the probable fate of an ancient and now stagnant
civilization, is well exemplified by the concluding passage of one
of his articles on China in the late 1850s:

> While the semi-barbarian stood on the principle of morality, the
> civilized opposed to him the principle of self. That a giant em-
> pire, containing almost a third of the human race, vegetating in
> the teeth of time, insulated by the forced exclusion of general
> intercourse, and thus contriving to dupe itself with delusions of
> Celestial perfection—that such an empire should at last be over-
> taken by fate on the occasion of a deadly duel in which the repre-
> sentative of the antiquated world appears prompted by ethical
> motives, while the representative of [the] overwhelming modern
> society fights for the privilege of buying in the cheapest and sell-
> ing in the dearest markets—this indeed is a sort of tragical coup-
> let, stranger than any poet would ever have dared to fancy.[19]

This elegiac note is struck repeatedly in the writings he devoted
to China in 1858-1859, while the struggle to "open up" the
Treaty Ports was in progress, but it is only towards the end of
this period that Marx—by now in the throes of drafting his
major economic work and with the *Critique of Political Economy* already behind him—pulls the strands of his theoretical argument together:

> It is this same combination of husbandry with manufacturing in-
> dustry which for a long time withstood, and still checks, the ex-
> port of British wares to East India; but there the combination was

[17] *Ibid.*
[18] Cf. *Vorlesungen über die Philosophie der Weltgeschichte*, ed. Lasson
(Leipzig, 1920-1923), especially I, pp. 232 ff., II, pp. 275 ff.
[19] NYDT, published as an unsigned editorial, September 20, 1858; cf.
Marx on China, p. 55; *Gesammelte Werke* (Berlin, 1961), 12, p. 552.

based upon a peculiar constitution of the landed property which the British, in their position as the supreme landlords of the country, had it in their power to undermine, and thus forcibly convert part of the Hindu self-sustaining communities into mere farms producing opium, cotton, indigo, hemp, and other raw materials, in exchange for British stuffs. In China the English have not yet wielded this power, nor are they likely ever to do so.[20]

Oriental society clearly is something more complex than a system of canals. It has to do, on the one hand, with centralized regulation of the basic economic functions and, on the other, with the prevalence of the self-sufficient village economy. But still the key, as we have seen earlier, has to be sought in the "absence of private property in land."

III

In January 1859, when writing the Preface to the *Critique of Political Economy*, Marx for the first (and last) time gave a summary of his method that indicates the exact relationship in which the economic process ("the mode of production of material life") stands to the historical process generally; and it is here, towards the close of the now classic formulation of the "materialist conception of history," that he introduces his four historical stages: "In broad outlines, Asiatic, ancient, feudal, and modern bourgeois modes of production can be designated as progressive epochs in the economic formation of society." [21] He was never again to display a similar degree of certainty in assigning their relative place to those forms of society which had embodied their characteristic features in definite stages of recorded history. Yet the general standpoint laid down in the Preface was not superseded or even substantially modified. (The qualifications introduced by Engels in the *Anti-Dühring* and the

[20] *NYDT*, December 3, 1859; cf. *Marx on China*, pp. 91-92; *Gesammelte Werke*, 13, p. 544.

[21] *Selected Works*, I, p. 363. The translation fails to convey the Hegelian ring of the original. Since an exact rendering of Hegelian thinking on world history into English is a stylistic impossibility, one is left with the bare statement that Marx echoes Hegel not only in distinguishing four major epochs of world history but also in the confident Europeanocentrism with which he pronounces sentence upon the three preceding ones.

Origins of the Family are not, in my opinion, of basic importance.[22]) There are four, and only four, major historical epochs,
the Asiatic being the first, and each corresponds to a definite
social order which in turn lays the foundation for the succeeding
one. These two aspects are internally related, but must nonetheless for analytical purposes be considered separately.

To start, then, with the "Asiatic mode" taken by itself, we
have already seen which features can be said to distinguish it. In
his unsystematic fashion, Engels had suggested two: climatic
conditions and the pervasive habits of an Oriental government.
Marx expanded these hints into a system by tracing the peculiar
character of Oriental society to the absence of private ownership
in land.[23] He related this to the overriding role of the central
government by suggesting that under the "Asiatic system" the
State was the "real landlord." [24] So far as private property in land
is concerned we are left in no doubt what Marx thought of its
role in dissolving the "Asiatic mode," since in the third and
concluding of his important *Tribune* articles on British rule in
India he expressly described it as "the great *desideratum* of Asiatic society," [25] for the sake of which the infamies practiced by
the Indian *zamindar* and *ryotwar* systems, "abominable as they
are," should nonetheless be regarded as a step towards the
emancipation of Indian society. Now what of the role played by
the State? That in Asia it was the "real landlord" Marx never
doubted. For proof we have the passage in *Capital*, volume III,

[22] For a different view, cf. Wittfogel, *op. cit.*, pp. 382 ff.
[23] Engels' notion that the failure of Oriental society to develop private
landed ownership was "mainly due to the climate" is a trifle naïve, and
looks back to Hegel or even Montesquieu: one of the many instances of
his tendency to relapse into ordinary cause-and-effect explanation, in the
manner of the Enlightenment. The point cannot be pursued here; the
reader of Hegel's *Vorlesungen*, I, pp. 178 ff., can easily discover where
Engels obtained his basic notions about Oriental history. Marx, though
equally inclined to take a Hegelian view of the historical process, relied
for his factual information upon the classical economists, down to and
including J. S. Mill, and upon British Blue Books and other official or
semi-official sources.
[24] *NYDT*, August 5, 1853; cf. *Gesammelte Werke*, 9, p. 218; this
article has for some reason not been included in any English-language
collection known to the writer.
[25] *NYDT*, August 8, 1853; cf. *Selected Works*, I, p. 353.

where he refers to the situation of the producers being confronted not by a private landowner, "but rather, as in Asia, under direct subordination to a State which stands over them as their landlord and simultaneously as sovereign." [26] These characteristics of "Asiatic society"—State control over the producer, and absence of private property in land—are presumably related to the strategic role of the central government in administering the irrigation system, but how does this complex interrelationship come about *historically?* Engels never bothered about such difficult questions, but from Marx we are entitled to expect an answer. Let us see how far he has provided one.

An indirect clue is afforded by his observation that where the small peasants "form among themselves a more or less natural production community, as they do in India . . . the surplus labour for the nominal owner of the land can only be extorted from them by other than economic pressure, whatever the form assumed may be." [27] This is followed by the remark about the State-sovereign doubling as landlord, so that taxes and ground-rents coincide. Marx then continues: "Under such circumstances there need exist no harder political or economic dependence than that common to all subjection to that State. The State is then the supreme lord. Sovereignty here consists in the ownership of land concentrated on a national scale. Conversely, no private ownership of land exists, although there is both private and common possession and use of land." [28]

Does this point in the direction of a theory of conquest or some other form of political usurpation which blocks the emergence of true "private ownership" of land, leaving the subject peasant population only with "possession and use"? The puzzling thing is that the immediately following sentence states: "The specific economic form in which unpaid surplus labour is

[26] Quoted after the Moscow, 1960, English-language edition, p. 771.

[27] *Capital*, III, p. 771. Marx here appends a footnote which adds: "Following the conquest of a country, the immediate aim of the conqueror was also to convert its people to his own use. Cf. Linguet. See also Möser." It is not quite clear whether this refers to Indian conditions or whether it is meant to stand indifferently for all cases where peasant proprietors fall under some form of non-economic exploitation.

[28] *Ibid.*, pp. 771-772 (cited after the German text).

pumped out of [the] direct producers determines the relationship of rulers and ruled, as it grows directly out of production
itself and in turn reacts upon it as a determining element. Upon
this, however, is founded the entire formation of the economic
community which grows up out of the production relations
themselves, (and) therewith simultaneously its specific political
form." [29] Other parts of the same chapter refer to serfdom and
similar forms of socio-economic bondage.[30] It must be borne
in mind that vol. III of *Capital* was pieced together by Engels
from unfinished drafts. Even so it remains uncertain how
Marx envisaged the historical genesis of a relationship which
counterposes the State as supreme landlord to the peasant-
producer. He makes it quite clear, however, that it is the domi-
nance of the State which excludes genuine private ownership of
land, *i.e.*, the precondition of feudalism. If anything defines
"the Orient" according to Marx (and Engels) it is this supremacy of the State, which reduces the landowners to the role of
merely "nominal landlords" as Marx calls them.[31] There cannot
then have been any genuine Oriental feudalism, at any rate not
in India and China, the two Asian countries to which Marx had
given some systematic attention. That he regarded their problems as broadly similar appears from a passage in *Capital*, vol.
III, where he refers to the impact of European commerce upon
Eastern societies:

> The obstacles presented by the internal solidity and organization
> of pre-capitalistic, national modes of production to the corrosive
> influence of commerce are strikingly illustrated in the intercourse
> of the English with India and China. The broad basis of the
> mode of production here is formed by the unity of small-scale
> agriculture and home industry, to which in India we should add
> the form of village communities built upon the common owner-

---

[29] *Ibid.*, p. 772; for the original text, cf. *Das Kapital* (Berlin, 1949),
III, pp. 841-842. The authorized English translation published in Moscow
is both wooden and inaccurate.

[30] *Ibid.*, pp. 772-774.

[31] The context makes it clear that this refers to the original pre-
conquest Indian landowners, and not only to the *zamindars*, as might be
supposed from Marx's characterization of the latter as tax-gatherers imposed by the British government upon the wretched Bengali peasants (cf.
NYDT, August 5, 1853).

ship of land, which incidentally was the original form in China as well. In India the English lost no time in exercising their direct political and economic power, as rulers and landlords, to disrupt these small economic communities. English commerce exerted a revolutionary influence on these communities and tore them apart only insofar as the low prices of its goods served to destroy the spinning and weaving industries which were an ancient integrating element of this unity of industrial and agricultural production. Even so this work of dissolution proceeds very gradually. And still more slowly in China, where it is not reinforced by direct political power. The substantial economy and saving in time afforded by the association of agriculture with manufacture put up a stubborn resistance to the products of the big industries whose prices include the *faux frais* of the circulation process which pervades them. Unlike the English, Russian commerce, on the other hand, leaves the economic ground-work of Asiatic production untouched.[32]

The interest of this passage is that it shows Marx, in the 1860s and while at work on *Capital,* reverting to the theme of his early newspaper articles. He does so also in a footnote in which the "absurd (in practice infamous) economic experiments" conducted by the British in India are duly condemned, with special reference to the creation of "a caricature of large-scale English estates" in Bengal.[33] Yet we have seen that in 1853 he had described private property in land as "the great *desideratum* of Asiatic society," and expressly mentioned the *zamindars.* There is of course no contradiction if one bears in mind that for Marx the rupture of India's ancient stagnation involved the payment of a terrible price in exploitation and dislocation. But the new stress in *Capital* on the futility and absurdity of these "economic experiments," together with the reference to the solidity

[32] Cited after Moscow edition, pp. 328-329; Engels' qualifying footnote (appended in 1894, *i.e.*, almost thirty years after Marx had written these lines), about Russian commerce having in the meantime become genuinely capitalistic, does not affect the substance of the argument. Incidentally, the Soviet translation is not merely scandalously bad but in parts positively misleading, *e.g.*, the key sentence really ought to run as follows: "Insofar as their commerce here revolutionizes the mode of production, it does so only as through the low price of their merchandise they destroy the spinning and weaving which constitutes an ancient and integrating part of this union of industrial-agricultural production and thus disrupt the communities."
[33] *Loc. cit.*, p. 328n.

of the ancient social structure built upon the union of farming and handicrafts, does strike rather a different note. When he remarks that "in the north-west they (sc. the English) did all they could to transform the Indian economic community with common ownership of the soil into a caricature of itself" [34] he seems to be saying, or at least hinting, that but for this outside interference the village community might have evolved in a sounder direction. Then there is the passing reference to the economic savings inherent in small-scale enterprise, as against the *faux frais* of modern large-scale industry—this last a familiar theme in socialist literature since Fourier, but one to which Marx normally did not give a great deal of attention. Altogether the tone of this passage seems to anticipate his well-known observations upon the prospects of the Russian village community in the 1880s: there is a hint of "Narodism" about it. [35]

It is, I think, a fair inference from these passages that while in the 1850s Marx was inclined to emphasize the progressive role of Western capitalism in disrupting Oriental stagnation, by the time he came to draft his major economic work he was less certain that traditional society embodied no positive factors. At any rate, it may be said that by the 1860s his attitude had become ambivalent. We now find him remarking upon the stability of the ancient village communities, in a manner suggesting that he saw some genuine virtue in their peculiar mode of life. At the same time his hostility to capitalism had deepened. This is worth stressing as a qualification of the familiar statement that he had by the 1860s lost some of his early revolutionary ardor. If one has in mind his former attachment to a rather Jacobinical view of the coming European revolution, it is true to say that he grew more moderate in the measure that he became the theorist of a genuine labor movement with democratic aims. But at the

[34] *Ibid.*

[35] For Lenin's view on this issue, which of course was central to the gradual emergence of Russian Marxism from its Populist chrysalis, see his rather agitated defense of the "real" Marx against the Narodniks (who naturally quoted *Capital*, volume III, when it suited them) in *The Development of Capitalism in Russia* (1900; new ed., Moscow, 1956), pp. 310 ff.

same time he sharpened his critique of bourgeois society and the operation of capitalism as an economic system. The *Manifesto*, rather paradoxically, had celebrated the triumphant march of capitalism at the same time that it proclaimed the proletariat's coming victory. By the time Marx wrote *Capital* he was more concerned with factory legislation than with the proletarian revolution, but this did not make him more tolerant of "the system"; rather less so. The note of indulgence has vanished, and the tone has become one of unqualified hostility and contempt. In 1847 the bourgeoisie still gained some plaudits for battering down the Chinese walls of barbarism; by 1867 even the "Asiatic mode" comes in for favorable comment, at any rate so far as the village community is concerned: it is valued as a bulwark against social disintegration.

IV

Here, then, is something like a hiatus in the argument. To some extent the difficulty arises from the fact that the more strictly historical part of Marx's theory of Oriental society is to be found in the posthumously published draft for *Das Kapital*, the so-called *Grundrisse*.[36] Before turning to this theme it may be as well to note where he departs from his predecessors. There was an eighteenth-century and early-nineteenth-century view of Asian society with which Marx was thoroughly familiar. It is briefly but succinctly set out in the *Wealth of Nations*, and it is amusing to find that Smith, like Marx, refers to Bernier's travels as a source.[37] Chinese isolationism and indifference to foreign trade attracted the unfavorable attention of Smith who thought

[36] Cf. *Grundrisse der Kritik der politischen Ökonomie (Rohentwurf)* 1857-1858 (Berlin, 1953); originally published in two volumes (Moscow, 1939-41); part of this draft (over a thousand pages in print) was revised and published by Marx in 1859 under the title *Zur Kritik der politischen Ökonomie*; the bulk was reworked from 1863 onwards into what is now called *Das Kapital*.

[37] Cf. *Wealth of Nations* (New York, 1937), p. 688, where the title of Bernier's *Voyages contenant la description des états du Grand Mogol*, etc. (Amsterdam, 1710), is given as *Voyages de François Bernier*.

that "upon their present plan they have little opportunity of improving themselves by the example of any other nation; except that of the Japanese":[38] a nice example of historical foresight. China is classed with "ancient Egypt and Indostan," and Smith makes the pertinent point that in both these countries the government paid much attention to the canal system.[39] He also observes that "the sovereigns of China, of ancient Egypt, and of the different kingdoms into which Indostan has at different times been divided, have always derived the whole, or by far the most considerable part, of their revenue from some sort of land-tax or rent. . . . It was natural, therefore, that the sovereigns of those countries should be particularly attentive to the interests of agriculture, upon the prosperity or declension of which immediately depended the yearly increase or diminution of their own revenue." [40] Later he remarks that "the sovereigns of China, those of Bengal while under the Mahometan government, and those of ancient Egypt, are said accordingly to have been extremely attentive to the making and maintaining of good roads and navigable canals, in order to increase, as much as possible, both the quantity and value of every part of the produce of the land. . . ." [41] He then goes on to discuss "the loss of the sovereign from the abuse and depredation of his tax-gatherers" and the interest of "the Mandarins and other tax-gatherers" in maintaining system of payment in kind that enabled them to fleece the peasants and defraud the central government.[42] There are the elements here of a theory of Oriental society, but it cannot be said that Smith makes much of them. He is content to register various features of Indian or Chinese administration, without inquiring to what extent they constitute a whole. In the following generation, we find James Mill, in his *History of British India* (1820), referring to an "Asiatic model of government," [43] while John Stuart Mill already employs the term "Ori-

---

[38] *Ibid.*, p. 645.
[39] *Ibid.*, p. 646.
[40] *Ibid.*, p. 647.
[41] *Ibid.*, p. 789.
[42] *Ibid.*, p. 790.
[43] I, pp. 175 ff.

ental society" as distinct from European.[44] Marx was familiar with these writers. Where does he diverge from them?

Principally, it seems to me, in expanding their hints into a theory that is both historical and sociological.[45] Unfortunately the theory was never formulated in systematic fashion, but has to be pieced together from his published and unpublished writings, notably the *Grundrisse* of 1857-1858, where it is, however, chiefly employed to bring out the contrast between Oriental society and Greco-Roman antiquity. By drawing upon all these scattered sources (including a very early work, the *German Ideology* of 1845-1846, which throws out some interesting hints about slavery and feudalism), we arrive at something like the following:

The various stages in the development of the social division of labor correspond to different forms of property.[46] The "first form" is communal and proper to "the undeveloped stage of production where a people sustains itself by hunting and fishing, by cattle-raising or at most by farming." [47] At this stage, the division of labor is rudimentary and consists for the most part in a further development of the primitive division of functions inherent in the family. "The social order therefore limits itself to an extension of the family: patriarchal tribal chiefs, below them the members of the tribe, finally slaves. The slavery latent in the family develops gradually with the growth of population and needs, and with the extension of external intercourse, both of war and barter trade." [48] This primitive tribal or communal organization is succeeded historically by a "second form" which in the 1845-1846 sketch is equated with "the communal and state property of antiquity." This is said to arise particularly "from

---

[44] *Principles of Political Economy* (1909 edition), p. 20; Marx on the whole prefers the term "Asiatic Society," perhaps first used by Richard Jones in *An Essay on the Distribution of Wealth* (1831); cf. Wittfogel, *op. cit.*, p. 373.

[45] The originality of Marx's approach, and the basic difference between his theory and the unsystematic hints thrown out by his predecessors, seems to me to have been understressed by Wittfogel.

[46] Cf. *Die deutsche Ideologie*, MEGA, V, pp. 11 ff.

[47] *Ibid.*

[48] *Ibid.*, p. 12.

the union of several tribes to a city through contact or conquest, and while retaining slavery. Side by side with communal property, mobile and subsequently immobile private property develops, but as an abnormal form subordinated to communal property. The citizens of the state possess power over their laboring slaves only collectively, and for this reason alone they are tied to the form of communal ownership. It is the joint private property (*das gemeinschaftliche Privateigentum*) of the active citizens who are compelled *vis-à-vis* the slaves to remain in this primitive (*naturwüchsige*) manner of association. Hence the entire organization of society based thereupon, and therewith the power of the people, decays in the same degree in which especially immobile private property develops. The division of labour is more highly developed. We already find the contrast of town and country. . . . The class relationship as between citizens and slaves is fully developed." [49] Marx notes as a possible objection that "the fact of conquest appears to contradict this whole conception of history," and goes on to demonstrate that "for the conquering barbarian people, war itself is . . . a regular form of intercourse, which is exploited all the more energetically the more the growth of population together with the traditional . . . primitive mode of production arouses the demand for new means of production." [50] This organization finds its ultimate development in Roman society, where "slavery remains the basis of the entire production" and the plebeians "stationed between free citizens and slaves never got beyond a *Lumpenproletariat*." It is succeeded by the "third form" of property, namely, "feudal or estate ownership." [51] In other words, by the European Middle Ages.

In 1845-1846 Marx had not yet discovered Oriental society and the "Asiatic mode"; consequently he mentions only three pre-modern stages: tribal society is succeeded by classical antiquity founded on slavery, and the latter by European feudalism. By 1859 the Preface to the *Critique of Political Economy* pre-

[49] *Ibid.*
[50] *Ibid.*, pp. 12-13.
[51] *Ibid.*, p. 13.

sents four stages corresponding to different forms of property: Asiatic society, antiquity, feudalism, and modern bourgeois society. Tribal society has disappeared, to be subsequently resurrected by Engels.[52] Now the 1859 work is based on the unpublished *Grundrisse* of 1857-1858, and when we turn to this much neglected source we obtain some light on how Marx had in the meantime come to regard the relationship of the Orient and the "Asiatic mode" to primitive tribal society on the one hand, and to classical antiquity and European feudalism on the other. His economic studies had acquainted him with the researches of the British school, and what we now get is a picture in which the skeleton of the "materialist conception of history" is fleshed out with economics.

True to his method, the approach remains historical. Marx begins by asking what are the "forms which precede capitalist production," [53] and he replies that the historical presupposition of the latter is the "separation of free labour from the objective preconditions of its realization. . . . Hence above all separation of the toiler from the soil as his natural laboratory: thus dissolution of small free landed property, as well as of the joint [*gemeinschaftlichen*] landed property resting upon the Oriental commune." [54] "In the first form of this landed property there appears a primitive [*naturwüchsige*] commonwealth as the precondition: [the] family and its extension to the tribe . . . or a combination of tribes. . . ." "Tribal community [*die Stammgemeinschaft*], the natural community, appears not as the result but as the precondition of joint appropriation . . . and utilization of the soil." "The earth is the great laboratory, the arsenal, which provides the means as well as the materials of work, and

---

[52] Cf. the latter's *Origin of the Family* (1884). In passing it may be observed that Marx's sketch of 1845-1846 supplies a very realistic hint at the emergence of slavery from within the tribal organization. Compare this with Engels' account of how and why "the old classless gentile (*i.e.,* tribal) society" with its "simple moral grandeur" succumbs to "civilized" pressure from outside; cf. *Selected Works*, II, p. 231.

[53] *Grundrisse*, p. 375. Cf. E. J. Hobsbawm, ed., *Karl Marx: Pre-capitalist Economic Formations* (London, 1964), esp. pp. 67 ff.

[54] *Ibid.*

likewise the location, the basis, of the community." [55] The individual participates in ownership of the soil and the instruments of production only insofar as he is a member of this primitive commonwealth held together by the ties of consanguinity. "The real appropriation through the process of labour occurs under these presuppositions which are themselves not the product of labour, but appear as its natural or divine preconditions. This form, based on the same primitive relationship, can realize itself in many different ways. Thus it is not contradicted by the fact that in most of the Asiatic patterns [*Grundformen*] the encompassing unity, which stands above all these small communities, appears as the superior or as the sole proprietor, [and] the real communities only as hereditary possessors. Since the unity is the true owner and the real precondition of common ownership, it can appear as a particular something [*als ein Besonderes*] above the many real particular communities, where the individual is then in fact without property, or property . . . appears as though mediated for him through a grant by the total unity [*der Gesamteinheit*]—which is realized in the despot as the father of the many communities—to the individual through the intermediacy of the particular community. The surplus product . . . thus belongs inherently to this supreme unity. In the midst of Oriental despotism, and of the absence of ownership [*Eigentumslosigkeit*] which juridically seems to obtain therein, there thus exists in fact as the basis this tribal or communal ownership, generally produced by a combination of manufacture and agriculture within the small community, which thus becomes entirely self-sustaining and contains within itself all the conditions of reproduction and surplus production. Part of its surplus labour belongs to the higher unity which at last exists as a person, and this surplus labour makes its appearance both in tribute, etc., and in common works for the glorification of the unity: in part the real despot, in part the imaginary tribal being, the god." [56]

[55] *Ibid.*, pp. 375-376.
[56] *Ibid.*, pp. 376-377.

This kind of common ownership, held together at the top by the "higher unity which at last exists as a person," appears under different historical variants: either the small communities maintain a separate existence and the individual works his plot independently, together with the members of his family; or again, "the unity may extend to communalism at work itself, which may be a formalized system, as in Mexico, notably in Peru, among the ancient Celts, [and] some Indian tribes. Further, the communal form [*die Gemeinschaftlichkeit*] within the tribal organization may appear realized in a head of the tribal family, or rather as the mutual interrelationship of the heads of families. Thence either a more despotic or more democratic form of this commonwealth. The common preconditions of genuine appropriation through labour, *waterworks* [Marx's emphasis], very important among the Asiatic people, means of communication, etc., thus appear as a work of the superior unity, the despotic government suspended above the small communities. Towns come into existence here only where there is a particularly favourable location for foreign trade; or where the head of state and his satraps exchange their revenue (surplus product) against labour, expend it as labour-funds." [57]

As against this centralized system—historically typified above all by the various Oriental despotisms—Greco-Roman antiquity, with its development of private property in land, represents what Marx describes as "the second form" wherein the original communal (tribal) organization raises itself to a higher sociohistorical level. The lengthy process whereby the urban patriciate of independent landowners, which here monopolizes political power, builds up its peculiar institutions (ultimately resting upon slave labor, and constant war to acquire more slaves) and eventually brings about its own downfall, is described with many fascinating details, and—quite in accordance with Hegel, but also with Niebuhr and nineteenth-century historiography generally—the decline and fall of antiquity leads straight on to the Germanic Middle Ages:

"An [other] form of ownership by the labouring individuals,

[57] *Ibid.*, p. 377.

self-sustaining members of the community, of the natural conditions of their work, is the *German*. Unlike the specifically Oriental form, the member of the community is not as such a co-
owner of the communal property . . . nor, unlike the Roman
or Greek form . . . is the soil occupied by the community.
. . ." (follows a brief analysis of the *ager publicus* as the specifically Roman institution, whereby the individual Roman citizen exercises his sovereign ownership over a particular area
of Roman soil).[58] As against these earlier forms, "the German community"—which is treated by Marx as the original cell
of the medieval body politic—represents something new: "Ancient classical history is a history of cities, but of cities founded
upon landed property and agriculture; Asiatic history is a kind of
indifferent union of town and country (the great cities are to be
regarded merely as princely camps, as superfetations above the
economic construction proper); the Middle Ages (German age)
starts from the countryside as the seat of history, whose further
development then proceeds through the antagonism of town
and country; modern (history) is urbanization of the land, not
as in antiquity ruralization of the town." [59] Among the Germans,
the coming-together of the clan chiefs does not subvert their
original independence: "The community appears as association,
not as union [*als Vereinigung, nicht als Verein*]," the (originally
tribal, later feudal) landowners constituting themselves as "independent subjects." [60] "The community does not therefore in
fact exist as a *state* . . . as in antiquity, because it does not exist
as a *city*. For the community to come into real existence, the
free landed proprietors must come together in a meeting,
whereas, e.g., in Rome it existed apart from these meetings, in
the being of the city itself and the officials standing at its
head." [61] True, the medieval Germans also had their *ager publicus*, their commons, but it did not, as in Rome, appear "as the
peculiar economic existence of the state, side by side with the
private owners." It merely served as a "supplement to individual

[58] *Ibid.*, pp. 380-381.
[59] *Ibid.*, p. 382.
[60] *Ibid.*, p. 383.
[61] *Ibid.*

ownership" and thus represents a profound contrast to the "Asiatic form" where the individual has "no ownership, only possession";[62] but it also contrasts sharply with the Greco-Roman system, where the city has a life of its own, being the collective organization and quasi-ideal representation of the citizens in their public capacity, as distinct from their private existence. Thus, in the European Middle Ages, private property predominates from the start. "The community exists only in the mutual relation of these individual landowners." [63] Our modern liberties (Marx might have added, but did not) have their roots in the Germanic forests.

What he does add is an extremely interesting and subtle analysis of tribal and communal ownership in antiquity, interlarded with polemical excursions against Proudhon[64] which need not concern us here. When he returns to his original theme—tribal organization as the source of the subsequent threefold differentiation into Oriental, Greco-Roman, and German-medieval forms of private and common ownership—it is to emphasize once more that the tribal system, "wherein the community originally dissolves itself," recognizes no property save that held by members of the tribe, so that conquered tribes are automatically deprived of it. "Slavery and serfdom are thus only further developments of the property rooted in the tribal system. They necessarily modify all its forms," though least of all in the "Asiatic form," with its "self-sustaining union of manufacture and agriculture on which this form rests." [65] What Marx describes as "the general slavery of the Orient" (as distinct from the personal slavery of classical antiquity) appears as a special case of the institution of property. The latter—"in its Asiatic, Slav, antique, German, form" [66]—originally signifies "the relation of the labouring [producing] . . . subject to the conditions of his production or reproduction." [67] Historically this relationship takes

[62] Ibid.
[63] Ibid., p. 384.
[64] Ibid., pp. 384-392.
[65] Ibid., p. 392.
[66] Ibid., p. 395.
[67] Ibid.

different forms, depending upon the existence of the individual "as a member of a tribe or community (whose property he is up to a certain point)": an interesting hint which hardly squares with the rather more idyllic picture subsequently painted by Engels. Man originally makes his appearance on earth as part of a primitive collective: "a generic being, tribal being, herd animal —though by no means a *zoon politikon* in the political sense." [68] He individualizes himself through the historical process, which is primarily a process of evolving various forms of communal and private property, *i.e.*, various ways of organizing his social intercourse with nature and the—natural or artificial—preconditions of work. The different forms of this metabolism correspond to different stages of society, among which Oriental society is historically closer to man's primitive origins, having conserved some elements of primitive communism "in the midst of Oriental despotism." Hence the succession of stages—Asiatic, antique, feudal, modern—mirrors the gradual dissolution of the "primitive unity," and the evolution of private ownership properly so called. The forcible disruption of the Indian or Chinese village community by European capital completes the process by rendering it truly global.

V

With this historical sketch in mind we can now return to our starting point and try to establish whether Marx's and Engels' utterances on the subject of Oriental society are reducible to a consistent pattern.[69]

The picture in some ways is a puzzling one. Reference has

[68] *Ibid.*, pp. 395-396.

[69] I express a mere personal opinion when I say that the argument outlined in pp. 375-396 of the *Grundrisse* seems to me to be among the most brilliant and incisive of Marx's writings. Unfortunately it remained a mere sketch and, what is worse, it did not see the light until 1939-1941. Had it been published around 1900, instead of remaining unknown until our days, one may suppose that Max Weber and his school would have found even better reason for relating themselves to Marx's researches. Marx in fact anticipated a good deal of what Weber had to say about Oriental society.

already been made to the gradual change in Marx's attitude towards the Asian village community and its resistance to the battering rams of Western capitalism. Now when one turns to the other structural element of the "Asiatic mode of production," the centralized governmental despotism, it would seem as though Marx and Engels gradually deepened their hostility to this form of rule, to the point of discovering some positive virtues not only in private property but even in European feudalism and the Germanic Middle Ages. How else account for Marx's 1859 statement about "Asiatic, ancient, feudal, and modern bourgeois modes of production" being "progressive epochs in the economic formation of society"? It must be remembered that these words were written shortly after he had composed his unpublished draft of 1857-1858, with its quasi-Hegelian stress on the element of personal freedom inherent in the rude institutions of the European Middle Ages. It must also be recalled that for Marx "progressive" does not signify "whatever happens to be going on," as it later did for his more thoughtless followers. "Progress" in his sense stands for the unfolding of man's dormant powers. European feudalism is "progressive" compared with Asiatic or Greco-Roman society because, thanks to its relatively healthy starting point, it embodies new potentialities of growth and human development; in Hegel's terminology, it represents "a new principle." These potentialities clearly have to do with a circumstance to which Marx alludes in passing in the *Grundrisse*: the fact that among the Germans political power did not at first exist separately from the individuals, but was simply the result of joint decisions taken in public. Engels was subsequently to go further by implying that the German barbarians rejuvenated Europe by infusing the remnants of their clan organization into the decaying fabric of the Roman Empire.[70] Sound Teutonic orthodoxy, one might say, as well as containing an indubitable amount of truth.[71] But exactly how does it relate to the more strictly theoretical concepts formulated by Marx and Engels?

[70] *Origin of the Family*; cf. *Selected Works*, II, p. 277.
[71] Cf. Marc Bloch, *Feudal Society* (London, 1961), pp. 145 ff.

There is no question that both men maintained and even accentuated their original aversion to Oriental rule considered as a political system. As we have seen, their first tentative utterances go back to the 1850s, when Marx was still inclined on occasion to play off the moral superiority of the decaying Confucian empire against the crude materialist aims of the encroaching Europeans. These polemical sideswipes are, however, scarcely to be taken seriously. They relate back to the familiar eighteenth-century habit of contrasting the virtuous Chinese with the hypocritical Europeans: an amiable fantasy which Marx commonly ranked with other childish naïvetés of the Rousseauist age. When he speaks as a theorist, the term "semi-Asiatic" carries connotations which are both precise and unflattering. Moreover, it was gradually extended to Russia and became the standard reproach addressed to the government of that country. In this respect Engels took the lead [72] but Marx followed suit in contrasting "Russia" with "Europe," [73] and thereafter consistently referred to the Tsarist government as a despotism suspended above an unfree peasantry. The references are too numerous and familiar to need citing. Later in 1875 we find Engels classing Russia with the "Asiatic mode" in an article where incidentally he comments on the village community.[74] The same point is briefly made in a better-known work, the *Anti-Dühring*: "Where the ancient communes have continued to exist, they have for thousands of years formed the basis of the most barbarous form of state, Oriental despotism, from India to Russia." [75] Lastly, there are Engels' writings of the 1890s, in which it is indeed suggested that Tsarist despotism is crumbling (and even that "the young Russian bourgeoisie has the State entirely in its power"),

[72] The article in the *New York Tribune* of April 19, 1853, in which Russia is first described as "semi-Asiatic," was signed by Marx, but actually written by Engels; cf. *Gesammelte Werke*, 9, p. 23.

[73] *NYDT*, August 5, 1853; cf. *Gesammelte Werke*, 9, p. 215.

[74] "Such a complete isolation of the individual [village] communities from each other . . . is the natural foundation of Oriental despotism, and from India to Russia this societal form, wherever it prevailed, has always produced despotism and has always found therein its supplement." Cf. *Internationales aus dem Volksstaat* (1871-5) (Berlin, 1894), p. 56.

[75] *Anti-Dühring* (German ed., Moscow, 1935), p. 165; cf. Foreign Languages Publishing House ed. (Moscow, 1954), p. 251.

but here too the surviving "despotic autocracy of the Tsar" is related to "the old communistic village community"—now in process of breaking up.[76]

In between, he and Marx had, however, given qualified support to the notion that the village community might become the starting point of a socialist development. How was this to be accomplished? We have two statements by Marx, both regrettably brief. In his letter to Vera Zasulich of March 8, 1881, we find him ready to go some distance in accepting the Populist notion that the resistance of the village community to private capitalism might offer the emerging socialist movement a unique opportunity; though after stating that "this community is the *point d'appui* of social regeneration in Russia," he is at pains to add that "the pernicious influences which attack it from all sides" must be eliminated, so as "to assure it of normal conditions for a spontaneous development." [77] Then there is the preface to the Russian edition of the *Communist Manifesto*, dated January 21, 1882, with the quasi-Trotskyist suggestion that "if the Russian Revolution becomes the signal for a proletarian revolution in the West, so that both complement each other, the present Russian common ownership of land may serve as the starting-point for a communist development." [78] These hints point in the direction of a controversy which was destined to convulse the Russian socialist movement for decades, but they do not contribute much to the strictly theoretical concept of the "Asiatic mode." At most they imply that for Marx socialism offered a way out of the uncomfortable dilemma suggested by his researches into Oriental society: the element of personal freedom, so plainly lacking in that society and equally so plainly at the roots of West European feudalism (and capitalism), might enter the system after the collapse of its "political superstructure." In different terms, the approaching fall of Tsarism

[76] *Werke*, vol. 18, pp. 663 ff., esp. p. 673.

[77] Full text in *Marx-Engels Archiv*, I (Frankfurt, 1926), pp. 309-42; cf. Blackstock and Hoselitz, *The Russian Menace to Europe* (London, 1953), pp. 275 ff.

[78] *Selected Works*, I, p. 24. In his 1894 gloss on this text, Engels pours a good deal of water into this heady wine; cf. "Russia and the Social Revolution Reconsidered," in Blackstock and Hoselitz, *op. cit.*, pp. 229 ff.

presented an opportunity to develop the healthy core of the ancient communal organization, instead of disrupting it completely in the interest of capitalism.

It is noteworthy that Marx—and to some extent Engels—saw such an opportunity latent in Russia, but not in India or China: presumably because Russia was only "semi-Asiatic." It was not a genuinely European country, but it nonetheless possessed the germ of development, whereas "the East" proper was stagnant. For the same reason, unfortunately, Russia was a permanent menace to Europe, and even its internal progress tended to make it more dangerous, because more aggressive and powerful.[79] The way out lay in a form of Europeanization which did away with the autocracy without—as the liberals would have it—simultaneously introducing Western capitalism. The commune—or what was left of it—was to be preserved as the future basis of a socialist society, or at any rate as an element of such a society. With this analysis the Populists were in agreement, and those among them who in the 1880s and 1890s gradually transformed themselves into Marxists could feel that they had not renounced the ideals and values which had originally brought them to socialism. Conversely, Marx for his part might think that by relating socialism back to pre-individualist, communal, forms of ownership, he had closed the circle of his argument: bourgeois society, so far from being "natural" and permanent, was revealed to be simply one socio-economic formation among others.

The unsolved, or half-solved, problem lay in the genesis of the Oriental state. In his writings of the early 1850s Marx had stressed both its centralized character and its independence from the vast mass of scattered village communes. In the 1857-1858 draft the roots of despotism in general are traced back to

[79] Cf. Marx, *Herr Vogt* (1859), in *Gesammelte Werke*, 14, especially pp. 497-498: "Incidentally, the emancipation of the serfs *in the sense of the Russian government* would multiply the aggressiveness of Russia a hundredfold. Its aim is simply the completion of the autocracy through the elimination of the barriers hitherto opposed to the great autocrat by the many little autocrats of the serf-based Russian gentry; as well as by the selfgoverning peasant communes whose material basis, the common ownership, is to be destroyed by the so-called emancipation."

the tribal organization, with its tendency to "realize" its internal unity in a personal ruler. Subsequently we find references to "the state" as "the supreme landlord," but no analysis of the means whereby the despotic sovereign builds up his power by surrounding himself with an administrative apparatus. From all this it is not difficult to conclude that Marx for some reason shirked the problem of the bureaucracy. Yet the latter's role is frequently alluded to in his other writings, notably in his diatribes against Bonapartism. His failure to make more of it in connection with the "Asiatic mode" remains an oddity. Perhaps the fact that he thought of it as a "caste" as distinct from a "class" of society lessened his interest in the subject; but though a possible explanation this is hardly an adequate defense.[80]

In this *Theories of Surplus Value* (1861-1863) Marx quotes Richard Jones to the effect that "the surplus revenue from the soil, the only revenues except those of the peasants of any considerable amount, were (in Asia, and more especially in India) distributed by the state and its officers." [81] Taken together with his own previous observations on the importance of centrally controlled irrigation in Asia, and with Engels' subsequent remarks (mainly in the *Anti-Dühring*) about the emergence of a ruling class from within primitive society, the elements of a complete theory of Oriental despotism appear to be present. Why were they not fully exploited? Perhaps an indirect answer is afforded by a somewhat lengthy passage from Engels which demonstrates at once the enormous advance in understanding he and Marx had actually effected in relation to earlier writers, and the point where their investigations tailed off into an uncritical acceptance of the prevalent Victorian attitude with regard to state and society:

[80] For a critique of Marx's and Engels' views on the subject of Oriental despotism, see Wittfogel, *op. cit.*, pp. 380 ff.; it seems to me, though, that Wittfogel overdoes the theme of Marx's alleged theoretical backsliding in his later writings. The most one can say is that the earlier suggestions were not systematically developed.

[81] R. Jones, *Literary Remains, Consisting of Lectures and Tracts on Political Economy* (London, 1859), pp. 448 ff.; cf. Marx, *Theorien über den Mehrwert* (Stuttgart, 1921), III, p. 501.

It is not necessary for us to examine here how this independence of social functions in relation to society increased with time until it developed into domination over society; how he who was originally the servant, where conditions were favourable changed gradually into the lord; how this lord, depending on the conditions, emerged as an Oriental despot or satrap, the dynast of a Greek tribe, chieftain of a Celtic clan, and so on; to what extent he subsequently had recourse to force in the course of this transformation; and how finally the individual rulers united into a ruling class. Here we are only concerned with establishing the fact that the exercise of a social function was everywhere the basis of political supremacy; and further, that political supremacy has existed for any length of time only when it discharged its social functions. However great the number of despotisms which rose and fell in Persia and India, each was fully aware that above all it was the entrepreneur responsible for the collective maintenance of irrigation throughout the river valleys, without which no agriculture was possible there. It was reserved for the enlightened English to lose sight of this in India; they let the irrigation canals and sluices fall into decay, and are now at last discovering, through the regularly recurring famines, that they have neglected the one activity which might have made their rule in India at least as legitimate as that of their predecessors.[82]

Setting aside the polemical glance at the British government in India, what does this passage suggest, if not that Engels—and by implication Marx, since he had seen the text before publication—thought of the "ruling class" in political terms, as the governing caste responsible for the exercise of those superior functions without which social life must come to a stop? The *Anti-Dühring* admittedly is a semi-popular tract primarily addressed to a working-class audience, but if Engels on this occasion expresses himself rather loosely, he does not contradict his or Marx's previous utterances. Political power arises from the exercise of a necessary social function: it then becomes independent of society (and of its own origins), but retains its roots in a collective need which it serves, *tant bien que mal*, until the social organism itself changes its character so as to require a

[82] *Herr Eugen Dühring's Revolution in Science* (Moscow, 1954), p. 249.

different kind of "superstructure." The state, in short, is an epiphenomenon. Although it does have a life of its own, it is subservient to the real basic needs of society; consequently the long-run process can be analyzed in terms of the latter.

In passing, it may be observed that Engels in the above passage identifies the "ruling class" so completely with the governing caste as to provoke the rejoinder that on his assumptions Bismarck might have claimed to be a more legitimate representative of German society than the elected Reichstag. It is not at all clear how Engels would have met the argument that the political elite of a given society is, and must always remain, something different from, and superior to, the socially dominant class. It is true that in nineteenth-century Germany—and to some extent in Victorian England—the two coincided, inasmuch as the landed aristocracy had retained its political and social role, while steadily yielding economic power to the bourgeoisie. But this symbiosis was a peculiarity of European history, and its roots—as Marx observed in his 1857-1858 sketch—lay in the relatively free and autonomous development of public life during the early Middle Ages. The Orient had never experienced anything of the kind, and since Engels had put his finger on the crucial role of the state—i.e., the bureacracy—in administering the central economic functions, it was really incumbent upon him to explain in what sense the governing caste was a "ruling class." Failure to clarify this topic was bound to obscure the entire problem of political power and the state in general.

At this point, however, we are on the threshold of the modern age, and for the same reason at the end of our investigation into the manner in which Marx and Engels, at the peak of the Victorian era, saw the problem of political power in an Eastern setting. It can hardly surprise a contemporary reader to find that they did not seriously examine the possibility of despotic rule in an industrial society: in other words, the problem of what we have learned to call totalitarianism. To have done so would have been to overstep the presuppositions they shared with their contemporaries: chief among them the confident belief that in modern society there was no longer a foundation for a new form of despotism. If we have in recent years begun to doubt this certainty, we may still extract what comfort we can from the notion that the inner principle of Western history has from the start been radically different from that of the East or of Greco-Roman antiquity.

part two

CONSERVATIVES AND RADICALS

Empire and After*

• In the spring of 1961 Dr. Arnold Toynbee spent some time at the University of Pennsylvania under the auspices of the Department of History. The event is likely one day to find its place in the revised Index of Dr. Toynbee's *Study of History*, which lists other important occasions in the life of the author (cf. Toynbee, Arnold Joseph: countries and places visited by). I make this confident prediction because Dr. Toynbee used the opportunity of his stay on the campus to deliver three public lectures, in which among other things he acquainted his hearers with the fact that they were now the owners and managers of a world empire in the succession of Rome.† At the same time that he made this disclosure, he voiced some uncomfortable doubts about the management of the estate, and even hinted that America might be losing the current popularity contest in the uncommitted world. The explanation he gave of this calamitous possibility must have made his hearers sit up, for it was quite out of tune with the rhetoric to which academic audiences are accustomed. After some polite talk about 1776 and all that, this is what the distinguished visitor had to say:

> Today America is no longer the inspirer and leader of the World Revolution, and I have an impression that she is embarrassed and annoyed when she is reminded that this was her original mission . . . America is today the leader of a world-wide anti-revolutionary movement in defense of vested interests. She now stands for what Rome stood for. Rome consistently supported the rich against the poor in all foreign communities that fell under her

---

* (Originally titled "Power and Ideology"), *Partisan Review* (Summer 1963).
† Arnold J. Toynbee, *America and the World Revolution* (London and New York, 1962).

sway; and since the poor, so far, have always and everywhere been
far more numerous than the rich, Rome's policy made for inequality, for injustice, and for the least happiness of the greatest
number. America's decision to adopt Rome's role has been delib-
erate, if I have gauged it right . . . yet, in the spirit that ani-
mates this recent American movement in reverse, I miss the en-
thusiasm and the confidence that made the old revolutionary
America irresistible. . . . Playing Metternich is not a happy role
. . . who . . . would have guessed that America, of all countries, would one day cast herself for Metternich's dreary part?
(pp. 16-17)

Now such remarks are clearly open to criticism. It can be argued that Dr. Toynbee spoke before the New Frontier had un-
folded its challenging vistas. It can also be objected that strictures of this kind come with diminished effect from the high
priest of High Toryism. All things considered, American imperialism (or what passes for such) has hitherto been somewhat
more progressive, or at any rate less unprogressive, than British
imperialism. Still, the charge of social conservatism must, one
imagines, have rankled with Dr. Toynbee's hearers because it is
so obviously true. It is not, of course, very original to say that
America has for some time been launched on the imperial path.
In substance it only repeats what Santayana said, in his usual
polite fashion, a good many years ago. But then Dr. Toynbee is
seldom original: his gift is for wrapping up commonplaces in
startling language. Moreover, when he descends from his usual
lofty heights to ordinary socio-economic reality, he intends to become less than infallible. His explanation of American conservatism is that all, or most, Americans are now well off, and thus
lack instinctive sympathy with poorer people. This kind of
amiable nonsense is to be expected from elderly historians unac-
quainted with economics. There is no need to pursue Dr. Toynbee's well-meant recommendations for making the United
States popular in backward countries: more missionaries, less
reliance on the local PX, etc. The Peace Corps can be trusted to
attend to these matters. Indeed it seems to have been specially
designed to cope with just the kind of problem that can be
solved with a little personal good will.

If Dr. Toynbee had taken his own assessment more seriously, he would not have devoted so much space to the minor misdemeanors of Americans abroad. Instead he would have expanded his warning of what may happen if America's allies become resentful of their present status:

> If it was reasonable . . . for Great Britain's thirteen colonies to insist on "no taxation without representation," "no annihilation without representation" seems an even more reasonable demand for America's allies to present to America today. To be taxed without being given a say was provocative, but to be annihilated without being given a say would be intolerable. (p. 33)

This is a bigger issue than rudeness to natives, and Dr. Toynbee felt impelled to recall "the history of Rome's constitutional relations with her Italian allies," which led to a civil war being fought before the "system of alliances between a paramount power and its satellites" was placed upon a more acceptable basis. "As you will see," he says with disarming candor, "I am suggesting that America has acquired an Empire and that, though this Empire is today still in an early stage of its development, it has been evolving, in some respects, along the same lines as at least one of the notorious empires of the past." This cautious formulation strikes the proper balance between Dr. Toynbee's basic commitment to Spengler's fatalism, and his occasional lapses into religious idealism: the future is not *quite* determined. The degree of indeterminacy (as we have heard by now) depends upon men's ability to raise themselves above the material level. "The true end of Man is *not* to possess the maximum amount of consumer goods per head." "See how Christian monks or Buddhist monks live. This will give you a fair measure of what the genuine necessities of life truly amount to" (pp. 68-9). If we restrict our "bogus wants," we can aid the poorer countries, regain their esteem, and perhaps save our souls in the bargain.

I I

It is fair to say, then, that Dr. Toynbee opened on a note of prophecy and concluded with a sermon. Something of its spirit is echoed in a tract for the times recently published by a distinguished representative of what for want of a better term must be called the American Establishment: Mr. Louis Halle.* A retired diplomat and a scholar, Mr. Halle embodies a well-defined tradition which the British used to think they had a monopoly of: that of the cultivated gentleman who in his leisure hours reflects upon the lessons of history and the meaning of events. Mr. Halle does not appear to be a philosopher by training, but neither was Arthur Balfour, whose writings—composed before he became Prime Minister—are still listed in reference books, though not perhaps very closely studied these days. Like Balfour, Mr. Halle is a gentleman-scholar with a skeptical turn of mind; also like Balfour, he is an instinctive conservative. Rousseau figures in his list of heretics immediately before Marx; Jacobinism appears as a peril scarcely inferior to Communism. Indeed the two are linked (as indeed they were, insofar as the Russian Revolution duplicated the French, though this scarcely exhausts the subject of Marxism). There are moments when one suspects that Dr. Toynbee may have had Mr. Halle in mind when he made his malicious remark about American conservatives having become pupils of Metternich.

However, there is no need to get annoyed with him. As conservatives go these days, he is a distinctly superior specimen: austere, learned, and almost excessively civilized. His refinement in fact worries me a little. If Dr. Toynbee is right, America now has an Empire, and every Empire must have an Establishment. Well and good: there is much to be said for Establishments. They rarely produce anything new and striking, but they are supremely competent when it comes to upholding standards, transmitting civilized values, and in general playing the part of culture preservers. I am all for having a genuine conservative

* Louis J. Halle, *Men and Nations* (Princeton, 1962).

Establishment (if only because it makes an ideal target for radicals), but I wonder if Mr. Halle may not have come on the scene a bit too early. There is something about his tone—urbane, patrician, melancholy, a trifle disconsolate even—that does not quite fit the circumstances. He would probably not resent being described as a spiritual descendant of Henry Adams. Now Adams could afford to be relatively complacent about the civilization of his day. In the first place he was an Adams; in the second place the world he lived in could be interpreted, more or less, in terms of his private philosophy. I am not so sure about Mr. Halle's relationship to *his* world. I suspect he is not merely out of tune with the present age—in which respect he must have the sympathy of every civilized person—but at a loss to account for its peculiar behavior. I was going to say that his style has an Augustan quality, but on reflection his manner strikes me as late-Roman. Now if Dr. Toynbee is right, and if we are witnessing the birth-pangs of the American Empire, there is something wrong with Mr. Halle's attitude. I confess I find his essay a bit disconcerting: it conveys the image of a cultivated gentleman, with private means and Stoic sympathies, whiling away the time under Caracalla, rather than an active participant in the Augustan enterprise. In short, I cannot help feeling that Mr. Halle has somehow strayed into the wrong epoch.

The thing that particularly disturbs me about him—always assuming that he ought to be doing a bit of spiritual empire building—is his defeatism about the modern world. After all, he is not the only traditionalist to remember better days and a stabler age. There is de Gaulle: my favorite conservative statesman, I have to admit. If we *must* have conservatism, let it be Gaullist, that is, intelligent, courageous, and frankly authoritarian. Then there was Churchill—a Liberal Imperialist (in British terminology) rather than a Tory, but distinctly a Burkean, and so a representative of the school Mr. Halle admires. Now the odd thing about Churchill and de Gaulle is that for all their basic conservatism they were remarkably successful in adapting to their age. I fancy this was partly due to their sense of the material possibilities opened up for their respective nations by science and technology. They were, in this sense, modern. Moreover, they were not distressed by the notion that democracy—in the full and original sense—is not workable: they never thought it was. This is the European cynicism that Americans get so angry with when they encounter it for the first time. Democracy is an American faith. Few Europeans have ever quite shared it, and even those who do usually concede that the system works best at the municipal level. Parliament is largely a sham which hides the reality of Cabinet government. The British have known this for a long time, just as they have long known that (in a phrase familiar to classicists) a democracy cannot govern an empire. It is one thing or the other: if you take your democracy seriously, you must resist the imperial temptation.

Is this why Mr. Halle sounds so melancholy, or is he unaware that he and his fellow thinkers are currently engaged on the important, and indeed overdue, task of providing the new American Establishment with an ideology suited to its current role in the world? To me he sounds like Marc Aurel when he ought to be sounding like Cicero. The burden of empire rests wearily upon his shoulders. Worse still, he conceives it his duty to impress upon his readers the importance of not taking the material world too seriously. His solution of the moral problem inherent in politics is a Platonist one. There are two realms: that of the senses, in which we unfortunately have to live, and that of spiritual ideas. Only the second is truly real. The material order is an inferior copy of the spiritual, or ideal, order. This can be proved by experience, even by experiment. "In human creation the idea always comes first." Religious conclusions naturally follow: "The Platonic view has its theological expression in the untranslatable first five verses of the Gospel according to John, in what is called the doctrine of the *Logos*: the idea came first . . . Christianity, as it was conceived by its founder, Paul, was rooted in this view." In the sublunary world, though, there are conflicting ideas: *e.g.*, "Nietzsche's idea of man does not agree with that of St. Francis, nor does Karl Marx's with that of St. Paul. . . . This is the human dilemma. . . . We live in two worlds, a primary world of perfect ideas and an imperfect world which imitates it." The imperfect world is that of ordinary human history, in which men are unable to agree upon ultimate aims. "The dual philosophy holds that, implicit in the order of nature from the beginning, there has been an idea of man that represents what he is intended to be. We ought to model ourselves on it, as Cicero and others have affirmed. But we are able to apprehend it uncertainly at best and cannot agree on it. In our ignorance and disagreement, then, some of us follow Nietzsche and some St. Francis, some Kipling and some Gandhi, some Tolstoy and some Hitler. Without knowledge of the ultimate, we are constrained to make do among conflicting opinions as best we can" (pp. 7-14).

Now this won't do at all. I am not here concerned with the substance of Mr. Halle's position. It has a respectable ancestry and doubtless it can be made plausible to people who are temperamentally disposed to such beliefs. But it is useless as an imperial creed, at any rate in the present stage, when the Empire still has to be constructed, and moreover must contend with an antagonist who believes firmly in the objective and universal import of *his* ideology. Mr. Halle must think again; or if he won't, someone else must. It is all very well for Professor Toynbee to be skeptical about ideal values: his own Empire (whose decline he has been celebrating in so many learned volumes) has virtually surrendered the ghost, and no longer needs a Public Philosophy to sustain it. But if America is to step into Britannia's shoes, its ruling elite will have to evolve a proper awareness of its role, and I don't see how Mr. Halle's blend of stoicism and skepticism can be much use to it. The less so since he is a nominalist and inclined to doubt the "real" existence of entities such as nations. "The existence of the individual is absolute and unmistakable. . . . A community, on the other hand, is a matter of degree" (p. 18). "Was Socrates a European, a Greek, or an Athenian? . . . What is a Jew? (p. 19) . . . What distinguishes German Jews from other Germans, perhaps, is simply an idea of Jewishness (p. 28). Mr. Halle has the courage of his convictions.

III

Philosophers of empire are made of sterner stuff. This is not to say that they must necessarily be reactionary or aggressive. There have been civilized exponents of the creed, including liberals and socialists as well as moderate conservatives. The failure to recognize this is among the numerous faults of the bulky textbook assembled by Professor Snyder.* Judging from his selection and the preface, he is one of those sound, forward-looking citizens for whom there are only two kinds of imperialism: reactionary (mainly British) and revolutionary (Russian). The United States, it appears, had a brief attack of the malady around 1900, but recovered with amazing rapidity, and has been healthy and virtuous ever since. This begs all the question, notably the question how the British managed to combine overseas expansion with economic liberalism. Of course if one defines "imperialism" to mean the kind of thing Britain practiced in India, France in Algeria, and Russia in Central Asia, everything becomes simple. One can then note with satisfaction William Jennings Bryan's rebuke to McKinley (p. 400), and conclude that the American people would have nothing to do with the doctrine expounded by Mahan and Theodore Roosevelt. And, needless to say, one can devote a sizable part of one's compilation to an indictment of the enemy, on the twofold ground that (a) Lenin's theory of imperialism is defective, and (b) Lenin's successors have become imperialists themselves. In which case we are back with the familiar equation: imperialism = domination over other people. But no one ever questioned that. The problem which other writers have been struggling with, and which Professor Snyder's anthology systematically obscures, is how and why imperialism survived into the modern age, when according to all the tenets of free-trade logic it should have withered away.

Now for one thing Professor Snyder does not play fair with his

* *The Imperialism Reader: Documents and Readings on Modern Expansionism*, ed. Louis L. Snyder (New York, 1962).

readers. He quotes out of context, selects what suits him, and overlooks (I had almost employed a less restrained term) inconvenient evidence. Thus by way of illustrating the thesis that European imperialism was closely tied to reaction, he cites the German Conservative Party's election manifesto of 1906 (p. 89), but says nothing about the colonialist propaganda of the Liberals who at that time had formed an alliance with the Conservatives. Elsewhere, Cecil Rhodes and Kipling duly appear as protagonists of British overseas expansion, while the far more influential Liberal Imperialists (and their Fabian allies) are ignored. Socialist pacifism before 1914 is illustrated by a bit of sentimental rhetoric culled from one of Jaurès' speeches on Morocco; nothing is said about Eduard Bernstein's public support for German colonial expansion and the acquisition of naval bases in China. Marxism is represented by Lenin, although his well-known pamphlet on imperialism (1916) merely vulgarized the work of more serious writers. Schumpeter's well-known essay of 1919 is quoted in such a fashion as to give the totally misleading impression that he denied the economic roots of modern imperialism; whereas in fact his account of the subject differs from the Austro-Marxist theory of Bauer and Hilferding only in unimportant details. This particular bit of "editing" really calls for something stronger than mere critical reproof. Scholars are free to indulge their political hobby-horses, but they are not supposed to tamper with the evidence.

But the chief fault of this tedious compilation is its mindlessness. A large-scale exercise in Cold War propaganda, elaborately dressed up as scholarship, might still have contained a few illuminating ideas. There are none, only a large and badly organized collection of snippets, and a parade of trivialities by the editor. Students curious to know what imperialism meant in its heyday before the First World War will do better to consult the case for the prosecution and the defense in two recent British publications: Bernard Semmel's *Imperialism and Social Reform* and A. P. Thornton's *The Imperial Idea and its Enemies*; the first a quasi-Marxist analysis of the forces underlying British policy, the second an eloquent apology of the imperial creed by one of its last defenders. For imperialism was more than a political maneuver. It was a movement, an ideology, almost a way of life. Its exponents included liberal aristocrats, Fabian Socialists, and neo-Hegelian philosophers, as well as militarists and racists. Above all, it was an international phenomenon. Its loudest and most eloquent protagonists were Anglo-American liberals. Mr. Halle, who (unlike Professor Snyder) is not disposed to conceal this awkward fact, quotes a characteristic utterance by the well-known liberal journalist William Allen White: "It is the Anglo-Saxon's manifest destiny to go forth as a world conqueror. He will take possession of the islands of the sea. . . . This is what fate holds for the chosen people. It is so written. . . . It is to be." [1] Of course this was at the height of the mania around 1900. The point is that, with few exceptions, the mood had taken possession of people who regarded themselves as advanced and progressive. The split within the Liberal Party in England (which finally wrecked it) is the best proof.

For obvious reasons, pre-1914 England was the country where the imperialist movement attained its fullest intellectual expression. England had the world's greatest empire, and it also had the world's most successful oligarchy. German imperialism was reactionary and racist. French imperialism was bourgeois and positivist. British imperialism was neither. Its exponents— whether they belonged to the Conservative or the Liberal Party —already possessed the ruling-class ethos which is the precondition of a fully developed imperial mystique. They represented a country governed on constitutional lines by an oligarchy drawn in part from the thirty thousand landowners who possessed 90 percent of Britain's soil. Most Americans have never seen a liberal oligarchy in action, and cannot imagine what it is like. They associate landowners with reaction. The smaller gentry were indeed Tories, but many of the great landed families were Whigs, and they dominated the Liberal Party down to the 1880s. What is more, they transmitted the ruling-class ethos to the wealthy patricians and solid professional men—Asquith, Haldane, Grey, and the rest—who succeeded them. The genuinely democratic,

[1] Halle, *op. cit.*, p. 177.

pacifist, anti-imperialist wing of the Liberal Party was never in control: its lower-middle-class, non-conformist, teetotaling, provincial earnestness made it appear ridiculous in the eyes of the ruling elite. These pacifist Liberals were the "Radicals" (in British parlance), and J. A. Hobson was their prophet. His well-known work entitled *Imperialism* appeared in 1902, and all the Socialists of the period, including Lenin, cribbed from it. But he never converted his own party, and Radicalism as a movement was a total failure. The only real leader it ever produced, Lloyd George, ran out on his followers in 1914 and—with the Liberal Imperialist Winston Churchill—became one of the two great wartime leaders Britain has had in this century.

The 1914-1918 conflict was a turning-point. It was the triumph of the imperialist movement, but also its Nemesis. As the war dragged on, the democratic and pacifist tide gained in strength, and by 1919 imperialism was on the defensive all over the Western world, and more particularly in Britain, where official Liberalism had split and thousands of pacifist Radicals streamed into the Labour Party. For the real heyday of the movement one must go back to the pre-war era, when popular feeling and imperialism marched hand in hand. Its first electoral triumphs occurred in the 1880s and then for a while indeed it was the Conservatives who profited most from it. They were traditionally the party of military rule, in India and elsewhere, and the "service classes" who read Kipling had their own vision of society. By then those strata of the middle class most closely connected with the military services and the colonial administration had assimilated the traditional ruling-class outlook and employed it as a justification for lording it over subject populations. Emotionally and intellectually, their creed envisioned an "ordered" hierarchical society, infused with feudal sentiments of mutual respect and obligation, though at the same time the new ruling elite would be self-made, not hereditary. It would govern the "lesser breeds" for their own benefit, and uphold the "law" taught in the great public schools. This was the ethos of Kipling, and by now everyone knows what to think of it. But what of Joseph Conrad?

The conquest of the earth, which mostly means the taking it away from those who have a different complexion or slightly flatter noses than ourselves, is not a pretty thing when you look into it too much. What redeems it is the idea only. An idea at the back of it; not a sentimental pretense but an idea; and an unselfish belief in the idea—something you can set up, and bow down before, and offer a sacrifice to. . . .[2]

Hardly an anti-imperialist utterance. Conrad in fact voiced the stoical sentiment in which middle-class liberalism adapted itself to the reality of Empire. It was there, and one had to make the best of it. The "idea" was what counted. There were others whose applause was more full-blooded. Lord Rosebery, a Liberal aristocrat and in 1894 Gladstone's successor as Prime Minister, had no doubt at all that the Empire was a great thing:

How marvelous it all is! Built not by saints and angels, but the work of men's hands; cemented with men's honest blood and with a world of tears, welded by the best brains of the centuries past; not without the taint and reproach incidental to all human work, but constructed on the whole with pure and splendid purpose. Human and yet not wholly human, for the most heedless and the most cynical must see the finger of the Divine.[3]

Rosebery, unlike Balfour, was no philosopher, and one hardly knows where he acquired these sentiments, but he could have obtained them during his stay in Oxford, then and for years a center of neo-Hegelianism. Balliol College, the "academy" of the Hegelians—Green, Bradley, Bosanquet and the rest—was also a nursery of statesmen and publicists: Curzon, later Viceroy of India; Milner, the great South African Proconsul and Lloyd George's colleague in the War Cabinet of 1916-1918; Asquith, Liberal Prime Minister from 1908 to 1916; Edward Grey; and Churchill's friend L. S. Amery. The link between Hegelian idealism and the imperialist movement was furnished by Hegel's theory of the State, which is anti-liberal and largely goes back to Burke. Its centerpiece is the notion that the institutions of

[2] Heart of Darkness.
[3] Cited by George Bennett, The Concept of Empire (New York, 1953), pp. 326-327.

society are the concrete embodiment of moral values which have a higher claim upon men's allegiance than the visionary utterances of the individual conscience. Morality consists in the discharge of man's duties in the narrow circle in which he actually lives—his family, his locality, his nation—not in running after cosmopolitan chimeras. Since Hegel had derived this conservative philosophy in part from Burke, it is hardly surprising that Hegelianism subsequently came to dominate Oxford, or that philosophers like Green and Bradley became the teachers of statesmen and administrators who then went out to govern an empire. But to suppose that all these men were Tories is to misunderstand the situation. The Hegelian philosopher T. H. Green was a faithful Liberal and an advocate of "three acres and a cow" radicalism, the program adopted by Joseph Chamberlain in 1885 when he was still a Radical and not yet the prophet of Empire. Bosanquet was another Liberal, and Arnold Toynbee, Sr., the friend of Milner, was even suspected of socialism!

Needless to say, Hegelian idealism was too esoteric to serve the purpose of the new imperialist creed in any but the most exalted circles. The middle class made do with popularized Darwinian notions and racial theories which preached the innate superiority of the Anglo-Saxons. But here again one must be careful: the Darwinians included Karl Pearson, and Pearson was a socialist who had come to the conclusion that Herbert Spencer and the other individualists were all wrong. Society was not just an assemblage of individuals; the "survival of the fittest" was a *collective* affair. A nation was "an organized whole . . . kept up to a high pitch of external efficiency by contest, chiefly by way of war with inferior races, and with equal races by the struggle for trade routes and for the sources of raw material and of food supply." [4] Its problems consequently had to be viewed in social terms. In order to be organized properly for the struggle against its neighbors, the nation had to be a "homogenous whole"; and, equally important, "we must not have class differences and wealth differences so great within the community that we lose the sense

[4] Karl Pearson, *National Life*, p. 46.

of common interest." This was National Socialism *avant la lettre*. Pearson had studied in Bismarckian Germany and knew what he was talking about.

IV

Against this stream of neo-Hegelian, neo-conservative, pseudo-liberal, racist, Darwinist, and National Socialist literature, which by 1900 had already become a veritable torrent, the surviving representatives of orthodox Liberalism conducted a hopeless defensive battle. Inevitably they were compelled, in the interest of self-preservation, to shift their center of gravity leftward, and eventually many of them broke with middle-class Liberalism altogether and joined the Labour Party. The interval was filled by Radicalism: the form in which Gladstonian (or Cobdenite) Liberalism finally gave up the ghost. Why was Radicalism a failure? For an answer one need go no further than to its theoretical Bible. Hobson's work was the credo of a manufacturing provincial middle class whose grandfathers in the 1850s had followed Cobden in his fruitless campaign against the Crimean War. (It is worth remembering that when it came to foreign policy, Cobden's failure was no less total than that of his descendants.) Hobson asserted that imperialism benefited neither the colonies nor the metropolis; the only thing that could benefit them was free trade. But in 1902 free trade was already becoming an unpopular doctrine, and moreover the camp of its defenders included the Liberal Imperialists, who agreed with the Tories on the need to prepare for the coming showdown with Germany. It also included the leading Fabians (notably Sidney and Beatrice Webb) who maintained the closest contact with the Liberal Imperialist group and furnished it with a good deal of intellectual ammunition. For the Webbs, with their faith in planning and a stronger state, Cobdenism was the enemy, and middle-class pacifist Radicalism a ghost from the Victorian past. In this attitude they were joined by the future Liberal War Minister, Haldane, and by the Tory Proconsul of Empire, Milner, who had started his career as a sympathetic student of socialism. The

London School of Economics was the great creation of the
Webbs, and the man they chose to direct it was the rabid imperialist W. A. S. Hewins. Another of their circle—informally
known as "the Coefficients Club"—was H. J. Mackinder, later
to become the founder of "geopolitics," a doctrine subsequently
propagated with great success in Germany by Karl Haushofer,
from whom Hitler acquired what little he knew about such matters. Mackinder, needless to say, was a prominent Liberal: he
succeeded Hewins as Director of the London School of Economics.

What did the Liberal Imperialists and their Fabian allies believe? In 1911 H. G. Wells drew a malicious portrait of them in
his *New Machiavelli,* where the group appears as the "Pentagram Circle." He makes the point that they thought war with
Germany was inevitable, as indeed they did. There was a subdi-
vision between Conservative protectionists and Liberal free-
traders, but as for defending the Empire against all comers they
were in agreement (except for Bertrand Russell, who resigned
from the club after a heated argument with Sir Edward Grey,
later Liberal Foreign Secretary, on the issue of military alliances
against Germany). Next, they had little use for democracy. On
this subject most of them accepted Sidney Webb's view that it
was a sham. Lastly, they thought that to become competitive,
Britain would have to adopt certain German institutions: notably social insurance for the working class, conscription for the
army, and the German educational system, which Haldane
thought was superior to the British and should be taken as a
model. In order to attain these ends they were prepared to
spend more money than financial orthodoxy in those pre-1914
days thought reasonable. Wells, who in 1911 stressed that the
"Pentagram" was "very keen on military organization," also
noted that "they were disposed to spend money much more
generously on education and research of all sorts than our formless host of Liberals seemed likely to do." The Webbs, who
stood at the center of this circle (which *inter alia* included a
Morgan partner and various Conservative journalists and politicians, some of them future Cabinet Ministers), supplied the in-

tellectual rationale for much of this agitation. Their private thoughts ran to confident forecasts that the coming war with Germany would necessitate a planned economy, hence Fabian direction and a measure of socialization: in which, however, they were largely disappointed so far as the *first* of the two German wars was concerned.

Bertrand Russell in his reminiscences (1956) has confirmed the essential accuracy of Wells's account, with special reference to the group's philosophical acceptance of the coming military showdown. "All the members except Wells and myself were Imperialists and looked forward without too much apprehension to a war with Germany." [5] On this issue Wells later joined the majority and became a notable exponent of the Wilsonian "war to end war" doctrine. This is relevant for an understanding of the Liberal Imperialist ideology which was so unlike the German variety. The latter never acquired a universalist character, but remained primitive, racist, and tied to its *völkisch* origins, hence repellent to other people (with the exception of the Japanese, who were even more committed to pre-modern myths). It is this which enables contemporary writers to treat imperialism as an essentially retrograde phenomenon, which it was not. Of course there were Liberals who resisted the pull, just as there were sections of the business class—notably among the financial community—who could see no sense in imperialism and clung to the hope that peace might be preserved. But they were conducting a rear-guard action, and for this it is not enough to blame the Germans. The pure logic of *laissez-faire* pointed towards pacifism and free trade, but *laissez-faire* made a diminishing appeal even in its British homeland.

In 1919 Mackinder—by now famous as the author of the strategic "Heartland" doctrine, which both the Germans and the Russians later tried to put into practice—published a volume entitled *Democratic Ideals and Reality* in which he summed up the quarrel between protectionists and free traders, pronounced

[5] Bertrand Russell, *Portraits from Memory* (London and New York, 1956), p. 77.

it unimportant, and went on to stress that the imperialists of both schools had been essentially "organizers" and patriots, whereas their opponents, the Cobdenite Liberals, were "idealists" and "internationalists," "in futile revolt against all organization." The doctrine of the "organizer" views men as "existing for the State," while the democrat is "thinking of the rights of man." This does not mean, though, that "the organizer" (a generation later James Burnham rediscovered him and called him "the manager") neglects the welfare of men. "On the contrary, he regards . . . society as so much man-power to be maintained in efficient condition." The rule of "the organizer" is "the Nemesis of democratic idealism," for democracy and efficiency are incompatible. This was the doctrine Mackinder had been taught by the Webbs, and which years later they were pleased to find embodied in Stalin's Russia. Mackinder also believed that democracy was incompatible with imperialism, though "even democracies are compelled to annex empires." [6] Were the British then doomed to lose their freedom? In 1902, while teaching geography at Oxford, he had suggested that British democracy and imperialism could coexist because of "the intervening ocean." In 1924 he still thought that "the separation of the tropical Empire from the European island" had the advantage that "imperial rule in the dependencies has not corrupted freedom at home," while on the other hand "those who exercise that rule, go out . . . with the spirit of justice and trusteeship ever renewed from their free homes and schools." [7] Sir Halford Mackinder wrote these lines after having briefly served as British High Commissioner for South Russia in the civil war year 1919: an experiment in governing part of the East European "Heartland" he had described in his geopolitical essays fifteen years earlier. He was not to know that two decades later another geopolitician would come a cropper in Southern Russia; or that his own former employers, the Webbs, would hail the Russian victory at

[6] H. J. Mackinder, *Britain and the British Seas*, p. 342. Cf. Semmel, *op. cit.*, pp. 175-176.
[7] H. J. Mackinder, *The World War and After* (London, 1924), p. 266.

Stalingrad as a world-historical turning point, and a confirmation (naturally) of their own faith in rational organization. Such are a few among the avatars of a creed whose impact is not yet exhausted.

Two Revolutions*

• The neo-conservative vogue in political writing is now al-most exhausted. Like other intellectual fashions, it drew its strength from passing circumstances, while resting its appeal upon supposedly self-evident truths and eternal principles. The circumstances were bound up with the Cold War in the particu-lar form it had assumed in the 1950s, when the Soviet-American antagonism called for a statement of principles, at any rate on the Western side (the Russians already possessed a coherent body of dogma and needed only to refurbish it in a few particu-lars). The principles invoked were substantially those which had validated the Anglo-American war effort against Germany, save that in those innocent days the USSR officially counted as a "democracy." The discovery that Soviet totalitarianism repre-sented something definite, not to be conjured away by the enun-ciation of Four Freedoms, Atlantic Charters, or United Nations platitudes, came as a shock. Worse followed when some of the new nations went over to the Soviet camp, while others assumed a neutral pose. Faced with these disappointments, liberal-ism fell silent, while its critics were able to ring the changes upon the half-forgotten theme of traditionalism: revolutions (unless consecrated by religion) are subversive of the natural order. The Russian Revolution, being self-avowedly atheist, not only lacked such consecration, but had from the start condemned itself to absurdity by trying to found a commonwealth of unbelievers— something even Robespierre had thought impossible. To resist its claims was to rediscover the perennial truths that inspired the founders of the Greek *polis* and the Roman Republic. In our

* Originally titled "Varieties of Revolutionary Experience"), *Partisan Review* (Summer 1964).

epoch the only surviving embodiment of spiritual health was located in the Anglo-American tradition, and particularly in the United States Constitution; the lesser breeds (specifically the French and other Latins still dazzled by the false glow of 1789) must rest content with an approximation. Their sins, it was suggested, might be forgiven them, on condition that they repented their original presumption. (This, it may be noted, was also the opinion of Pétain and the noble band of self-sacrificing public servants who sustained his devoted labors during the years when the Vichy regime set about dismantling the godless system of civil liberties established by the Republic.)

The part played by ordinary hysteria in the propagation of this faith is a matter for conjecture. One surmises that the echo it found among people who normally content themselves with plainer intellectual fare had something to do with the concurrent spread of purely political anxieties. On the face of it there was no compelling reason why the well-known differences between the American and the French tradition should be inflated into a doctrine tending to divorce the United States from half its actual and potential allies. As Hannah Arendt pertinently remarks in her new work,* "even revolutions on the American continent speak and act as though they knew by heart the texts of revolutions in France, in Russia, and in China, but had never heard of such a thing as an American Revolution" (p. 218). There are reasons for this, some of which she mentions in passing, notably the American habit of equating freedom with "free enterprise." One can only regret that while Miss Arendt dissociates herself from this thoughtless equation, she has gone the neo-conservatives one better by treating the difference between American and French interpretations of democracy in quasi-theological terms. To genuine Tories, the two revolutions have always looked remarkably alike, and even at the present day one finds a Burkean Whig like Michael Oakeshott deploring the Declaration of Independence in terms usually reserved for Rousseau's spiritual progeny. Among European theologians, Karl Barth thought there was not much difference between the

* *On Revolution* (New York, 1963).

classic manifestoes of 1776 and 1789, though he preferred the American version, for the obvious reason that theology had not been completely extruded and there was some talk of duties as well as rights. Whether this amounts to a difference in principle so great as to warrant the assertion that the French in 1789 made a complete break with the past, is a question for philosophers, not for historians. The historian can only register the fact that, by comparison with the French Revolution, the American has remained an isolated phenomenon. It is none of his business to discover philosophic origins for this circumstance, since on any interpretation of what either history or political science is about, such origins do not account for politically relevant happenings in the short run. To take a currently topical example: the recent tentative rapprochement between the Vatican and the Kremlin cannot sensibly be discussed in terms of Thomist and Leninist philosophy, although it is a fact that both have a common source in Aristotle, and that Lenin's writings on the subject sit better with some contemporary Catholics than with most Western liberals. The two themes are not closely enough related to permit any meaningful inference to be drawn from such evidence.

I have purposely applied this seemingly farfetched comparison because Miss Arendt, throughout her writings and more than ever in her latest offering, shows an inclination to discuss political topics in philosophical terms, and vice versa, until the distinction between metaphysics and politics is lost or dimmed in a twilight zone where it no longer seems to matter whether we are dealing with actual events, contemporary beliefs about these events, or subsequent reflections upon them by thinkers motivated by convictions and interests quite foreign to the participants. At some stage a writer has to decide whether the discussion is to be about the political realm ordinarily so called, or about the most general principles regulating human behavior. It is no use asserting that this distinction was overcome once and for all by Aristotle and his successors. (Who are they? Do they include the medieval Aristotelians who no longer had a *polis* to reflect upon?) Since the seventeenth century (or according to

some writers, since Machiavelli) the classical tradition has
ceased to be binding upon political theory. Those who do not
regard political philosophy as a body of truth revealed once and
for all to the Greeks, and embellished since then only in unimportant respects, have tended to infer from their own reading
of history that "revolutions" in human society (*e.g.*, the Industrial Revolution) are something quite different from the kind of
cyclical movement with which the ancients were familiar. The
decline of the city-state is itself not explicable on the assumptions entertained by Aristotle or any other classical thinker—not
surprisingly, since they lacked the necessary perspective. If there
are permanent principles to be derived from their writings, they
can only bear upon certain very general notions, *e.g.*, the rule of
law. To suppose, as Miss Arendt does, that "the phenomenon of
revolution" can be meaningfully discussed in suprahistorical
terms such as "violence," or related to mythical events ("Cain
slew Abel and Romulus slew Remus"), is to obliterate several
centuries of thought starting with Vico if not Machiavelli. This
is not conservative empiricism but mere dogmatism—as doctrinaire as anything produced by the most extreme rationalists.

Once the discussion is brought down from the metaphysical
heaven to the profane earth on which ordinary mortals dwell,
the question that puzzles her—why the "disastrous" French
Revolution has been so much more influential than the beneficial
American one—finds a ready answer, and this quite irrespective
of a circumstance to which she herself draws attention: namely
that over much of Europe absolutism had established a pattern
which positively cried out for violence. Setting this familiar
fact aside, the French Revolution was more *radical* than the
American in the fundamental sense of the term: it went closer
to the roots. For example, it did away with slavery, while
the American Revolution confirmed it (thereby condemning a
later generation of Americans to the ordeal of Civil War). It
also (for a time) did away with theology, but then even quite
conservative Protestants have acknowledged that this was simply
the penalty visited upon the Catholic Church for its antecedent
attempt to stamp out all other forms of thought, including rival

brands of Christianity. In short, the French Revolution was more "total" because the *ancien régime* was more coherent (and more despotic) than its Anglo-American counterpart.

These considerations are not irrelevant to the theme of a philosophical essay which sets out to interpret the phenomenon of revolution in the post-medieval age, with a mimimum of historical reference and a maximum of emphasis on the thought processes of those concerned (notably the professional ideologists among them). Since Miss Arendt is, to put it mildly, no historian, it is no great matter that the events themselves remain in the background, or that she occasionally gets lost in unfamiliar territory, as for example, when she suggests that the Levellers whom Cromwell put down were radical democrats (they were nothing of the sort). So far as France is concerned, it may seem unkind to suggest that the Revolution (as distinct from what some people at the time said and wrote about it) is a closed book to her, but certainly the reader of Georges Lefebvre's great work on the subject will have difficulty relating his account of what actually occurred during those years to Miss Arendt's interpretation of what presumably went on in the heads of the participants—or at least the more prominent and literate among them who had the means for recording their illusions and disappointments in writing. All this is relatively unimportant, as is the somewhat confused presentation of the argument, which eschews chronology and wanders back and forth between the Greek concept of the good life (democracy = community) and the modern attempt to fashion a rule of law for people not held together by ties of consanguinity or physical cohabitation in an area small enough for all active citizens to assemble in the market place. There is, after all, little new to be said about the problematic nature of Rousseauist (or, for that matter, Jeffersonian) notions about politics. But why are we told so little about the religious background? The fundamental fact about the American Revolution surely is that it occurred in a Protestant country with an Anglo-Saxon tradition of limited self-government. Miss Arendt makes much of the contrast between the misery of the French peasant and the relative prosperity of the American farmer; but this is merely the reverse side of the medal. No Protestant population could ever have been beaten down to the French (or Spanish or Latin American) level. Even the serfs of Prussia were not reduced to quite the existence of the peasant helotry in neighboring Catholic Poland. In the nineteenth century the landless English farm laborer had a pretty thin time, but it was the Irish peasantry that actually starved en masse. These historic circumstances are not irrelevant to Miss Arendt's work, just as it is not immaterial to the theme of her concluding chapter that in present-day Europe the two largest Communist parties are those of France and Italy (or for that matter that Hitlerism arose in Catholic Austria and Bavaria, not in Lutheran Prussia). There are of course sound practical reasons for keeping quiet about this explosive topic, notably in the United States. But a political philosopher who wields so ruthless a scalpel in dissecting the smallest logical flaw in the writings of Rousseau or the speeches of Robespierre might have been expected to cast a little light on so large and important a theme. The modern age—if one is going to talk in these terms—begins with the Reformation. Once Northern and Southern Europe had gone their separate ways (Germany as usual was partitioned), all the rest followed, at any rate if one takes the traditional view that the Dutch Rebellion and the English Civil War set the stage for the American Revolution. Is the traditional view wrong? If not, why is there no mention of Holland—the cradle of the modern world? And why the desperate attempt (p. 36) to persuade the reader that the English Revolution of 1640-1660 was not a "real" revolution, because, if you please, the participants at first thought they were restoring the ancient order? What else did the French of 1789 think?

Practically speaking, all this is irrelevant. The French Revolution needs no defense, least of all in an age that has witnessed the German Counter-Revolution. What France might have become if it had not—at great cost admittedly—broken out of the medieval prison-cage can be studied in contemporary Spain. Incidentally, the endless Iberian and Latin American cycle of bloodletting over the past century and a half is much closer to what the Greeks called *stasis* than anything that has occurred in France since 1789. A writer domiciled in the United States might also have reflected upon the curious circumstance that France's relations with her former colonies—including Algeria— are decidedly better than U.S. relations with Latin America (even setting aside the distressing Cuban experience). It seems the Messianic and universalist spirit of the French Revolution, however confusing and even dangerous in the short run, is still paying dividends. This pragmatic argument should appeal to readers brought up in the decidedly unmessianic spirit of Ben Franklin. Whether it will appeal to Miss Arendt, I doubt. Her cast of mind is un-pragmatic and bears a close resemblance to that of some contemporary European ideologists. It is the more remarkable that she has found a spiritual resting place among the classic statements of the American faith in reasoned progress and constitutional liberty.

These statements have never escaped criticism even from writers who were otherwise in sympathy with the aims expressed in 1776. Bentham thought the Declaration of Independence a "hodge-podge of confusion and absurdity" (*Works*, Vol. X, p. 63), but then Bentham had a poor opinion of any document not composed by himself. On the whole, French, English, and American liberals and radicals have over the years worked out a community of mind that transcends their earlier divergencies, and of late this spirit has even shown a capacity for assimilating people brought up to regard *all* statements of the liberal faith as so much antiquated nonsense. Against this background one may question the relevance of an attempt to treat the American experience as an embodiment of traditions and principles foreign to Europeans (with the possible exception of the English). Not that there is any doubt as to the more radical and universal character of the formulation which the common faith received in eighteenth-century France. The French had come on the scene at a moment when the compromise solution worked out by the British in 1688—constitutional government under oligarchic control—no longer satisfied thinking people who had dimly begun to sense that democracy might become an actual possibility. Along with this went the first stirrings of the industrial revolution and hence the "social problem" in its modern form. Leslie Stephen, in his great *History of English Thought in the Eighteenth Century*, put the matter in words with which we may conclude:

> Locke expounded the principles of the Revolution of 1688 and his writings became the political bible of the following century. They may be taken as the formal apology of Whiggism. He gave the source from which later writers drew their arguments, and the authority to which they appealed in default of arguments. That authority vanished when the French Revolution brought deeper questions for solution, and new methods became necessary in politics as in all other speculation (II, p. 114).

Rousseau and de Maistre*

• There is a story, perhaps apocryphal, of an eighteenth-century Italian nobleman who fought fourteen duels in defense of the proposition that Tasso was a greater poet than Ariosto, yet confessed on his deathbed that he had never read a line of either. True or not, the anecdote would have amused Voltaire (if indeed he is not the inventor). It would have made no appeal to Rousseau, that most solemn and humorless of moralists. In this assumed contrast there lies buried something of the pathos which after two centuries still clings to the name of Jean-Jacques Rousseau; something too of the attraction he continues to hold for poor, proud, and ambitious men everywhere. For his earnestness was the secret of his power in an age which had begun to tire of its own frivolity. And it is because, for all his perversities and inconsistencies, he came to incarnate something of the puritan spirit that his image still confronts us with that curious gaze of mingled pride, resentment, and melancholy which so fascinated his contemporaries and made even his enemies reluctant to strike at him.

Jean Guéhenno's massive biography† has the prime virtue of bringing its difficult subject to life, and the excellence of the translation preserves the peculiar cadence of his style, a style plainly fashioned on that of his hero. For M. Guéhenno is himself something of a Rousseauist, as befits a writer who in his own person consciously exemplifies the provincial virtues (Breton in his case). One senses his instinctive liking for the champion of rural simplicity—an honest man in a corrupt society, contemp-

---

* *New Statesman* (16 September 1966).

† Jean Guéhenno, *Jean-Jacques Rousseau*, trans. by John and Doreen Weightman (London, 1966).

tuous of the glitter of wealth and fashion. Yet he is painfully
aware that Rousseau fell short of his self-created standard, that
the image contained an element of unconscious pose: the
"Citizen of Geneva" did not disdain the help of enlightened
and influential patrons; the moralist for a number of years
frequented the salons; the author of *Emile* sent his five
illegitimate children to the orphanage and kept his faithful
Thérèse busy in the kitchen, while he made love to married
and titled ladies. M. Guéhenno wrings his hands over so much
vanity and self-deception, and despairingly asks himself and the
reader whether Rousseau can have been sincere. The reply he
gives, after much heart-searching and minute exegesis of the
sources, amounts to a qualified "yes." Jean-Jacques, we are told,
remained true to his deepest convictions, those implanted in him
during the comparatively blameless years of his childhood and
adolescence. But these convictions were fully compatible with
the artistic credo which enjoined upon him the supreme duty of
getting on with his work. That work indeed contained an element of simple craftsmanship—music and the drudgery of mu-
sical copying—for Rousseau believed in the importance of exercising an honest trade or profession. But he was no Spinoza, and
the pose of rigorous independence from wealthy patrons looks
unconvincing when examined against the record of his fashionable middle period. For some years at least he had his circle of
influential friends, including Grimm, Holbach, and Diderot;
and if his closeness to the leading Encylopedists did not improve
his relations with Voltaire, the tone of their correspondence
suggests that envy and resentment on his side had a major share
in the estrangement.

Personal motivation of course ceases to be relevant when
placed in the context of a major cultural reorientation. The ple-
beian in Jean-Jacques had his reasons for disliking Voltaire, and
they were not all discreditable. Karl Barth, himself a Swiss Calvinist and severely critical of Rousseau, remarked that he had at
least one thing to his credit: he went mad in an age of which
Voltaire had become the admired symbol. One need not share
Barth's theological assumptions to see the point. Whatever his

own faults, Rousseau was genuinely shocked by the frivolity of
his admired contemporary. Behind the mordant wit he sensed a
fundamental lack of seriousness.

The point is connected with Rousseau's place in the Romantic movement, of which he was a forerunner rather than a true
progenitor. Perhaps there were no genuine Romantics in eighteenth-century France, or indeed anywhere outside Germany; it
depends on how one defines Romanticism. Certainly the new
creed involved more than the "cult of the heart," or the dichotomy of urban corruption and rural innocence. If a true Romantic is one who believes that discursive reasoning cannot establish
valid truths about man and society, then Rousseau does not
qualify. But who in the eighteenth century did, save for Ha-
mann and his progeny? Irrationalism of this sort was not to be
found in Western Europe—at any rate not among writers, however unorthodox. It is worth remembering that Rousseau contributed to the *Encyclopédie* and did not at first greatly mind
when d'Alembert, in the *Discours Préliminaire*, mildly rebuked
him for his attacks on science. The dispute between moralism
and scientism was a private quarrel among humanists, and
Rousseau never intended his critique as more than a corrective
to the dominant mode of thought. He believed—with good reason—that the official culture of his day had become seriously
unbalanced, and in his sentimental fashion he proposed "nature" as an archetype capable of healing the injury done to man
by "civilization." It was left to the German Romantics of the
Napoleonic era—and still more to imbecile savages like Bakunin
in the generation following—to inaugurate the revolt against
civilization as such.

So far as the immediate consequences of Rousseau's preaching were concerned, it is evident enough that his personal eccentricities concealed more than they revealed. As a pre-Romantic
he was a precursor, and thus shared the usual fate of those who
are ahead of their age: that of having to struggle with formless
(because uncomprehended) elements in his own makeup. Politically speaking, he was likewise out of step, since as a Swiss he
looked back to an age of genuine self-government among free

burghers and peasants, while in his capacity as a naturalized Frenchman he anticipated the upheavals of 1789 and 1793. It was not in his power to discern what has since become a commonplace: that his teachings were to furnish the staple of both nationalism and democracy. Neither of course was compatible with Voltaire's aristocratic libertinism, or for that matter with Montesquieu's anachronistic longing for a pre-absolutist age of rule by the gentry. That as a prophet he was highly effective even his critics could not deny. One may regret that French democracy came to birth in the sign of Rousseauism; one can hardly dispute that it did. The Jacobins were his pupils, and Robespierre might have claimed the honor of having died for the faith of Rousseau (after guillotining others for clinging to the spirit of Voltaire).

However one chooses to regard these matters, Rousseau's private quirks have little interest for the historian, and the same applies to his doctrinal eccentricities. It is hardly worth establishing once more that the Social Contract was a myth. The important point is that on French soil the doctrine had an explosive effect which it noticeably lacked in America. But then the French were faced with an absolute Monarchy, not a parliamentary one, and with a Church which took its claims to omniscience seriously. Insofar as Rousseau's personal fate inserted itself into that of his adopted country, his Genevan origins were doubly relevant: his original monarchism, real or feigned, was at best lukewarm, and the effect of his Calvinist upbringing was never lost (though his formal reconversion in middle age was clearly prompted by nothing more exalted than the desire to have a home). Geneva indeed, no less than France, rejected him when the storm broke over his head in 1762: the faith of the *Vicaire Savoyard* was not compatible with that of Calvin. But the Republic could afford to shrug him off—there was no political tinder lying about its tidy streets. France was another matter, for here the *ancien régime* was about to crumble and the Catholic Church was deeply involved in its fate. That is why Rousseau's Genevan origins were to prove more than a personal matter: the spark he had accidentally struck helped to set off an explosion possible only in a Catholic country. In the sixteenth century France had narrowly missed the Reformation. It was now about to undergo the experience of the Revolution. The Bourbon Monarchy had anyhow become discredited, but its replacement by a Republic modeled on Rousseauist principles was not written in the stars or inherent in the logic of social development.

Less than a generation after Rousseau's death this became the principal theme of de Maistre, a selection of whose writings is now available in an edition useful to students, though rather too skimpy to convey a rounded impression of the man.* De Maistre's paradoxical relationship to Rousseau is well brought out in Mr. Lively's introduction. Both men were in a sense provincials—the Savoyard aristocrat no less than the "Citizen of Geneva." Both, though for different reasons and in different directions, rebelled against rationalism. There the resemblance ends, for de Maistre combined the hardheadedness of the eighteenth century with the shocked and frightened authoritarianism of the nineteenth. His appeal is to tradition, authority, hierarchy. Established institutions (the Catholic Church above all, with the Monarchy next in order) are worth preserving and defending simply because they *are* established. They need no other defense, least of all that of reason. It is enough that they exist—shields of order, bulwarks erected by God and man against the ever present danger of chaos.

De Maistre has no faith in sociability and precious little in the people, though he is willing to make room for an element of popular representation (if granted from above, by the King, not demanded as of right). He is a consistent authoritarian. Order rests on fear of the Executioner. Government is a device for holding back the flood of murder and destruction lurking in the heart of Rousseau's model citizen. The Revolution, "Satanic in its essence," is an uprising not merely against the established regime, but against social morality, and ultimately against the divine order. Regicide is a crime against heaven. "Each drop of

* Jack Lively, ed, and trans., *The Works of Joseph de Maistre* (London, 1966).

Louis XVI's blood will cost France torrents; perhaps four million Frenchmen will pay with their lives for the great national crime of an anti-religious and anti-social insurrection crowned by a regicide." And so on. Compared to de Maistre, Burke is a liberal. Indeed he never got rid of the Whig tradition, while the French had to wait for another generation before Tocqueville revived the dormant Whiggery of Montesquieu. In the meantime there was de Maistre to lend point to the ideology of the counter-revolution. He if any man put into words what the leaders of the Vendée were fighting for.

At our present distance from the scene it is nonetheless apparent that Rousseau and de Maistre have something in common. Both are totalitarian in the sense that they draw no distinction between religious faith and civic obligation. For de Maistre as for Rousseau, the social order rests upon the recognition by all of certain self-evident truths: without such unity of belief, society cannot stand and the nation cannot discover its true self. Moreover, both hold that it is the duty of the government to define the dogmas governing the correct behavior of the citizenry. In the age of Mao Tse-tung none of this sounds unfamiliar, and indeed the totalitarian assumption crops up of necessity in every great revolution. It has taken our own civilization several centuries to evolve beyond the point of enforced unanimity about first principles. By one of those ironies of which Hegel was so fond, the French Revolution helped to promote this outcome, though neither the Jacobins nor their enemies had willed it. By a further irony the Germans, who in those stirring days were content with the platitudes of conservative traditionalism, were destined to endure the debased Romanticism of the Third Reich. On balance one may feel that the French were more fortunate and that in this context even Rousseau stands in the Enlightenment tradition. Nor is de Maistre a genuine irrationalist. They are both pre-Romantics, busy pouring the new wine into the ancient rationalist container. The real revolt against reason, and against the idea of humanity as a reality over-arching the varied splendors of race and nationhood, had to await the coming of the Germans.

The Politics of
Conservative Realism*

• When a writer of Hans J. Morgenthau's standing assembles three stout volumes of essays† published over the past quarter century, he places the reviewer before a dilemma: a summary judgment would be almost an impertinence, yet some attempt must be made to come to terms with the author's central thesis. How else is one to thread one's way through the labyrinth of an argument that unwinds at majestic length across the entire land-scape of public debate: from the principles of politics to the pursuit of tactical advantages in the Cold War, and back again to the general ideas underlying the conduct of statesmanship? The reviewer must take his choice. If he shares with the author an interest in political theory (not to mention the accident of a common background) he will treat this bulky work as a state-ment of faith ultimately derived from a particular philosophy of history. And it may then occur to him that this philosophy in turn has its source in certain European attitudes and as-sumptions: specifically those prevalent in nineteenth-century and early-twentieth-century Germany. It thus becomes a subsidi-ary, but not uninteresting, theme to inquire into the theoretical status of these assumptions and their relevance to current Anglo-American thinking. Fortunately this procedure is in tune with Mr. Morgenthau's own approach, so that no violence is done to his work by asking how far it echoes recent European experi-

---

* *Commentary* (June 1963).
† *Politics in the Twentieth Century:* Volume I, *The Decline of Demo-cratic Politics;* Volume II, *The Impasse of American Foreign Policy;* Volume III, *The Restoration of American Politics* (Chicago, 1963).

ence. The "Atlantic" current is strong, and even those who question the practicality of an "Atlantic Community" may share the feeling that diverse intellectual traditions are about to be fused into a larger whole.

Even so, it is not altogether easy for a critic to cope with a writer who deals specifically with the problems of American foreign policy; and the difficulty is not materially diminished by the author's casual acceptance of the need for a supranational approach. For it must be said that on this subject Mr. Morgenthau is not quite consistent. The reader of his reflections on "Nationalism" in the opening volume of his trilogy will discover that he regards the nation-state as a survival from the pre-nuclear age. Yet his policy recommendations are necessarily addressed to the leaders of what is now the dominant nation within the Western alliance, and his explicit aim is to induce the United States to take up positions all over the world which will enhance America's influence, and diminish the power and prestige of its rivals.

The dilemma is inescapable; it can be eluded only with the aid of a utopian idealism of which Mr. Morgenthau is rightly critical. Policy must be formulated by governments, and Mr. Morgenthau for the past quarter century has been addressing his advice to those who may be thought to have some influence on the conduct of one particular government, namely that of the United States. Moreover, he is convinced that Americans tend to blind themselves to the realities of the world, and their own place in it, when they pretend that America is not a Great Power like others; that its past history has not been one of conquest and annexation wherever possible; and that it can afford to adopt moral attitudes radically different from those of other powers. He has denounced as a self-evident absurdity the flattering notion that America's past record is somehow more virtuous than that of Europe, and for the present he insists that the only thing to be done about "power politics" is "to live with them and still remain civilized; that is, we must make the best of them." [1] There is much to the same effect in the eloquent essays

[1] *The Decline of Democratic Politics*, p. 321.

on "Nationalism" and "The Problem of National Interest" which lend weight to the introductory volume (the most theoretical of the three). There is even some rhetoric about "the territorial integrity of the nation and . . . its survival as a free country" (as against the utopian idealism of the "Atlantic Charter" and the "Four Freedoms") which conservatives will doubtless read with pleasure. Yet they should note that it comes from a writer who elsewhere affirms his belief that nuclear power has made an end of the self-sufficient nation-state as the supreme political entity.

The nation-state is obsolete, and we in the Western world are saddled with it, although it has ceased to protect us. The dilemma—it is not of Mr. Morgenthau's making, but he gives eloquent expression to it—runs through his pragmatic policy recommendations. It is well formulated in an essay in the third volume entitled "Is the United Nations in Our National Interest?" The answer appears to be a qualified yes; the question has doubtless been deliberately phrased to underline the author's commitment to the brand of political thought known as "realism." There is to be no nonsense about altruistic purposes: "The U.N., seen from the vantage point of the United States, is as much an instrument of American foreign policy as are diplomatic negotiations and alliances, and these instruments must be continuously subjected to the pragmatic test of their usefulness for the national purposes which the United States happens to pursue at the moment." A subsequent essay makes the point that "the United States and its allies have a vital interest in an effective U.N." primarily because it is "an obstacle, weak in actual performance but endowed with untried and intangible potentialities, that stands in the way of the Communist bloc." America and its allies "want what the U.N. must want: the preservation and strengthening of international law and order and, more particularly, the protection of the territorial status quo from violent change." This is as much as to say that the West should back the principle of a world authority only insofar as it stands (or can be made to stand) for "law and order," traditionally a conservative interest. From this one may infer that if the U.N. should one day acquire a majority hostile to the status quo, it would have to be abandoned. Presumably Mr. Morgenthau would not flinch from this conclusion: it is his peculiar intellectual distinction that he makes explicit what the policymakers cannot say out loud, and what liberal ideologists dare not admit to themselves.

If one takes issue with this kind of thinking, it is not for the sake of scoring points, or because one shares the naïve expectations of pacifists, world federalists, and assorted utopians. Mr. Morgenthau's brand of conservative realism is proof against the standard arguments employed by such sentimentalists, just as it is superior to the short-sighted pragmatism of the New Frontier, with its pseudo-toughness, its faith in technical gimmicks, and its breezy indifference to history. Intellect, experience, and a certain ingrained pessimism about men and affairs combine to raise him above the level where breathless commentators, or self-deluded world saviors like Bertrand Russell, frantically scan the headlines for signs of yet another exercise in summitry. In turning a cold eye upon these trivial excitements, Mr. Morgenthau performs an important and necessary service. Leisured consideration of his more strictly topical writings confirms the impression one had on reading them for the first time. Though devoted to the passing moment, they stand up well to the inevitable second thoughts, and their subsequent publication in book form justifies itself by reason of their consistent adherence to a definite set of principles. These essays are lucid, hardheaded, perceptive, sustained by wide reading and the constant application of a mind at once reflective, critical, and disillusioned: the mind not of a practitioner, but of a theorist aware of the maze of conflicting and often insoluble problems that dog the statesman's heels. If the tone is rather bleakly rational, that is no harm in an environment where rhetoric too frequently takes the place of argument. Indeed, there is a no-nonsense air about Mr. Morgenthau's writings which can be appreciated even by the critic who proceeds from quite different assumptions.

Prestige aid has this in common with modern bribes that its true purpose, too, is concealed by the ostensible purpose of economic development.

A nation may . . suffer from human deficiencies which preclude economic development. As there are individuals whose qualities of character and level of intelligence make it impossible for them to take advantage of economic opportunities, so are there nations similarly handicapped. To put it bluntly: as there are bums and beggars, so are there bum and beggar nations.

A civilization such as the Burmese, which deprecates success in this world because it stands in the way of success in the other world, puts a cultural obstacle in the path of industrial development which foreign aid by itself cannot overcome.

One begins to see why the author is a favorite consultant of Senatorial committees investigating the wasteful use of public funds and past errors of foreign policy.

There is no occasion to deplore either these sentiments or their somewhat authoritarian mode of deliverance. In bringing together his scattered essays, Mr. Morgenthau has placed both the public and the critics under an obligation, for he represents an attitude that needs to be taken seriously. This is true even of his miscellaneous excursions into minor scandals and other topical affairs—occasional pieces which serve to flesh out a body of thought best described as conservative realism. Like other intellectual dispositions this mode of thought, too, has its unexamined premises, and an inquiry into their nature may cast some light on the practice they are intended to support.

I I

First, then, the theoretical framework within which the discussion of current affairs is placed throughout these three volumes. Its guiding lines are traced in the more philosophical sections of Volume I and elaborated in subsequent essays dealing with the principles of politics and diplomacy. The political realm—both internally and internationally—is defined by Mr. Morgenthau as a world of autonomous and conflicting power units. The theory of politics has to do with power, as that of economics has to do with wealth. The constituent members of a particular society are individuals and groups subordinated to a sovereign power. The constituents of the international order (or disorder) are nation-states not subjected to such a sovereign. "What sets international society apart from other societies is the fact that its strength—political, moral, social—is concentrated in its members, its own weakness being the reflection of that strength." [2] The term "international relations" denotes relations among autonomous political units or their individual members, and these units have throughout recorded history displayed certain consistent patterns of behavior, "whether entered into by hereditary monarchs or elective governments, cities or nation-states, continental empires or tiny principalities, ecclesiastic or secular rulers. The consistency of patterns beneath the variety of historic manifestations makes both historic understanding and theoretical analysis of international relations possible." [3] "The dynamic force that molds international relations is to be found in the aspirations for power of autonomous political units. These aspirations crystallize into three basic patterns: to keep one's power, to increase one's power, to demonstrate one's power. From these patterns three basic types of policy ensue: the policy of the status quo, the policy of imperialism, and the policy of prestige." [4] International relations may accordingly form themselves into multiple, bipolar, or imperial systems, as exemplified throughout ancient, medieval, and modern history.

The contemporary crisis springs from the growing technological unification of the world and the incidental disappearance of the frontier between limited and total war. The traditional system of international relations has thereby been rendered inoperative, for war—the *ultima ratio*—becomes irrational when it involves the total destruction of the participants. The resultant dilemma points to such differing solutions as international organization transcending the nation-state, or alternatively "the

2 *Ibid.*, p. 55.
3 *The Restoration of American Politics*, p. 167.
4 *Ibid.*, p. 168.

abolition of international relations itself through the merger of all national sovereignties into one world state which would have a monopoly of the most destructive instruments of violence. Both kinds of solution are supported by the awareness of the unity of mankind underlying the inevitable fragmentation of international relations." If and when realized in one way or another, these conflicting solutions will at last result in the establishment of a supranational political order. There is some prospect of this happening, for the urge toward such an order, "in times past mainly a spiritual or humanitarian impulse, in the nuclear age has been greatly strengthened by the desire, innate in all men, for self-preservation." [5]

The immediate situation is, however, characterized by the unfortunate circumstance that the unification of the planet is being attempted—in conformity with the usual bipolarity of politics—by two antagonistic groups or coalitions of states, namely the Western alliance and the Sino-Soviet bloc. The Western world is held together by certain commitments which it cannot surrender without falling under the domination of the rival bloc, whose way of life is incompatible with its own. The United States, as the leading or hegemonial power within the Western camp, is obligated so to conduct its affairs that its interests are seen to mesh with those of its allies. These allies are for the most part wealthy, industrialized, and conservative powers, as indeed is the United States itself. ("It is a conservative power both domestically and internationally, and must so appear particularly to the underdeveloped nations.") America and its allies are likewise handicapped by their democratic pluralism, and by the absence of a simple message wherewith to revolutionize the backward countries. In this respect the United States is on the defensive, whereas the Communist powers are able to direct world-wide revolutionary movements; in addition, their own internal problems "are more meaningful, at least on the surface, to the underdeveloped nations than are ours." With the best will, aid to the backward countries can only be a holding operation until they have learned to solve their problems.

[5] *Ibid.*, pp. 173-175.

For the rest, the United States "must . . . [wage] the competitive struggle with the Communist bloc without at the same time increasing the risk of war." [6]

In order to pursue their task with any hope of success, the policy-makers need guidance, and this guidance in the last resort must come from philosophy, which invariably underlies the secondary constructions of political science—for even the most empirical kind of political thinking is rooted in philosophical assumptions. Now it so happens that in politics the correct assumptions have to do with the concept of power. "By making power its central concept, a theory of politics does not presume that none but power relations control political action. What it must presume is the need for a central concept which allows the observer to distinguish the field of politics from other social spheres. . . . As economics is centered upon the concept of interest defined as wealth . . . so political science is centered upon the concept of interest defined as power. . . ." Yet since it deals with the problem of rational action—i.e., action properly adapted to means and ends—a theory of politics also contains a normative element.[7] This is important, for political theory must show itself capable of adapting to novel situations, such as the present post-liberal situation, which is "characterized by the interaction between the political and economic spheres. This interaction runs counter to the liberal assumption and requirement of actual separation, which is reflected in the academic separation of the two fields. This interaction reverts to a situation which existed before political science was established as an academic discipline." We no longer live in the liberal age, and its assumptions have in part become inconsistent with the rise of giant collective power organizations—corporations, labor unions, the modern state itself —which tend to unify the political and economic spheres.[8]

What political science needs above all is a firm commitment to "the truth about matters political for its own sake." This

6 Ibid., pp. 266-267, 304.
7 The Decline of Democratic Politics, pp. 48-49 ff.
8 Ibid., p. 51.

truth articulates itself into a certain number of particular truths, which in the course of time were discovered and stated by the great thinkers to whom we give our reverence. "It may be pointed out in passing that all great contributions to political science, from Plato, Aristotle and Augustine to *The Federalist* and Calhoun, have been responses to . . . challenges arising from political reality. They have not been self-sufficient theoretical developments pursuing theoretical concerns for their own sake." [9]

Why then are we going through an intellectual crisis? "Since in every epoch political thought is but the particular manifestation of . . . a general philosophy, this destruction of the political tradition must be seen in the context of the general intellectual trend of the times. What Rousseau and Marx did to politics, Kierkegaard did to religion, Nietzsche to philosophy, and Freud to the image of man. These attacks upon the very foundations of Western civilization have left the received systems of thought empty of content and, in any event, without conviction." [10] Political theory must set itself the task of restating "the perennial truths about politics." Contemporary political thought is unable to pose and answer the relevant questions. "Its relativism prevents it from raising the perennial problem of the distinction between truth and opinion." [11] There are certain permanent truths about human nature and political life whose recognition is essential to the health of the body politic. It is the task of philosophers to state them, and of public men to apply them so far as possible. This can never be easy. "Of the tasks political philosophy must perform, that of restoring a defective political order is the most precarious," as Plato and others discovered to their cost. Yet though philosophy is too abstract and rational for the contingent world of politics, it can help the actors to understand what they are doing. "Political philosophy can hold up to society the mirror of its ills and contrast it with the ideal picture of health, hoping to mold thought and inspire

[9] *Ibid.*, p. 47.
[10] *Ibid.*, pp. 2-3.
[11] *Ibid.*, p. 131.

action." [12] It must not, however, strive to usurp the place of the public man: philosopher-kings are rare; the most one can normally hope for is that the king (under modern conditions the elected ruler) will allow the philosopher to do some of his thinking for him.

That, more or less, is the intellectual framework. What is one to make of it?

First of all, it must be said that when it suits him, Mr. Morgenthau is not above playing fast and loose with his own categories. Thus in Volume III he has a brief essay on "The Revival of Objective Standards," where he rebukes Mr. Walter Lippmann for placing his faith in the restoration of what Lippmann for some reason calls "the public philosophy," *i.e.*, the doctrine of Natural Law. The "public philosophy," Mr. Morgenthau points out (quite rightly) "was not destroyed by its own rational deficiencies or by the hostility of the intellectuals, but . . . by the modern conditions and problems of life which the public philosophy, as it has come down to us, is unable to reflect and solve." So it seems after all that Rousseau and Marx, and all those other revolutionaries, were not solely responsible for the overthrow of the old order. Then again, the "public philosophy" had another awkward weakness: it was an ideology of the particular society which the democratic revolution subverted: ". . . natural law, the form in which the public philosophy has been transmitted to us, has not only been the reflection of the objective standards of politics, but it has also always been a political ideology, and predominantly an ideology of the status quo. In other words, the existing political order was identified with the objective and rational order. Yet when the existing political order lost its viability, natural law . . . became a mere ideological tool by which partial interests and subjective opinions tried to establish their universality and objectivity. We cannot forget that experience, and no self-contained intellectual movement can obliterate its philosophic effects." This candid assessment does not leave a great deal of the traditional conservative posi-

[12] *The Restoration of American Politics*, p. 67.

tion intact, yet commitment to the *philosophia perennis*, and therewith to Natural Law doctrine, is implicit in Mr. Morgenthau's own approach. The contradiction is not resolved; it takes the form of an intellectual dilemma of which Mr. Morgenthau is aware and which he does not hesitate to admit, therein differing—to his advantage—from other conservative writers who commonly make do with an inferior degree of intellectual rigor. "We" (the Western world) need something like a Natural Law doctrine, but if we are honest "we" also know that traditional Natural Law has been devalued and shown up for what it is (and always was): the intellectual counterpart of a particular social order. This is "our" dilemma, and "we" have to live with it as best we can.

It is perhaps noteworthy that on this issue Mr. Morgenthau occupies a position not shared by liberal democrats who have accepted the French Revolution. For him, Marx simply continued the work of destruction which Rousseau had begun. This assessment results in a drastic narrowing of the ground on which the modern conservative is supposed to take his ideological stand. How drastic, one may gather from his Introduction, where the entire political and technological upheaval of the past two centuries—in other words, the democratic revolution, taking the term in its widest sense—is treated as a challenge to "the Western tradition"; while the accompanying intellectual revolution—from Rousseau (why not Voltaire?) to Freud—is described as an attack on "the tradition of Western political thought."

Mr. Morgenthau in fact shares with Niebuhr and others the habit of appealing to something called "the Western tradition" which on inspection turns out to be the conservative tradition. Its chief pillars are Aristotle, the Church Fathers, and the theorists of absolutism, down to and including Hobbes, plus of course Edmund Burke. Among the moderns he includes the German exponents of *raison d'état*, notably Meinecke (who lived to regret his passionate absorption in *Realpolitik*) and his predecessor Ranke, though for some reason not Hegel, from whom Ranke and Meinecke acquired whatever general notions they possessed. All radical thinkers are ipso facto outside "the Western tradition." As for liberalism, it stands revealed as an illusion, and for the rest it is to be considered as a bourgeois ideology. Mr. Morgenthau has this to say (in an essay on "The Tragedy of German-Jewish Liberalism"):

> The liberation of the Jew was a by-product, and in a sense an inevitable by-product, of the rise of liberalism, and the rights of Jews in the Western world stand and fall with the belief in, and the practice of, liberal principles. For once you assume that men are not endowed with inalienable rights which require that with regard to their social and political positions they be treated as equals, you have already left behind the basic principle upon which the rights of Jews depend. . . . However, it so happens that the philosophy and the institutions of liberalism are not the expression of eternal verities. That philosophy and those institutions arose under certain historic conditions and hence were bound to disappear under different historic conditions. It is not by accident that the rise of liberal philosophy and of liberal institutions is intimately connected with the rise of the middle classes. The liberal philosophy is the philosophy par excellence which expresses the interests of the middle classes, and the liberal institutions are the bulwarks safeguarding their position in society. . . . German Jews, being predominantly middle class in social composition and liberal in political and philosophic outlook, shared to the full the optimistic mood of the liberal middle classes. . . . The rise of Nazism to power is obviously connected with the economic, social, and moral decline of the German middle classes. . . .[13]

The notable thing about this passage is not its employment of a somewhat popularized form of Marxist sociology (quite common since the early twentieth century in the German academic milieu, once Max Weber had rendered it respectable), but its unrestrained relativism. For if liberalism can be dismissed as a transitory ideology, there is really no stopping. Yet the reader who expects Mr. Morgenthau to be equally ruthless with other ideologies is in for a disappointment. It is true that now and then (e.g., when it is a question of Natural Law, with its uncomfortable Thomist implications) he wavers a little. But some

[13] *The Decline of Democratic Politics*, pp. 247 ff.

things, it turns out, are sacred after all: not only the eternal verities of Aristotelian politics, but even the common decencies of everyday life. The Van Doren case roused the moralist in Mr. Morgenthau, and once roused he was not easily quieted. Let the reader consult his "Epistle to the Columbians on the Meaning of Morality" (an open letter to some students of Columbia University who expressed reservations about the resignation of Charles Van Doren from the teaching staff of that institution). He will there find that when it comes to something really serious (such as cheating on a TV quiz show) there is no sterner judge of morals, and none less given to cultural relativism, than Mr. Morgenthau. Mr. Van Doren had admitted having cheated, and the authorities had hurriedly arranged for him to resign. To the protesting students Mr. Morgenthau replied:

> You must have smiled indulgently or shrugged with impatience when you saw me refer to the sanctity of the moral law. Is not morality, so you might ask, a relative thing, the ever changing result of environment and circumstances? If this were so, let me ask you, how do you explain that we can not only understand the moral relevance of the Ten Commandments, originating in a so- cial environment quite different from ours, but also make them the foundation of our moral life? How do you explain that the moral ideas of Plato and Pascal, of Buddha and Thomas Aquinas, are similarly acceptable to our intellectual understanding and moral sense? If the disparate historic systems of morality were not erected upon a common foundation of moral understanding and valuation, impervious to the changing conditions of time and place, we could not understand any other moral system but our own, nor could any other moral system but our own have any moral relevance for us.[14]

The naïve reader may perhaps scent the germ of a contradic- tion in the contrast between this passage and the remarks on Jewish emancipation cited above, but then he must remember that Plato, Aquinas, and Pascal—unlike Rousseau, Nietzsche, and Marx—are part of "the Western tradition." Liberalism, that is to say (and *a fortiori* radicalism), may be treated as an ideology (born "under certain historic conditions and hence

[14]*Ibid.*, p. 372.

bound to disappear under different historic conditions"); but traditionalism and moral authoritarianism may not: they have, so to speak, a privileged ontological status which renders them immune to the flux of time and circumstance. Like Aristotle's notions about politics, they share in the eternal verities. I am afraid this won't do. It smacks of party propaganda in the guise of philosophy—the sort of thing Burke practiced with such success at a time when the foundations of the traditional social order were under attack. But then Burke was a political pamphleteer, and his inconsistencies may be thought pardonable. His modern disciples are called upon to display greater logical coherence. To do Mr. Morgenthau justice, his occasional lapses from logic occur when he is roused to strong emotion by a particularly outrageous happening (such as the spectacle of a junior academic teacher trifling with the truth), and even then they relate to the metaphysical underpinnings of his system, not to that system itself. At the level of reflection upon politics he is perfectly consistent, though this does not necessarily render his thought immune to criticism. The critique, however, must try to penetrate to what lies behind his thinking, to the social reality upon which he reflects, and whose material contradictions make their appearance in the shape of unsolved (and insoluble) theoretical difficulties.

III

In an interesting and revealing essay in Volume I on "The Problem of the National Interest," Mr. Morgenthau dissociates his attitude from that of the thinker who clearly has had the greatest influence upon his own theorizing, namely Hobbes. "I have always maintained that the actions of states are subject to universal moral principles," he writes, "and I have been careful to differentiate my position in this respect from that of Hobbes." The evident truth of this statement is not affected by the consideration that Mr. Morgenthau's mechanistic view of politics, as a chessboard of predictable power moves, does not in practice leave much room for morality. A theorist may take a Hobbesian

143 : *The Politics of Conservative Realism*

view of the political universe and still retain a hankering for the moral certitudes embodied in Natural Law. The resolution of the dilemma may be found in the Hegelian doctrine that the institutions of society are the concrete embodiment of ethical values which have a claim upon our allegiance: to serve the state is to obey the moral law. Mr. Morgenthau does not expressly invoke Hegel—a philosopher with a notoriously bad reputation in the English-speaking world—but his qualified defense of Hobbes's "extreme dictum that the state creates morality as well as law" is in tune with the Hegelian tradition of nineteenth- and twentieth-century German thought: "Universal moral principles, such as justice or equality, are capable of guiding political action only to the extent that they have been given concrete content and have been related to political situations by society." [15]

One may suppose Mr. Morgenthau is aware—even though he does not go out of his way to say so—that this doctrine played its part in undermining the Natural Law tradition in nineteenth-century Germany. Presumably he also knows that in the later nineteenth century its spokesmen displayed a "realistic" outlook which suited the tendencies of the Wilhelminian age and in the end created a gulf between Germany and her neighbors. His difficulty in this respect is that, while committed to the defense of "Western values," he regards the liberal philosophy as naïve and intellectually inferior to the "tragic" realism of Hobbes and (though he does not mention him) Hegel. These thinkers portray the world as it really is, whereas liberalism embellishes the picture by making unsound assumptions about human goodness and rationality. The problem then consists in formulating a theory of politics which will be realistic without being cynical. In confronting this urgent task, Mr. Morgenthau—like every theorist who assumes the fixity of "human nature"—finds himself thrown back upon the familiar dichotomy of conservative realism and liberal utopianism:

> The history of modern political thought is the story of a contest between two schools which differ fundamentally in their conception of the nature of man, society, and politics. One believes that

[15] *Ibid.*, p. 106.

a rational and moral political order, derived from universally valid abstract principles, can be achieved here and now. It assumes the essential goodness and infinite mallcability of human nature, and attributes the failure of the social order to measure up to the rational standards, to lack of knowledge and understanding, obsolescent social institutions, or the depravity of certain isolated individuals or groups. . . . The other school believes that the world, imperfect as it is from the rational point of view, is the result of forces inherent in human nature. To improve the world one must work with those forces, not against them. This being inherently a world of opposing interests and of conflict among them, moral principles can never be fully realized, but at best approximated through the ever temporary balancing of interests and the ever precarious settlement of conflicts. This school then . . . appeals to historic precedent rather than to abstract principles, and aims at achievement of the lesser evil rather than of the absolute good.[16]

One catches the familiar echo of Burke inveighing against radical sophists, and indeed in a later essay in Volume I ("The Escape from Power") we are told: "Any realistic conception of politics must start with an assumption which is the exact opposite of Rousseau's. It must assume that man is born and lives in chains . . . freedom is a condition not of his empirical existence but of his moral existence. Man lives in chains, but everywhere he wants to be free." This statement, though, might win assent from some radicals, and as for the distinction between utopianism and realism, it is not obvious why one needs to be a conservative to grasp the point about the world being made up of opposing interests and conflicting forces. What else is Marxism about? The real ground of Mr. Morgenthau's pessimism about reforming movements comes out in a passage from another essay in Volume I ("The Commitments of Political Science") where, instead of merely invoking "human nature," he tells us what this nature is:

Why is it that all men lust for power; why is it that even their noblest aspirations are tainted by that lust? Why is it that the political act, in its concern with man's power over man and the concomitant denial of the other man's freedom, carries within

[16] *Ibid.*, p. 80.

itself an element of immorality and puts upon the actor the
stigma of guilt? Why is it, finally, that in politics good intentions
do not necessarily produce good results . . . and why is it conversely that evil men have sometimes done great good in politics,
and improvident ones have frequently been successful? Here we
are in the presence of the mystery, the sin, and the tragedy of
politics. . . .

The quasi-theological tone of this passage serves as a reminder
that one has heard similar utterances from Niebuhr. It is now
the fashion in American literature (as it was in German literature on the eve of 1914, when Germany braced itself for its
"tragic destiny") to describe history as inherently sinful, and
politics as subject to insoluble moral dilemmas. I confess to an
unworthy suspicion that talk about the "tragic dilemma" of politics will shortly become part of the official cant. How long will
it be before the more literate politicians discover the intellectual
attraction of decking out their maneuvers and compromises in
this kind of language? But let that pass. The important question
is this: what is it that lends to this language an air of profundity
lacking in the utterances of the liberal school? Why is it that
people are ready to agree that talk about the evil propensities of
human nature, and the essential sinfulness of "the political act,"
plumbs greater depths than are reached by the common-sense
language of rationalism? Furthermore, what is the link between
a theory of politics which makes "power" its central concept,
and a doctrine of human nature which asserts that the lust for
power is both universal and inherently destructive of human solidarity? Is the Hobbesian view of man and society so self-
evidently true as to impose itself upon us when we allow our
critical faculties free play? Or is not perhaps its plausibility secured by assumptions self-evident only to a theorist whose imagination is bounded by his own culture, and whose gaze is fixed
upon one particular aspect of modern history?

The word "modern" needs to be underlined in this context,
for it is part of Hobbes's distinction that he was the first important thinker to provide a coherent account of society which
broke with the standard medieval assumptions about the social

order. It is a commonplace of intellectual history that he did this by developing certain individualist notions already implicit in medieval nominalism; also that his thought represents a break with the Natural Law doctrine which the schoolmen had derived from Aristotle. It was this which made him seem alarming, as it had earlier caused the outcry against Machiavelli. Parenthetically one sees here why a modern author who constantly appeals to "the Western tradition"—*i.e.*, the Natural Law tradition—is bound to differentiate himself from Hobbes, whose thinking was subversive of that tradition. The fact remains that Mr. Morgenthau's political universe is that of Hobbes, though he affirms (on what seem to be extra-rational grounds) that "the actions of states are subject to universal moral principles." This appears to signify no more than that we may moralize about them: it is not intended to suggest that the actual behavior of states and nations can be deduced from an effective moral principle embedded in the natural order of things (or the natural *ratio* of men), for in that case we should be back with the Natural Law tradition. It is inherent in the Hobbesian view of civil society that the political order is amoral, if not actually immoral. Its only unifying principle is self-preservation—that is, the fear of death. In the words of a sympathetic exponent of Hobbes's thought, namely Professor Michael Oakeshott (in the Introduction to his edition of the *Leviathan*): "There is in this society no concord of wills, no common will, no common good; its unity lies solely in the singleness of the Representative, in the substitution, by individual acts of will, of his one will for the many conflicting wills."

Is this an accurate account of the manner in which society actually operates, apart from those periods of acute crisis (one of which Hobbes lived through) when it is in the grip of panic? Is Mr. Morgenthau justified in suggesting that a realistic view of the political order requires as its philosophical correlative a theory of human nature which recognizes no effective bond between man and man save that of fear? It should be clear at any rate that even on Aristotelian principles—derived from the practice of a commonwealth of slaveholders, armed to the teeth, and ready for constant war against rival city-states—there is something seriously deficient about a theory of politics which reduces "the political act" to the exercise of one man's power over another. (Elsewhere Mr. Morgenthau refers to the unbridgeable gap between Christian ethics and "the great commandment of politics: 'Use thy neighbor as a means to the ends of thy power' ": which, to say the least, discloses an odd notion of how society actually operates.)

Politics has always, among other things, been a means of establishing a social consensus and a mechanism for harmonizing conflicting interests. It could not have performed this function if its practitioners had not shown some desire and capacity for attending to communal tasks, organizing joint enterprises, balancing individual and social claims, taking care of minority interests, and in general serving (or at least pretending to serve) the common good. A society constituted on Hobbesian principles would instantly fall apart, which is among the reasons why Hobbes's detailed prescriptions have never been taken seriously by any political school (his general principles survived in a watered-down form in Locke's system, but by that time his frantic appeal for an autocratic and self-perpetuating sovereign had been dropped). The Hobbesian universe is a philosophical extravaganza. It is plausible only as long as one does not remind oneself that even in the seventeenth century it was not in the end possible to clamp a despotic authority upon a completely atomized society of selfish individuals. The reason—as Professor C. B. Macpherson has recently shown in an important study of the subject—is that Hobbes had overlooked the reality of effective social solidarity among both the exploited and the privileged classes of seventeenth-century society, the factor which subsequently enabled Locke to construct a rather more workable theory. Individual selfishness and the demonic lust for power turned out after all to be controllable. The social order could be held together without recourse to despotism, because all those individuals and groups who then counted for something (mere wage earners were by tacit consent not full citizens) had a common interest in supporting a regime which guaranteed public order, while leaving the propertied classes free to attend to their private concerns, of which the chief was the maximization of economic gain. This could be done even though absolutism had been abandoned. In short, Hobbes—appalled as he was by the birth trauma of the new order—had misread the nature of bourgeois society, and Locke had to correct his error before the basic elements of his system could enter into the Benthamite calculus.

The peculiarity of modern conservative "realism" lies in the fact that its theorists have reverted to Hobbes at a time when even Locke is out of date; for the universe of "possessive individualism" can now be transcended in theory and practice alike. Since he is not a socialist, Mr. Morgenthau cannot be expected to see this. The strength of his position derives from his willingness to dispense with those Lockean assumptions which are in fact no longer tenable, and to revert to the pessimistic authoritarianism of Hobbes which corresponded to an earlier crisis of modern society. But this "realism" is backed by philosophical generalizations which abstract from the social situation that originally attended their birth. Authoritarian thinking overlooks the plain truth that the Hobbesian system was unworkable and had to be amended before it could be utilized. The fact that the optimistic liberal amendments have now in turn been invalidated by the collapse of the social environment whose permanence Locke took for granted, lends a spurious air of toughness to the neo-conservative critique of liberal democracy, but it does not help to get us out of the crisis. At most it supplies intellectual ammunition for parties and movements which expect the breakdown of liberal democracy to result in the establishment of a self-perpetuating authoritarianism, backed by copious appeals to Natural Law and the inherent wickedness of human nature. Such an outcome is by no means impossible, but that is another matter. What must be resisted is the intellectual arrogance of a school which—while it promotes one particular solution—asserts that its philosophy embodies the only eternally valid insight into human nature.

In reality the Hobbesian view of "human nature" rests upon a conflation of metaphysical and social assumptions: the former derived from theology, the latter projected into political theory from the unexamined premises of a particular social order. Since this order no longer functions in accordance with classical liberal precepts—on this point the new authoritarians are right—the fashionable picture of "human nature" takes on a darker and more pessimistic coloring than it did in the nineteenth century, when the liberal integration was fully effective. Yet conservative authoritarianism is still tied to the social situation which Hobbes encountered when he sketched the first rough outline of his philosophy: the unleashing of uncontrolled private appetites by the operation of a market economy. Its basic assumptions in consequence are still those of the thinker who first laid it down that man is a wolf to his neighbor. Never mind that Hobbes went wrong when he asserted that men had nothing in common save fear of death (today he might add that nations have nothing in common save fear of nuclear obliteration). The relevant point is that he was first with the announcement that man is autonomous and owes nothing to society, *i.e.*, to his fellow men. The announcement was factually true for his own age and for those individuals whose experiences he generalized into a system. Its limited factual truth has always been the strength of a certain kind of middle-class conservatism. Against the liberal idealism of academic theorists, this conservatism stands pat on the discovery that, in a society dominated by market relations, only the independent proprietor is a full citizen, *i.e.*, one able to resist the selfish claims and lusts of other men, and make use of the power of the state (which latter exists for the purpose of protecting the proprietors from each other as well as from the lower classes).

Liberalism sublimated this reality by establishing a kind of majority consensus. Now that the erosion of the liberal compromise translates itself into the crisis of liberal democracy, conservative "realism" acquires fresh intellectual prestige, and simultaneously proclaims its own metaphysic of human nature: why not recognize that men are inherently evil and must be held in check by superior power? We are back with Hobbes. Politically this is the natural recourse for all those groups and individuals who can see in the present crisis only a threat to "order." At the philosophical level it takes the form of pessimistic reflections upon the eternal tragedy of "human nature": a nature viewed as a permanent threat to the existence, and the rights, of other men. Having read their current preoccupations back into nature, the theorists of the new authoritarianism are able to present themselves as custodians of the eternal verities. It does not occur to them—or to their admiring public—that the very notion of a fixed and unchanging human nature represents a prejudice. If the status quo has to be frozen, we may as well start believing that what the authoritarians tell us about mankind is true and not subject to historic change. In which case we had better not ask indiscreet questions about the social origins of the Hobbesian world-view.

For better or worse, however, there are two sides to this dispute and their differences relate not only to the question of what is to replace the liberal-democratic integration, but also to the position of man in society. On this issue, conservatives and radicals do indeed part company. To Mr. Morgenthau's rhetorical question "Why is it that all men lust for power?" the answer is: "Some don't." And to his implied assumption that all thinking people, whatever their differences, must at any rate concede the truth of the Hobbesian world-view, the answer is that it has now become historically possible for rational men to reject the basic assumptions of the social order which made Hobbes's account of political behavior plausible. To do this they need not take refuge in utopia. They need only generalize from their own daily practice, which could not sustain itself for an hour without the constant exercise of simple, ordinary human solidarity, as exemplified in the ability to work together rather than against one another. A social order which utilizes these capacities more fully than the existing one can ever hope to do, is not beyond the realm of possibility, and its attainment is the cure for theoretical dilemmas which at the present level must remain unanswerable.

Leviathan*

• It is rare for a book to change the intellectual landscape. It is even more unusual for this to happen when the subject is one that has been thoroughly investigated by generations of philosophers and historians. The English Revolution of the seventeenth century is such a subject, as is its intellectual accompaniment: the philosophical revolution inaugurated by Hobbes and given final form by Locke. Until the appearance of Professor C. B. Macpherson's work,† it seemed unlikely that anything radically new could be said about so well-worn a topic. The unexpected has happened, and the shock-waves are still being absorbed. To judge from the reserve with which his study has been received in some quarters, the specialists may need time before they forgive the author for upsetting their professional applecart. Meanwhile students of philosophy and history alike have reason to be grateful.

Professor Macpherson, who holds the chair of political science at Toronto, has done something very unusual: he has treated the crisis of the seventeenth century as a single phenomenon encompassing both a political upheaval and an intellectual reconstruction; and in so doing he has shed new light on topics as disparate as Hobbes's doctrine of human nature and Harrington's scheme for a new commonwealth. On the conventional view these subjects either have nothing to do with each other, or else it is assumed that the ideological issue is to be regarded as a pale reflection of the "real" conflict proceeding somewhere behind the scenes. As to the latter, it is commonly supposed that

---

* *New Statesman* (6 September 1963).
† *The Political Theory of Possessive Individualism: Hobbes to Locke* (London and New York, 1962).

at any rate the factual circumstances are fully known and properly understood. Now Macpherson has shown that this cannot be taken for granted. Thus he has conclusively demolished the legend that the Levellers stood for political democracy based on manhood suffrage. After all that had been repeated by writers on this subject, it really seemed that there was nothing further to be said. Yet so distinguished a historian as Mr. Christopher Hill has now acknowledged that (in common with his fellow scholars) he had been mistaken on this important point. In future it will not be possible to go on treating the Levellers as precursors of the Chartists. Professor Macpherson has gone over the evidence and the actual social background with a magnifying-glass, and made it clear that the projected Leveller commonwealth was one where power would have lain with a propertied minority. The Levellers, it turns out, were forerunners of Locke and the Whigs, "radical liberals" rather than "radical democrats."

> For they put freedom first and made freedom a function of proprietorship. . . . They can claim the distinction of being the first political theorists to assert a natural right to property for which the individual owes nothing to society and which entails none of those duties entailed in the earlier doctrine of stewardship (p. 158).

By placing property rights at the center of their advocacy of popular representation (for their proposed constitution, which was too radical for Cromwell, excluded wage earners), "they made it easy for Locke to confuse . . . the equal right to property with the right to unlimited property, and thus to harness democratic sentiments to the Whig cause. The confusion was not repaired for two centuries." Not, that is to say, until socialism had appeared on the scene.

If Professor Macpherson had merely established this challenging thesis, his book would already consitute an event in historical scholarship. In fact he has done a great deal more. In the light of his extremely detailed and subtle investigations into the meaning of what he calls "possessive individualism," the whole of seventeenth-century political philosophy takes on a new look.

It becomes clear that Cromwell, Harrington, Hobbes, Locke, and the Whigs were all struggling with the same problem: that of political freedom *for a minority* under the conditions of a competitive society which had disrupted the old hierarchical status order. Hobbes is no longer simply the theorist of absolutism: he appears as an important precursor of Bentham. And the demonstration does not hinge upon his explicit social and political views: it is effected by a close analysis of his basic philosophical concepts, notably his interpretation of "nature" and "human nature." The Hobbesian world-view is shown to embody a mental image which Hobbes had read back into nature from the society around him. His psychology is brought into relation with the actual psychological determinants of individuals set free from inherited social obligations. "The state of nature is a deduction from the appetites and other faculties not of man as such but of civilized men."

It is true that earlier students of the period had already moved towards some such conclusion. Professor Leo Strauss (in his recently republished *Political Philosophy of Hobbes*) suggested as far back as 1936 that Hobbes's system had an implicit social content. He even went so far as to assert that "the genesis of Hobbes's political philosophy is nothing other than the progressive supplanting of aristocratic virtue by bourgeois virtue." Coming from an Aristotelian like Strauss, whose detestation of post-medieval philosophy explicitly embraces Hobbesian and Lockean individualism, this was not intended as a compliment. Professor Macpherson, whose unspoken commitments clearly place him in the Marxist camp, does not dissent from the characterization of Hobbes's value-system as "bourgeois," though in general he avoids the term and speaks of "possessive individualism" instead. Where he differs from Strauss is in treating as relatively unimportant Hobbes's observations on man's innate desire for unlimited power over others. As he shows, such an assumption, even if it could be substantiated by reference to the "state of nature," would hardly account for the characteristically Hobbesian doctrine that individuals *in society* are in constant rivalry, and in equally constant danger from each other. Setting

THE CONCEPT OF IDEOLOGY

aside Hobbes's tendency to read social assumptions back into his psychological postulates about the "state of nature," one has to relate his model of society to the individualist concepts which he shared with his contemporaries (including the Levellers). This Macpherson has accomplished in a manner which appears conclusive. It is difficult to see how anyone will ever again be able to think of the subject in terms that antedate his analysis.

The originality of this achievement is not diminished by its concordance with the established view of Hobbes as the founder of modern political philosophy. Why should it be? It is, after all, one thing to say that Hobbes is the ancestor of all later individualism (and indeed more radical in this respect than Locke, who merely rendered his system acceptable to middle-class opinion). It is quite another matter to link his conceptual model of man and society to the actual circumstances of his day, by showing how the very notion of autonomous man—man who owes nothing to his fellow men—represents a break with the traditional assumptions proper to a "status society" in which customary social obligations are taken for granted. This Macpherson has done through an analysis of Hobbes's (and Locke's) fundamental concepts. It is naïve to object (as has been done by one critic) that these writers were not concerned with "bourgeois nature" but with "human nature." This is to take at face value the conceptual language every thinker has to employ in dealing with the problems of his age. It is on a par with the illusion of some contemporary sociologists who imagine themselves to be saying something about "social structure" in general when in fact they are describing (not always very clearly) the structure of modern industrial society.

Hobbes and Locke at least had the excuse of writing at a time when this particular form of self-delusion had not yet been subjected to critical treatment. Its current revival testifies to a residual unwillingness to accept the principle that suprahistorical generalizations about society must either be platitudes or illegitimate extrapolations of social concepts to the realm of nature. As a philosopher, Hobbes reflected on man and society in general. As a political scientist—the founder indeed of political science—he laid bare the nature of *modern* society. His greatness is not diminished thereby, and it is quite gratuitous to defend him against the imputation of being no more than the theorist of a particular social order. As if any serious thinker could ever be anything else!

The implications of Macpherson's work for contemporary political theory are evident, and they relate in a somewhat disturbing manner to the question he raises in his concluding pages: namely whether modern democracy can continue to function on a liberal-individualist basis, now that its inherited social framework has largely disappeared. The problem arises from the fact that, as he puts it, for a completely secularized doctrine of political obligation (*i.e.*, one not dependent upon appeals to God or Nature) to be acceptable, men must be able to see themselves "as equal in some respect more fundamental than all the respects in which they are unequal." This condition was fulfilled from the seventeenth century to the nineteenth by the operation of a mechanism which subordinated the individuals to the determination of a market-centered society. In these circumstances, a rough equality of opportunity was actually felt to exist. At the same time political cohesion was guaranteed by the effective limitation of power to a property-owning minority. The erosion of this environment has made it questionable whether liberal democracy can continue to function, and indeed Macpherson suggests that democracy may have to cease being liberal (in the classical sense), on pain of being superseded altogether. It must, he thinks, evolve a new intellectual justification, for the inherited doctrine will not do any longer.

> Either we reject possessive individualist assumptions, in which case our theory is unrealistic, or we retain them, in which case we cannot get a valid theory of obligation.

Studies of political thought come in all shapes and sizes. Professor J. W. Allen's standard work on the sixteenth century (originally published in 1928 and reprinted as a paperback in 1960) covers a comparatively brief period in some five hundred closely printed and heavily footnoted pages. Mr. John Plamenatz has allotted himself a wider span. His two-volume work *Man and Society* is subtitled *A Critical Examination of Some Important Social and Political Theories from Machiavelli to Marx*. It has the virtues of clarity, urbanity, and readability. Written up from lecture notes, it avoids technicalities and maintains an agreeably leisured pace. The tone is conversational. Students may find it useful as an introduction to the subject, though it lacks the usual apparatus; there are only the barest references and no bibliography at all.

What the text lacks is rather more serious. Mr. Plamenatz adheres to the conventional notion that the proper way of dealing with a thinker is to expound his doctrines and then compare them to the teachings of other thinkers. His expositions are invariably clear, fair-minded, and a little shallow. He avoids conceptual difficulties; he also steers clear of modish innovations, such as social history or intellectual history. The reader is warned that he has not tried to write a history of political thought or to explain how one theorist influenced another. Nor is he interested in the social matrix of thought. His critical analysis, he says, "scarcely looks at the circumstances in which this or that theory was produced." Some scholars nowadays tend to be a little apologetic about this sort of thing, but Mr. Plamenatz is not one of them. History is none of his business. He is concerned with what his authors thought, and whether they were right or wrong. When he thinks they were wrong, he does not hesitate to tell them off.

He also shows no embarrassment about admitting that some things are too difficult for him—Hegel's metaphysics, for instance. Hegel, it appears, lacked common sense: he believed in something called the concrete universal, which Mr. Plamenatz says he does not understand. Furthermore he believed (as did Plato) that philosophy represents man's awakening from the dream of existence. Mr. Plamenatz has no use for such fancies and treats Hegel with a good deal of severity, though he rightly defends him against the fashionable charges of willful obscurity and intellectual fraudulence. All in all, Hegel puzzles him. One

157 : *Leviathan*

feels that he would have been happier with Kant, but Kant is not discussed at all.

This is not the only major omission. In general Mr. Plamenatz proceeds in chronological order, as textbook authors should, but there are large gaps in the story. A number of writers usually regarded as important are left out or mentioned only in passing. Thus Machiavelli is discussed, but not Vico; Bodin, but not the Protestants. Spinoza is briefly mentioned as an advocate of toleration, and then drops from sight. There are chapters on Montesquieu and Burke, nothing on the American Constitution; yet it is arguable that the *Federalist* contains better reasoning than Burke's writings. The Scottish historians (other than Hume) and the French Encyclopedists are not considered at all. Perhaps news of them has not reached Oxford?

Since Mr. Plamenatz does not believe in writing social history or intellectual history, he is not bothered by troublesome questions over which other writers have lost sleep, such as the relation of cultural change to theoretical problems. Indeed he is not so much concerned with problems as with personalities. Every thinker gets a self-contained chapter or subsection, and is then dismissed to make room for another. People who did not write books, Cromwell for example, do not come in at all, not even in connection with authors of books such as the *Leviathan*. Mr. Plamenatz does not believe in confusing the reader by relating history to philosophy. Thus Hobbes is discussed without reference to the Civil War, Rousseau without reference to the French Revolution, Marx without reference to the Industrial Revolution. There are two lengthy chapters on Marxism; from them the student will gather that Marx and Engels were wrong about practically everything, but he will not learn how Marxism arose, or why it has been influential. Nor will he find any mention of the 1848 upheaval, or of German and European history since that date. Instead there is a lengthy discussion of what Marx meant by "ideology." This always fascinates academic writers, but it is not central to the understanding of Marxism.

Like most people who specialize in a subject, Mr. Plamenatz

is best on what is closest to home. Easily his most informative chapter is that on Bentham. Here he is on familiar ground and moreover is able to draw upon his own earlier work. Bentham gets thirty-six pages—twelve times more than Spinoza. Mr. Plamenatz explains Utilitarianism, and then indicates what are its logical flaws. This has been done before, but he does it very well. His chapters on Hobbes and Locke are less successful. Unlike Professor Macpherson, he is not concerned with the political problem in its social setting, and so misses the point of what Hobbes and Locke were trying to do. He also misses the point about Marx, on whom he has written an earlier book. Marx, unlike Hegel, was not a metaphysician, and thus offers fewer intellectual difficulties; but he was an economist, and Mr. Plamenatz confesses frankly that this subject is outside his range. Instead he concentrates on Marx's theory of the state. Unfortunately Marx had no theory of the state. He was not interested in the state; he was interested in society. He was also interested in history, which does not interest Mr. Plamenatz. In consequence, his treatment of Marx is not very illuminating and does not reach the level of his chapter on Bentham, who of course is easier to understand. Perhaps the moral is that if one dissociates history from philosophy, one is unlikely to make much sense of either.

Tyrants Ancient and Modern[*]

• The reappearance in print of Professor Leo Strauss's well-known study[†] derives its special interest from circumstances only indirectly connected with the original publication. In 1954, France's leading Hegel scholar, Alexandre Kojève (in private life a high official in the French administration), published a critical study entitled *Tyrannie et sagesse* in which he dealt in the grand Hegelian manner with Strauss's work. Translated as *Tyranny and Wisdom* for the volume under review, his essay of forty-five printed pages drew a lengthy rejoinder from Strauss, originally published in French and later included in the collection of papers issued by the Free Press in 1959 under the title *What Is Political Philosophy?* In the volume now before the public all these writings have been brought together in a very attractive format, not omitting thirty-three pages of Notes to Strauss's interpretation of Xenophon's *Hiero* which makes up the bulk of Part One. It has been necessary to dwell on these externals because they are in fact closely related to the topic of the dispute. Strauss is so completely under the spell of the Greeks in general, and Xenophon in particular, that he presents his argument in the form of an eighty-page analysis of Xenophon's text (a new translation of which was commissioned by Agora Editions, the editors responsible for the book, to enable the reader to follow the finer points of Strauss's analysis). For such perfectionism no praise can be too high. If Xenophon is a school classic, and if Strauss is on his way to becoming a modern university classic, then the least one can say is that both authors have been fortunate in their publishers. As for Kojève, it

[*] *Commentary* (November 1963).
[†] *On Tyranny* (New York, 1963).

was time he was introduced to the Anglophone public. His *Introduction à la lecture de Hegel* (Paris 1947) is caviar for the general, and moreover shows no sign of being translated. Apart from this one major work, he has written—or at any rate published—very little, and even in France is known mainly to a small circle of initiates. His influence has, however, been considerable, not least in starting the post-war Hegel renaissance.

After these preliminaries, can we at last get down to the real topic? Unfortunately the answer is no, and for this Strauss must take the responsibility. What is really of importance in the matter emerges from his controversy with Kojève, but before he arrives at this point the reader has to make his way through Xenophon's *Hiero* and Strauss's detailed exegesis of this rather slight and inconsequential piece of writing. I am of course aware that in saying this I am offending against the accepted canons of literary decency and good taste. I am also offending against Strauss's basic assumption, which is that Wisdom is encapsulated in the classical texts he has chosen to interpret. Being in this matter on Kojève's side, I shall compound the original felony by suggesting that the full meaning of Xenophon can be grasped by an intelligent schoolboy at the first reading. This is such an outrageous statement that I shall make no effort to defend it. I merely observe, in passing as it were, that Xenophon has always been a favorite with schoolmasters (though less so with their pupils).

The *Hiero* (in case some of my readers have been unjustly deprived of a classical education) takes the form of an imaginary dialogue between the tyrant Hiero and Simonides, a "wise man come from afar" (like Strauss) to instruct the wretched tyrant in the arts of government. Hiero is wretched because, as he explains to Simonides at considerable length, a tyrant is necessarily unloved and in constant fear of his life. Simonides, who is not a tyrant, merely a poet and wandering scholar with no public responsibilities, thereupon informs Hiero that, while remaining a tyrant—*i.e.*, not a legitimate ruler, but one governing by fear—he can nonetheless make himself more popular by various devices whose nature has not greatly changed since those days.

161 :   *Tyrants Ancient and Modern*

The argument prefigures the wisdom of Machiavelli. In fact—
not to put too fine a point on it—it *is* the wisdom of Machiavelli. Strauss, who dislikes Machiavelli and moreover credits him
with a specifically modern viewpoint, is constrained to note that
"the *Hiero* marks the point of closest contact between pre-
modern and modern political science." A writer less enamored
of the Greeks might have put it differently, perhaps even going
so far as to hint that the politics of Athens were not really all
that remote from those of Florence: especially after democracy
had collapsed in both places, and cynical young aristocrats
(Xenophon, though less amusing than Alcibiades, clearly is a
horse from the same stable) had discovered the secret of im-
posing upon their fellow citizens.

However this may be historically (Strauss is not greatly interested in history), the reader is treated to a subtle distinction
between "good" and "bad" tyrants. Xenophon's Simonides sets
out to show Hiero how he can "rule as a virtuous tyrant" (p.
96), and his learned exegete by implication subscribes to this
noble enterprise. The reader must decide for himself whether it
is feasible. There have of course been enlightened despots,
though even at their peak, in the later eighteenth century, they
frequently disappointed their tutors. In his reply to Kojève,
which makes up the concluding part of this fascinating volume,
Strauss concedes (pp. 199-201) that, on the evidence presented
by Xenophon, Hiero does not sound like a very promising pupil.
Yet on an almost despairing note he inquires whether this may
not have been due to an accidental failure to ask for the proper
advice on how to become a "good tyrant." This is followed by a
passage in which Strauss observes: "The general lesson is to the
effect that the wise man who happens to have a chance to influence a tyrant should use his influence for benefiting his fellow
men. One may say that the lesson is trivial. It would be more
accurate to say that it was trivial in former ages, for today such
little actions like that of Simonides are not taken seriously because we are in the habit of expecting too much" (p. 201).
What we are in the habit of expecting is not having to bother
about tyrants. If this is unwarranted, as Strauss appears to be-

lieve, it is at any rate an attitude firmly established in countries where constitutional government has been the rule.

So far as political understanding goes, there is not much to be got out of Xenophon or any other minor Socratic. The *Hiero* in fact is trite. This point leads to a consideration of Kojève's essay, which is by far the most brilliant part of the book, and the element that raises it above the level of mere exegesis. Although Strauss is an Aristotelian, it takes the challenge of the Hegelian Kojève to bring out his full commitment to Aristotle, which is why his rejoinder to Kojève is a more interesting and incisive piece of writing than his original study of Xenophon. Kojève fortunately wastes no time over Xenophon's inanities, but comes straight to the point. Strauss had demanded to know how a wise man can live under tyranny. Kojève replies that it is his own fault if he has no influence over the tyrant, since the latter is in fact dependent on his advice, for he sees the whole picture (in Hegelian terms, "the truth in its concreteness"), while the statesman—who need not be a tyrant—never sees more than what is immediately relevant to his purpose. Moreover, no regime can get on without general ideas which are ultimately supplied by philosophy. A reign of "pure terror" is unthinkable, since no one can personally terrorize more than a handful of people. Loyalties are essential to every form of government, and the concept of loyalty leads back to philosophy, which is the vision of the historical process as a whole. Thinkers rather than poets are the unacknowledged legislators of the world. Kojève cites Alexander's relationship to Aristotle, which prompted the conqueror's revolutionary aim of transcending the *polis* in the direction of a universal empire. He also drops a tantalizing hint about Hegel, who admired Napoleon and whose acceptance of enlightened autocracy has had practical consequences in our own day. At this point Kojève runs into the difficulty of having to make room for the kind of tyrant who places himself in the service of a revolutionary idea. Strauss promptly picks up the challenge by reminding him of Stalin. The rejoinder is legitimate, but Strauss goes on to suggest that on Hegelian principles, which he traces back to Machiavelli and

Hobbes, there are no moral bounds to tyranny. This is inexact, for Hegel would have recognized that (to cite a topical example) the destruction of Germany as a nation was the price paid by the Germans for allowing Hitler to come to power.

Kojève and Strauss enter into a fascinating dispute over the philosopher's role in the "city." The burden of Strauss's original argument had been that, under a constitutional government, or even under a "virtuous tyrant," the proper role of the philosopher is to attend to the eternal verities which are perceived in contemplation. Kojève points out that this attitude renders the philosopher not merely politically impotent, but even useless as a thinker, since as an isolated spectator confined within his four walls he cannot get beyond subjective certainty, which is no guarantee of the truth. Left alone with his untested notions he is not distinguishable from "the lunatic who believes that he is made out of glass, or who identifies himself with God the Father or Napoleon." In order to test the validity of his thoughts he must leave his study—or his Epicurean "garden"—and venture out into the market place, where he will encounter other men, not all of them philosophers. He will then have joined the "Republic of Letters" whose constant sociability is at least a cure for solipsism and "a sufficient guarantee against the danger of lunacy." Permanent residence in the Academy, or Republic of Letters, however, has the drawback that it shuts the thinker off from the political sphere where ideas are clothed with flesh. If he decides to break through this barrier, he will naturally be drawn to tyrants, as being more likely that ordinary statesmen to cut the Gordian knot with some energetic stroke. Kojève presents a sophisticated apology of this situation, on the grounds that "the conflict of the philosopher faced with the tyrant is nothing else than the conflict of the intellectual faced with action . . . the tragedy of Hamlet and of Faust" (p. 177). This is a very Hegelian notion which Strauss, not unreasonably, finds alarming. It is in fact the reflex of a passing situation similar to the Napoleonic age, and as such perhaps chiefly relevant as a reminder that Europe has already once before passed through a revolution which issued in dictatorship.

While Kojève and Strauss clash at practically every point, their deepest difference relates to what Strauss calls "historicism," and what Kojève describes as the understanding of history. For Kojève the very existence of philosophy is an historical factum which may be brought to an end by the practical realization of those ultimate aims that make their appearance in the great utopias of literature. Strauss, who thinks in terms of archetypal situations which the classics have described once and for all, denounces the very notion of such an outcome. For him, the human situation is fixed eternally in the classical (Biblical and Socratic) texts, and the modern attempt to disregard these verities represents a monumental aberration, for which the world may have to pay by sliding into universal tyranny. His disagreement with Kojève is particularly acute at this point because it ties in with the Hegelian depreciation of classical wisdom. Although Hegel was himself in the classical tradition—the "German Aristotle" quite deliberately went back to Plato for some of his basic concepts—he tended in his historical writings (e.g., in his lectures on the history of philosophy) to treat the ancient world in a somewhat condescending manner, as a preparatory stage to subsequent revelations. From the Hegelian viewpoint—which on this topic was indeed the modern viewpoint—the classical world was a kind of intellectual nursery which Europe had outgrown. This attitude became fixed among his followers who substituted "Europe" for "Christendom." To Strauss it is intolerable because it undercuts his profound conviction that eternal truth is to be found in the classics, with their Natural Law doctrine, and nowhere else. The movement of thought since Machiavelli (he does not mention Vico) is for him a movement away from the truth.

The sharpest reproach Strauss can urge against Kojève (and Hegel) is that of atheism. At least since Hobbes and Spinoza almost every major thinker has been an open or concealed atheist. Yet Strauss—while well aware of this fact and deeply alarmed by it—refers to atheism with horror, as though it were some kind of obscene disease caught by infection, instead of being the characteristic attitude of modern man. Doubtless the fact of something being the typical modern attitude does not render it immune to criticism, but Strauss meets the challenge not at its deepest level, but at the level of alarmist forecasts concerning the results to be apprehended from the world-wide triumph of a totally secularized outlook. Even if the consequences are in fact going to be as disagreeable as he thinks, his readers are unlikely to heed his call for a return to the past. It is a necessary aspect of the modern commitment to intellectual honesty that such appeals must be dismissed. A philosophy which flinched away from its own insights, as being too bleak and comfortless, would scarcely be worth having.

Hegel*

• If civilization is wiped out in a nuclear war between East and West, it is quite likely that Hegel will be among the few authors to survive the holocaust. His writings are currently being studied in places as remote as Ghana and Cuba. He is part of the curriculum in Samarkand, and Mao Tse-tung has seen to it that Chinese schoolboys are imbued with a proper respect for the official philosopher of Prussian conservatism. There are bearded sages in Central Asia for whom he has taken the place of Aristotle (the only other philosopher to have come to their notice). Africans who study in Paris cannot fail to return with potted fragments of Hegel in their mental baggage, though they may think of themselves as followers of Marx or Sartre. All in all, Hegel has made good. The only considerable area of contemporary civilization where he remains taboo is the Anglo-American academic world.

The appearance of a critical commentary on Hegel by Professor Walter Kaufmann† provides a welcome opportunity for examining some of the reasons for this cultural lag. The most important of them is obvious. The Anglo-American school of philosophy has been hard at work since the First World War trying to make people forget its own previous indebtedness to Hegel. Green, Bradley, and McTaggart in Britain, Royce and Dewey in America, had been deeply influenced by him. Indeed the whole idealist movement down to 1914 owed its peculiar cast of mind to the impact of the Hegelian tradition. Penance was called for, and Hegel was duly exorcized, along with Nietzsche (with whom he had literally nothing in common). In later

* The New York Review (July 15, 1965).
† Hegel: Reinterpretation, Texts, and Commentary (New York, 1965).

years the rise of Communism and Fascism—both ostensibly linked to Hegel—sharpened the antagonism. By 1945 the educated public was ready for Professor Popper's furious vituperation in *The Open Society*. In vain did the surviving academic Hegelians, with G. R. C. Mure of Oxford in the lead, point out that Popper clearly had not read Hegel properly, let alone understood him. The general reader was impressed by Popper's authoritative tone and reluctant to credit the notion that he might be talking through his hat. Only when Professor Kaufmann some years ago, in a lengthy and effective polemical essay, demolished Popper's criticism, did it become possible once more to get the debate back on dry ground.

What Kauffmann has now done in his new book is decidedly original. He opens with a brief biography of Hegel, and then goes on to a discussion of some of the more difficult texts, principally the *Logic* and the *Phenomenology*. In addition he has provided a full translation of the lengthy and important Preface to the latter work, with a textual commentary on facing pages. There he not only clarifies Hegel's famous obscurities, but offers the reader a guide to the often very puzzling connotations of Hegel's elaborate punning in German. No translator can do full justice to the *Phenomenology*—the most poetic, as well as the most difficult of Hegel's voluminous writings—but Kaufmann at least gives the student who has no German a glimpse of the fascination of the original. He clearly takes Glockner's view that "whoever has understood the preface to the *Phenomenology* has understood Hegel," and his lengthy commentary is a minor masterpiece of concise and erudite interpretation. This is a welcome departure from the lazy habit of pretending that Hegel was an obscure pedant who fortunately left some quite readable lectures on the philosophy of history. In fact the famous lectures (as Kaufmann points out) were put together after his death, and the editing left much to be desired. It will not do either to follow the other fashionable direction and confine oneself to the *Philosophy of Right*, where Hegel expounds his political doctrine; or to his minor political essays (recently published in T. M. Knox's translation, with a Preface by Mr. Z. A. Pelczynski). From these writings one may gather that Hegel was a conservative, but one will not learn why radicals like Marx took him seriously. Even less will one understand why he has been called the German Aristotle. To grasp what Hegel was really trying to do, one has to confront his metaphysics, and thanks to Kaufmann this can now be done even by the philosophical novice.

The editor, however, has not simply popularized his subject. He has indeed provided an introductory essay in *haute vulgarisation*, but even at this level he writes as a specialist (and as a trenchant critic of previous editors and translators). Moreover, it is just not possible to discuss Hegel's early work without plunging into the celebrated German metaphysical fog, never thicker than in the early years of the nineteenth century. The *Phenomenology of Spirit* is as romantic and chaotic as Goethe's *Faust*, the first part of which was published almost in the same year (1807-1808). Maddeningly obscure, it is also lit up by sudden flashes of almost superhuman illumination. Decked out with stylistic gargoyles, it is at the same time loaded down with oblique allusions to classical and modern drama, from Sophocles to Schiller. It is in fact a work of art—the greatest in the history of modern philosophy. The editor himself suggests that Hegel, like Wagner half a century later, was trying to produce "a *Gesamtkunstwerk*, leaving out little but music." An earlier German biographer spoke of Hegel's "romantic masquerade." It is a fact that he alludes in passing to such varied themes as the death of Socrates, the Antigone, medieval Christianity, the French Revolution, Diderot's *Neveu de Rameau*, and the writings of Kant— always in such a way as to leave the reader in doubt as to his precise meaning. Anything that served his purpose was stuffed in, whether it was Goethe's Iphigenia or his own sister. There is even an obscure reference to Macbeth.

That a writer who first made his mark with such a work should have come down to posterity as a dry German professor tells one something about the way history gets written, but it is also part of Hegel's own tragedy. A romantic in his youth, and quite actively concerned with public affairs—when Napoleon's invasion of Germany wrecked the university of Jena and halted his academic career, he made a living for a while as a newspaper editor—he gradually turned into the stiff, elderly pedant who from his professorial chair in Berlin laid down the law to colleagues and students alike. Even then (if one can believe Heine, who studied under him) he was capable on occasion of sudden flashes of rationalist cynicism, at least in private and on the subject of religion. But the mask had stuck. He had become the official apologist of Prussian conservatism, though the true reactionaries regarded him with unconcealed distrust, and after his death the aged Schelling was imported from Munich to grapple with the "dragon seed" of Hegelianism. The audience at Schelling's inaugural lecture in 1841 (which was generally voted a disappointment) included Engels, Bakunin, and Kierkegaard: fate (or revolution) knocking at the door.

Professor Kaufmann has comparatively little to say about that part of the Hegelian inheritance which was taken over by Marx and his followers. Perhaps he is wise. After all, one can have too much of a good thing, and this particular topic is now nearing exhaustion. I suspect, however, that his interest is not seriously engaged by the subject of history. He is more concerned to defend Hegel against Schelling's and Kierkegaard's strictures, and incidentally to make the point that some of Heidegger's innovations in 1927 were anticipated in 1807 by the *Phenomenology of Spirit*. This needed saying. I am less happy with his obstinate attempt to establish some sort of link between Hegel and Nietzsche. We all have our foibles. Professor Kaufmann's is an unshakable conviction that justice has not been done in Nietzsche's importance as a thinker. Instead of disputing the point I shall content myself with suggesting that Nietzsche's critique of religion would have seemed less original to his contemporaries if that rebellious Hegelian, Feuerbach, had not been so completely forgotten.

There remains the question of Hegel's contemporary relevance. This theme is rendered difficult by the conventional association of Hegelian thought with Marxism, and by the conviction of the Soviet Marxists that they are in possession of a "total" world outlook (known as "dialectical materialism") which is supposed to have come down to them from Hegel via Feuerbach and Marx. In actual fact, dialectical materialism was the invention of Engels, who on this point circumvented Marx and went straight back to Hegel, from whom in a sense he had never emancipated himself. One can be a Marxist without taking dialectical materialism seriously, though in Russia this is denied and most Communists still regard such statements as damnable heresy. In any case the whole issue has not the slightest practical relevance. No one—not even Hegel—ever tried to deduce the actual sequence of empirical events from the triadic march of logical categories. The Hegelian triad has no significance outside logic and was never intended as a universal key with which to unlock the mysteries of the universe. It is quite irrelevant how one rates Hegel's own performance in his *Logic*, of which Kaufmann gives a brief summary. On any interpretation, his conceptual scheme provides no access to discoveries not obtainable in principle by some other method. It is arguable that historians and sociologists owed much to Hegel, but their findings, once obtained, had to stand the critical test on their own merits. Kaufmann quotes Lenin's remark that one cannot understand *Capital* without having read the *Logic*. In a sense this is true, but plenty of people who had never read a line of Hegel proved perfectly competent to argue about Marx's economic work, though they may have had trouble with the Hegelian terminology of the opening chapter. It is a fact that Lenin (like Plekhanov before him) thought highly of Hegel, but so did some eminent Russian theologians. Indeed Hegel has been more influential in Russia than in Germany, among conservatives and radicals alike. This is because he was a metaphysician, and because the Russians, even more than the Germans, were hungry for metaphysics and contemptuous of positivism. Now that the Soviet Union is belatedly turning into a modern country, one may confidently expect that its philosophers will gradually become as empiricist and boring as the rest of us.

While no dialectical materialism can be found in Marx, there remains the question whether a species of dialectical theology is not to be found in Hegel. Kaufmann does not go into this subject, though he notes that German Protestant theology has since the nineteenth century been heavily indebted to Hegel. It may be said without unfairness that Hegel's employment of the term *Geist* (Spirit) enabled him to elude the difficult choice between a theological and a rationalist view of the world. It was after all his aim to "think the absolute in the form of subject," that is, to arrive at direct cognition of the supersensible reality whose self-generating movement was supposed to run through the phenomenal realm. The *Phenomenology of Spirit* is neither ordinary metaphysics nor psychology: it is both. The infinite spirit is encountered in the comprehension of the world by the finite spirit; the dialectical movement of concepts is held to mirror the ceaseless motion of the *logos* which is the common ground of being and thinking. The whole system constantly teeters on the brink of atheism, and the concluding passage of the *Phenomenology*, with its invocation of "the Golgotha of the absolute spirit," literally ends with the death of God. Yet Hegel managed to persuade himself—and numbers of theologians—that he understood Christianity better than its authorized exponents did. The Platonizing side of this thought found expression in the notion of Spirit's return to itself after passing through the lengthy travail of "estranging" itself in nature and history. In this manner Hegel maintained his hold upon the concept of philosophy as ontology: revelation of Being, albeit not to faith but to the contemplative mind. While treating theology as a propaedeutic to philosophy, he encouraged the theologians to believe that at the end of the journey they would find what they were looking for: proof of God's existence. He is the most ambiguous of the great philosophers, and it is his profound ambiguity which to this day has made it possible for men deeply divided over the most basic issues to find sustenance in his writings.

Metahistory*

• "The problem of the meaning of history is the problem of the meaning of man, the problem of a meaning of human life. We stand at the crossroad between the annihilation of the West and the unification of humanity. This is the time, if ever there was one, to raise fundamental questions."

These lines form the concluding passage of a learned, argumentative, often stimulating, but in the last resort somewhat puzzling tract for the times.† Its author belongs to that small group of contemporary thinkers for whom the term "philosopher of history" seems to have been specially invented, if only because if it did not exist, one would not know how to classify them. In Britain—if we can for a moment forget about Toynbee —Dr. Kahler's nearest counterpart is the Catholic historian Christopher Dawson. In Germany historical metaphysics are currently in bad odor, but though Spengler is discredited, a more traditional manner of philosophizing about history is part of the current effort to underpin the integration of Western Europe. Germany indeed is the home of this type of speculation. Long before Spengler there was Ernst von Lasaulx, a conservative pessimist of the mid-nineteenth century whose influential writings anticipated much subsequent talk about cultural decline and barbarian invasions. Lasaulx, a follower of Schelling and a relative of the mystical philosopher Franz von Baader, is not mentioned by Kahler, which seems a trifle odd, since Kahler's own thinking about history appears to an outsider to have something in common with Lasaulx: notably in the empha-

---

* (Originally titled "History as Philosophy"), *The New York Review* (May 28, 1964).
† Erich Kahler, *The Meaning of History* (New York, 1964).

sis he lays upon the unique significance of Christianity as a spiritual principle capable of regenerating the historical process: that is, starting a new "cycle" on European soil, after the preceding Hellenistic-Roman cycle of growth and decay had come to an end.

It will be seen that Kahler is in a distinguished tradition. It is a tradition for which, to be quite frank, I don't much care. Some of it derives from Hegel, but it is the aspect of Hegelianism that appeals to theologians rather than to historians. Although Kahler is a liberal (Lasaulx was a somewhat heretical Catholic for whom Socrates prefigured Christ), and an unabashed champion of the Renaissance ("the beginning of man's settling down on earth for good"), he tends to credit Christianity with the introduction of a new kind of historical consciousness which made it possible to break away from belief in eternal recurrence. He even goes so far as to assert that "only the sharp Pauline and Augustinian severance of spirit and body, and the ensuing release of purely secular interests and activities, made possible the kind of historical consciousness which we find evolving in men of the twelfth century." This, with all due respect, is circular reasoning. The "consciousness of the twelfth century"—meaning the consciousness of the theologians—was of necessity bounded by what the Church had retained of early Christianity. Approved writing consisted for the most part of learned commentaries on Paul and Augustine. From this it does not follow that Christianity had a built-in bias towards an open-ended and dynamic view of history. If such a bias existed, why did it not make itself felt when Paul and Augustine wrote? Because material conditions were not favorable? But if we are thus in the end referred back to ordinary history, why not begin with it?

The fact is that Kahler—like Schelling, Hegel, and the conservative Hegelians who dominated nineteenth-century German writing on the subject—operates with a dual concept of history. There is the gross, material, exoteric process which ordinary historians write about; and the inner, spiritual, esoteric story that consists in the dissemination of world-shaking Ideas. The Ideas —Hellenism, Judaism, Christianity—keep history going through the ups and downs of the external movement. The latter may be cyclical—cultures do grow and decay—but it also displays an underlying continuity. History, seen as the story of man, is developmental, in the sense that spiritual growth or evolution takes place, even though entire civilizations may disappear or be destroyed. The underlying movement can be described as "cyclic expansion," a concept which allows for dark ages and other retrogressions. The various religious and secular faiths are vehicles of this continuous movement, which is self-transcending and of its nature can have no final consummation. On the whole, then, Kahler takes the idealist view of history, though in a sophisticated form, as befits a modern, for whom optimism about man must always be tempered by awareness of the fragility of civilization.

In the concluding chapter the reader is warned that, though history will doubtless go on, *Western* history may already have passed its peak. It is interesting that Kahler (like Lasaulx) believes the future may belong to the Slavs, apparently on the grounds that their "basic human substance" is still unspent. But the "colored peoples of Asia and Africa" stand an even better chance. The "long dormant vital power of their masses," Kahler thinks, may "take up the torch and carry it further," though perhaps "after a new dark age." Not a very alluring prospect, but fortunately there is an alternative: "we, the West" may decide to "join forces with these peoples of the future, regardless of ideologies and leanings, and . . . all together, realize what potentially exists already, an organized, supranational world order." This—aside from being beneficial for obvious prudential reasons—would have the incidental advantage of investing History with a meaning: it would "mean the completed rounding of the cycle which began at the source of that Western civilization now shaping the population of the earth. It would confirm the meaning of *history as form*; at the same time, it is a *goal*, however transient." There are no *final* goals (except for the preservation of life itself), but there are intermediate aims which we may reasonably pursue since they are in tune with our own historical "cycle," the one that began in Greece and Judaea. I am not quite sure, though, why this particular tradition should be in danger of extinction: from a theological viewpoint this is surely a heretical notion. Conversely, if theology is abandoned in favor of anthropology, it is no longer quite so plausible to suggest that the uniqueness of Western civilization is due to the manner in which the Greeks and the Hebrews conceived the universe. We can all agree that Greece and Judaea have been uniquely important to the history of mankind. What seems questionable is Kahler's thesis that the source of the dynamic element in later Western culture is the Judaeo-Christian view of history as meaningful. He comes close to suggesting that history —what really happens—depends on men's notion of what is happening. What gives coherence to the whole process, it seems, is the manner in which it is experienced, first by privileged individuals and later by people in general. The Greeks— and in a different way the Jews—*discovered* history, and this is why "real" history begins with *them*.

I have some sympathy for this approach, if only because it is a useful antidote to Toynbee. It is nice, in this age of United Nations sentimentalism, to come across a writer who insists that Western history is unique; that cultures are of unequal value; and that an underlying continuity may be discerned through the turmoil of events. It is also refreshing to encounter a philosopher who has the temerity to dispute Professor Popper's dictum that history "has no meaning." For this alone Dr. Kahler deserves the gratitude of all practicing historians, not to mention intelligent laymen not yet brainwashed into unthinking obedience to the reigning orthodoxy. All the same, I cannot help feeling that he weakens his case, and hands arms to the enemy, by identifying "history" with "historical consciousness." He does not indeed go quite so far as Hegel, but near enough to alarm anyone who has learned from Marx to distrust such metaphysical constructions. Moreover, one cannot escape a feeling that he wavers between a genuine indeterminism, for which the future is truly open and ours to make, and a view of history as a continuum of which we are part and in which we are carried along willy-nilly. It is possible to reconcile the two concepts by

THE CONCEPT OF IDEOLOGY

placing them at different "levels," but this leaves it uncertain whether politics is carried on at the level of genuine freedom and indeterminacy, or whether the whole process is a shadow-play whose outcome is already determined. I am not sure either that I understand his toying with the notion that if we fail, the torch may be picked up by others. If Western civilization "represents . . . the leading strain of human evolution," one does not see how its disappearance could be anything but a catastrophe. Notwithstanding these reservations, it needs to be said that Dr. Kahler's essay is a distinguished piece of writing in a tradition which was once important, and which will perhaps disappear only with the culture that gave birth to it.

Forward to Utopia[*]

• The 1950s are disappearing from view, almost from memory. They turn out to have been an interlude between two periods of social strain and corresponding political unrest. The Cold War may turn into stalemate, but there is no let-up internally, and as for the "end of ideology," we shall soon have seen the end of *that* illusion! Western society turns out to be less affluent than one had supposed, and whatever the degree of material comfort it has secured for itself, there is a hungry world on its threshold: waiting to be helped, threatening to break out in destructive rebellion against the privileged minority (who in Afro-Asian eyes may already have come to include the Russians).

These stresses, and the intellectual problems to which they give rise are reflected in Professor Marcuse's new book,[†] whose somewhat puzzling title should not mislead anyone into mistaking it for yet another essay on Alienation. The author is at home with contemporary sociology and ready enough to particularize. An eloquent tract for the times, his work is also a stimulating piece of sociopolitical analysis. Since in what follows I am going to be critical, I had better begin by saying that it is an important book: both for the sake of its theme and because it comes to grips with fundamentals in a manner likely to stir the academic community to its shallow depths. Contemptuous of the accepted fossilized departmentalism, Marcuse ranges from metaphysics to politics and back again. Conventional wisdom suggests that philosophy is irrelevant to the conduct of public affairs. On Marcuse's showing it is rather the thinking epitomized

---

[*] *The New York Review* (February 20, 1964).
[†] *One-Dimensional Man: Studies in the Ideology of Advanced Industrial Society* (Boston, 1964).

in this belief that stands in the way of insight. Here is an author who defines his theme in the grand manner and yet is sensitively aware of the mechanical grind that makes up the life of the average citizen. If there is no "misplaced concreteness" in these tightly reasoned arguments, there is no evasion of empirical reality either. The analysis of abstract concepts, and the discussion of political problems, come together—as they should in the work of a Marxist. For it is a Marxist analysis that is offered here, though several light-years removed from what this term signifies east of what it is perhaps no longer fashionable to call the Iron Curtain. The proper terms of comparison are suggested by names like Merleau-Ponty, Lefebvre, Adorno, perhaps the early Lukács. This is a tradition which hitherto has had little impact in the English-speaking world, though it is now increasingly becoming associated with the New Left. As a contribution to the American discussion of neo-Marxism, or whatever one wants to call it, Marcuse's book thus possesses a cultural significance of its own. Here it is merely proposed to look at some of its main arguments, and if the following observations are largely critical, this is not because the reviewer fails to sympathize with the author's general intention.

One-Dimensional Man is several things, but above all it is a challenge to what Marcuse conceives to be the official ideology of present-day Western society. This theme is developed by way of analyzing certain prevalent opinions, e.g., the belief in the neutrality of science; but it also entails a critical examination of the manner in which society actually operates (at any rate in the United States). The political and sociological chapters are heavily dependent on the work of C. Wright Mills, whose "vital importance" to Marcuse's own analysis is duly stressed in the Introduction. The more strictly philosophical topics are developed along the lines of an argument already foreshadowed in the author's Eros and Civilization. The criterion here is human happiness and its denial by a repressive culture which takes away with one hand what it gives with the other. Modern technology has made us all potentially richer and actually poorer—by eroding individual freedom, by encouraging conformity, even by ruining the countryside. This state of affairs finds its ideological justification in what Marcuse calls "positive thinking and its neo-positivist philosophy." A chapter is devoted to the critique of Wittgenstein and his successors. The target here is not simply the hair-splitting that goes on among linguistic analysts, but the divorce of factual from value judgments. For all his commitment to Marx and Freud (or Marx plus Freud), Marcuse is basically in the Hegelian tradition. His defense of traditional philosophy against positivism rests upon the proposition that the truth about the historical situation is discovered by going beyond the limits of empirical thinking. As he put it in an epilogue (written in 1954) to the second edition of his important work on Hegel, *Reason and Revolution* (London, 1955): "Reason is in its very essence contra-diction [*sic*], opposition, negation, as long as freedom is not yet real. If the contradictory, oppositional, negative, power of Reason is broken, reality moves under its own positive law, and, unhampered by the Spirit, unfolds its repressive force. Such decline in the power of Negativity has indeed accompanied the progress of late industrial civilization." A decade later, his pessimism has reached the point of asserting that the very language of modern science tends to "close the universe of discourse."

Finally—as a by-product of the author's insistent critique of the status quo upheld by the current consensus in his country of adoption—he turns to a consideration of what is usually known as the Cold War. This particular chapter is not, in my judgment, the most successful part of the book, and there are aspects of it which may cause some eyebrow-raising even among readers well disposed to the author's general purpose. It is not, for example, altogether clear whether he approves of the post-1945 rise in living standards which has enabled the working class in advanced industrial countries to climb out of its former submerged existence. He does not indeed adhere to what might perhaps be termed the Baran-Sweezy syndrome: I mean the suggestion that the entire process has occurred at the expense of the backward countries, and is therefore to be deplored. But it is questionable whether he appreciates how great (and how recent) an achievement it is. Also that it is the precondition of all further political and social advance along democratic lines. Some of his observations could be read as an implied reproach to the working class for having ceased to be a proletariat in the nineteenth-century sense of the term.

This point is connected with another weakness of Marcuse's analysis which has some bearing upon his pessimistic view of the Cold War. He appears insufficiently concerned about political freedom. One understands his dislike of the reckless use made of the term "totalitarian," but it simply will not do to eliminate it altogether (or to muddle its meaning by suggesting that "the way it has organized its technological base" causes "contemporary industrial society" to develop totalitarian tendencies). If by "communism" is meant the political regime in the Soviet orbit—and what else can it mean?—then its antithesis is not "capitalism" (as it seems to be for Marcuse) but either "democracy" or "fascism," or some other political concept. For even if it were the case that modern society is potentially totalitarian by its very nature, the fact remains that it has so far assumed this shape (if one excepts the unsuccessful fascist experiments) only on one side of the great divide. This awkward circumstance is blurred in Marcuse's analysis. "Not only a specific form of government or party rule makes for totalitarianism," he writes, "but also a specific system of production and distribution which may well be compatible with a 'pluralism' of parties, newspapers, 'countervailing powers,' etc." I confess I am unable to assign any meaning to this statement. It seems to be self-contradictory, and—in its bland disregard of the "specific system of production" which underlies the Soviet regime—a trifle disingenuous as well. The Cold War is an area in which philosophers have difficulty keeping their balance, if only because they cannot always be quite up to date with their facts. In reading Marcuse's reflections on the subject, one is conscious of a tendency to make too much of the dialectical antithesis between the two systems now confronting each other. The evident bipolarity of world politics in our era promotes an inclination to think in terms of basic antagonisms. We are then all the more surprised (though the Chinese are not) when all of a sudden the U.S.A. and the U.S.S.R. show a tendency to get together. A different kind of misunderstanding may arise from the way in which "peaceful coexistence" (or what passes for such) is verbalized by politicians who have to explain it to the voters. Because there is in some areas peaceful rivalry between the two super-powers, it is tempting to suppose that they must be getting more alike. In some ways they are, in others not. They are not, *e.g.*, moving any closer as regards living conditions. Just because the Soviet leaders are fond of talking about "catching up with America," one must not make the mistake of thinking that they are actually capable of promoting such a development. The evidence is against it. At any rate, few economists believe that the Soviet Union is going to catch up with the United States in this century. It may catch up in steel production; but there are many things in life—even in economic life—besides steel. There is, for example, the little matter of food and clothing. There is also the accumulated dead-weight of rural backwardness, which in the U.S.S.R. still affects half the population. Russia is indeed advancing fast—from a very low level. Talk of catching up with America is moonshine; it is certainly not a matter for the present generation. If by 1980 the Russians have caught up with Yugoslavia (unlikely on present form), they will have done a great deal—more perhaps than can reasonably be expected. Personally I do not believe they will; I think it is going to take longer. Moreover, by the time they have got there, the West will have moved on, and the cleavage between the two worlds may have become even more pronounced.

Economics of course is not the whole of existence, but the political and intellectual gulf between the U.S.S.R. and the West (there is no point in dragging the backward countries in: comparisons would be unfair to them) is even wider than the economic. Marcuse does not really succeed in coming to grips with the realities of political and ideological control in the Soviet orbit. Where others (including some Soviet intellectuals, though not those in official favor) perceive a deep gulf dividing their country from the West, with its very different traditions,

he sees only gradations of unfreedom. But the disparities
are qualitative, not quantitative. The contrast between limited freedom and total suppression is fundamental, as is that
between limited sense and utter nonsense. "In both camps, non-
operational ideas are non-behavioral and subversive," he writes.
This is arguable, but a remark such as "the movement of
thought is stopped at barriers which appear as the limits of
Reason itself" seems ambiguous. We do not get a sense here
of the difference it would make to the mental climate of the
U.S.S.R. if the Soviet intelligentsia possessed even the limited
degree of freedom its ancestors had won for themselves in the
closing decades of the nineteenth century.

It is perhaps fortunate that this topic is marginal to the author's purpose. For the most part he is concerned with the
United States, and his critique of the official ideology—for it *is*
of course an ideology, though its spokesmen claim to have no use
for such constructs—is largely influenced by the work of the late
C. Wright Mills. This is not a safe topic for outsiders. One can
only register an impression that to some Americans who remain
critical of Mills's naïve populism it seems quite possible that
democratic institutions will come under an intolerably heavy
strain. One may respect their judgment, while feeling reasonably
certain that Western Europe has already passed beyond this particular danger zone. European countries, after all, are no longer
burdened by their former imperial responsibilities. Neither do
they have to worry about the impact of permanent unemployment upon racial animosities already rendered barely tolerable by slum conditions. These are problems specific to the
United States. Again, much of what Marcuse has to say about
thought control via the mass media seems to be an American phenomenon rather than something inherent in the character of modern industrial society. But even on the more pessimistic hypothesis to which, in common with much of the New
Left, he inclines, it does not by any means follow that the topic
can be usefully debated in terms relating to the East-West antagonism. If liberalism and Marxism face the same long-range

problems, then the real dividing line in the contemporary world must run elsewhere.

In fact, of course, as everyone knows by now, it runs between the advanced and the backward countries, or between those cultures which have now absorbed the Industrial Revolution, and those which have failed. Hence no doubt the increasingly casual fashion in which Indians, Chinese, and others speculate upon the chances of the U.S.A. and the U.S.S.R. blowing each other to bits. This is unlikely to happen, for self-preservation is a powerful motive-force, but if by mischance it *did* happen, there would be precious few tears shed in the "underdeveloped" parts of the world. Why then base one's analysis on an increasingly unreal competition for global control which each side in its heart already knows to be unattainable? The coming problems of world society are going to be pretty much the same on both sides of the political divide—if there is no catastrophe, as to which no prediction is possible.

This last indeed is the gravamen of Marcuse's charge: the world in which we live is irrational. But the irrationality is not the particular property of a society in which effective social control is not exercised from the center. In the U.S.S.R. there is such control, but no corresponding reign of wisdom: largely because the official ideology has an unchallengeable monopoly, so that everything depends on a handful of politicians seeing the light. Moreover, it is questionable whether the nuclear sword suspended over our heads is really the true symbol of civilization gone mad. It is a plausible notion, and Marcuse makes the most of it, but it is not self-evident to people living outside our culture. The truth is that being blown up is less disagreeable than starving to death or watching one's children starve, a common occurrence over large tracts of the globe. For most inhabitants of the planet it is still a question of crawling out of a subhuman form of existence. Our problems are not theirs, and we cannot share our worries with them. Most of these people would give their right arm for the privilege of being allowed to inhabit our comfortable madhouse, and if the whole gorgeous farce should come to a sudden and dramatic end for us, the spectators are likely to cheer. This is not to say that the whole subject can be shrugged off. There is every cause for concern, and philosophers do right to remind us that we have created a world which may come crashing down on our heads. But it is precisely this civilization, and no other, which will have to solve the problem of what Marcuse calls the "pacification of existence." There is nothing to hope for from the backward countries, now engaged in a race to copy our follies. The society which has given birth to the new technology will have to live or die with it, and if it wants to live, it will have to transcend its present limitations, of which national sovereignty and war are the greatest.

The problem of effecting this kind of transcendence, in an increasingly conformist culture which is progressively doing away with the class struggle in its old form, is at the core of Marcuse's analysis. It leads him to an interesting discussion of the social changes flowing from automation and the growth of technical rationality in general. What he calls "one-dimensional" thinking is one aspect of the growing domination of technology over the individual. While one may question his distinction between a "pre-technological" and a "technological" era (primitive technology could be pretty crushing and brutalizing—think of Chinese canals and Egyptian pyramids!), it is undeniable that there has been a qualitative change whereby the sheer size and complexity of the apparatus threatens to overwhelm the producers. Along with this goes a widening gap between the controllers at the top of the new hierarchy, and the "personnel" at the base. Now the point for a socialist is that mechanization increasingly does away with the input of sheer physical energy: what is commonly called labor. This has implications for theory, as well as for the political strategy of movements which have to attract white-collar support if they do not want to lose ground. As industry develops its scientific potential, the direct exploitation of living labor becomes a marginal phenomenon and the working class shrinks in relative size. None of this was wholly unforeseen: as Marcuse rightly points out, Marx predicted it over a century ago. He seems to have believed, though, that a state of affairs where "human labor, in its immediate form, has ceased to be the great source of wealth," was not likely to come about under capitalism. The discovery that it *can* happen (thought not under "free," unplanned, laissez-faire capitalism) is the new element in the situation.

This is connected with another development that has altered the traditional socialist picture, namely the steady rise in real incomes, at any rate for those in regular employment. Assuming that full employment can be secured—admittedly a large assumption for the United States, though quite reasonable in Western Europe, where public planning and the "mixed economy" have come to stay—the conjunction of these factors undercuts the notion that the changeover to a truly rational order must necessarily pass through a political upheaval. In fact it is likely to come about peaceably. This is so not only because economic planning is clearly rational and beneficial, but because organized labor, when effectively allied to the new technical intelligentsia, is strong enough to force it through by peaceful means: a possibility already envisaged by "revisionist" socialists early in this century, though for understandable reasons not before that date. Even now the division of the national "cake" takes the form of a share-out in which labor secures an increasing part of what Marx called "surplus-value"; for when items such as cars and refrigerators come to be included in the "customary standard of living," it is no longer a matter of people being on a subsistence standard. This does *not* mean that exploitation (in the Marxian sense) has come to an end, or that the working class has become a "middle class" (the "middle" position is now in fact occupied by the white-collar element, with the technological intelligentsia at its core). It *does* mean that the working class in advanced industrial countries (capitalist or socialist) has ceased to be a "proletariat," for it is part of the definition of this term that wage earners are permanently held down to a mere subsistence level. Hence no socialist in an advanced country can seriously contemplate the kind of political action that is still open to the poor and the exploited in the preindustrial hinterland.

The relevance of this topic to Marcuse's argument has to do with his insistent stress upon the dangers inherent in what he describes as the "containment" of potential rebellion against a welfare state which is also a warfare state. "Hatred and frustration are deprived of their specific target, and the technological veil conceals the reproduction of inequality and enslavement," as he puts it. Elsewhere he asks despairingly: "Is there any prospect that this chain of growing productivity and repression may be broken?" The danger, as he sees it, is that—labor having been tamed—there will be no one left to challenge the basic irrationality of the system. The latter "tends toward both total administration and total dependence on administration by ruling public and private managements, strengthening the preestablished harmony between the interest of the big public and private corporations and that of their customers and servants." Yet he also suggests that the system produces its own corrective. "Automation, once it became *the* process of material production, would revolutionize the whole society. The reification of human labor power, driven to perfection, would shatter the reified form by cutting the chain that ties the individual to the machinery— the mechanism through which his own labor enslaves him. . . . This would be the historical transcendence toward a new civilization." Presumably most socialists, and conceivably some liberals, would accept this, just as they would accept his remarks on the kind of rationalization that merely strengthens the hold of established authorities. Where they might differ is in being more hopeful about structural change coming about peacefully and democratically.

This is not the place to deal at length with what to Marcuse clearly matters most of all: his defense of traditional philosophy against positivist scientism. It must be sufficient to indicate the main line of the argument. Primarily, Marcuse is concerned to salvage those implicit "value judgments" that are inherent in the exercise of critical thinking: to reason is to commit oneself to belief in the importance of Reason. By eliminating the notion of transcendence, empiricism implicitly sanctions the status quo with all its built-in irrationalities. The impoverishment of thought and language inherent in much of modern sociology is the subject of some of Marcuse's most effective polemics. They should be pondered even by those critics who cannot follow him in all his diatribes against Wittgenstein and his successors.[1]

The loss of the philosophical dimension (whatever the motives that originally promoted it) leads to an absence of the historical dimension, and a consequent foreshortening of political perspectives. As the author remarks, this is not a party matter: the "old style" of political discourse is to be found in conservatives like Tocqueville and Burckhardt, and in liberals like Mill, as well as in Marx. Conversely, the jargon of contemporary scientism is subversive of *all* political philosophy. No doubt a price has had to be paid for the emancipation of science from theology and metaphysics, but the process has now got out of hand, and the threatened institution of a purely scientific worldview—along with a technological universe that has forgotten its own *raison d'être*—is a real danger. One doubts, though, whether it is more pressing in the West than in the East. The cult of "social engineering" has its counterpart elsewhere, as does the humanist revolt against it. A related difficulty, which can be mentioned only in passing, concerns the relation of this kind of philosophical critique to its roots in classical antiquity. Historically, the sort of thinking that lies at the root of Hegel's philosophy—and it is to Hegel plus Marx that Marcuse is ultimately working back—precedes the distinction between factual

---

[1] For a trenchant critique of Marcuse's rather old-fashioned notions about contemporary science, see Peter Sedgwick, "Natural Science and Human Theory," *The Socialist Register* (London, 1966), esp. p. 174. Coming from a socialist, this criticism should carry extra weight with some of Marcuse's readers, who may have too readily accepted his picture of a conformist science Establishment addicted to "operationalism" and "behavioralism." There is indeed something paradoxical about Marcuse's desire to remain in the tradition of Marx and Freud while rejecting such standard forms of scientific procedure as the construction of abstract models. Some of his arguments carry a distinct flavor of anti-Cartesian romanticism: a venerable relic from the age of German "natural philosophy," redolent of Schelling rather than of Marx.

and value judgments. Both were perceived in a single act of intellectual intuition, which at the same time fixed the timeless essence of things, and therewith the criterion for distinguishing between Reality and Appearance. In the history of European thought, Hegel is the last great representative of this tradition, some elements of which survived in Marx (though not in what is usually called Marxism). It is conceivable that we have now come to the end of the counter-movement, and that the patent sterility of the prevailing empiricist orthodoxy will promote a renewed attempt to unify (philosophical) theory and (political) practice: in other words, that men will once again try to realize ultimate aims. One is bound to be skeptical, though, about the notion that this can be done (even in thought) by extrapolating from historical tendencies. It seems more likely that the first step in the new direction will take the form of a decision to have nothing further to do with history and its decrees.

This qualification is not subversive of a humanism which seeks its justification in the fulfillment of actual (material and spiritual) needs, but it does involve a reconsideration of the status of guiding principles or *Ideas* (as distinct from mere *ideals*). In an interesting chapter on "negative thinking" Marcuse casually alludes to the "totalitarian universe of technological rationality" as "the latest transmutation of the idea of Reason." Now an "idea" which can transmute itself into a material universe of social relations is clearly something rather different from a mere "ideology." Marcuse traces the "logic of domination" back to its primary source in logic itself; that is, in the primary separation of Logos from Eros, intellect from feeling, functional manipulation from Intuition of Essence (to employ a vocabulary which is not the author's).

"Technological man" is seen to have emerged as the end product of a lengthy process which had its origin in the establishment of abstract generalization as the prevailing mode of discourse. "Dialectical logic," which implicitly corrects this one-sidedness, does so by "denying the concreteness of immediate experience." This experience is shown to be incomplete, self-contradictory, and potentially related to a dimension of the spirit transcending a world "where Reason is still Unreason, and the irrational still the rational." What "immediate experience" shows us is the need to master the realm of nature.

> But there are two kinds of mastery: a repressive and a liberating one. The latter involves the reduction of misery, violence and cruelty. In Nature as well as in History, the struggle for existence is the token of scarcity, suffering and want. They are the qualities of blind matter, of the realm of immediacy in which life passively suffers its existence. This realm is gradually mediated in the course of the historical transformation of Nature. . . . History is the negation of Nature. What is only natural is overcome and recreated by the power of Reason. The metaphysical notion that Nature comes to itself in history points to the unconquered limits of Reason (p. 236).

All this is in the tradition of German Idealism, and of Marx, whose scattered observations on the subject carry unmistakable echoes of a pathos that counterposes Mind to brute creation. But is it rationality that makes us (or some of us) wince at certain spectacles? In a finely worded passage Marcuse protests against the theological notion that animals have no claim on our sympathy because they have no "souls":

> Materialism, which is not tainted by such ideological abuse of the soul, has a more universal and realistic concept of salvation. It admits the reality of Hell only at one definite place, here on earth, and asserts that this Hell was created by Man (and by Nature). Part of this Hell is the ill-treatment of animals—the work of a human society whose rationality is still the irrational.

What lies beyond the instinctive brutality of Nature is here called Reason, though idealists are more likely to call it Spirit. Perhaps common ground can be found in saying that the "negation of Nature" which philosophy demands is at any rate not decreed by history, merely a historical possibility among others. Is it going to be realized? It is the measure of Marcuse's achievement that he has written a book which raises this kind of question.

part three

AFTER THE CATASTROPHE

Rosa Luxemburg[*]

• In the mythology of revolutionary socialism, east and west of the great divide, the name of Rosa Luxemburg (1871-1919) is indissolubly linked with that of Karl Liebknecht: victims of the Spartacist rising in January 1919 whose brutal suppression by soldiers nominally responsible to a Social-Democratic government sealed in blood the wartime split of the German labor movement. Nor is this familiar assessment confined to Communist literature. In Western historiography too, their names invariably appear as though joined together by history's decree. Every study of the Weimar Republic opens perforce with an account of the Berlin insurrection launched by the nascent Communist movement against the government of Ebert and Noske. And while the ceremonial linking of the names Liebknecht and Luxemburg by today's East German regime has long ceased to be anything but a gesture towards a dimly remembered past, the legend persists that German Communism conserves the heritage of this strange pair of martyrs: the solid lawyer and *Reichstag* deputy, suddenly catapulted into fame by his passionate wartime oratory in 1914-1918, and the brilliant Polish-Jewish woman revolutionary who appears in these accounts as his inspirer and companion. The fact that down to 1914 they had virtually nothing in common, that Liebknecht—by philosophical conviction a Kantian—was not even a Marxist, let alone a Communist, and that in 1919 he was merely the popular figurehead of a rebellion not effectively controlled by anyone, is seldom permitted to encroach upon the myth.

It is the great merit of J. P. Nettl's enormously detailed and

* *Encounter* (June 1966).

painstakingly scholarly work* that a serious study of Rosa Luxemburg's actual historical role is now at last available to the public. A biographer by choice and inclination, he is also in effect a historian of the East European socialist movement before 1914; and while his partisanship is never concealed, he has not on the whole allowed it to interfere with the analysis of personalities and events. The comparison with Mr. Isaac Deutscher's biography of Trotsky imposes itself. It works in Mr. Nettl's favor, if only because his intellectual apparatus includes economics and sociology, as well as the standard techniques of the historian. His grasp of Russian and Polish realities is the equal of Mr. Deutscher's, while in relation to Germany his understanding, if not quite flawless, is much superior to that of most writers whose primary background is East European. These are impressive qualifications, and they have resulted in the production of a remarkable work. Readers not put off by its formidable bulk (827 pages of text, plus two lengthy appendices, and 70 pages of bibliography in five languages, including Russian and Polish) can now at last find their way through the maze of political and theoretical conflicts from which in due course the Russian, Polish, Austrian, and German upheavals of 1917-1919 were to derive their shape.

What emerges from Mr. Nettl's analysis of the crucial role played by his heroine in these events is at first glance surprising. Those who had thought of Rosa Luxemburg as primarily a figure in German Socialist history will have to revise what they had gathered from earlier biographers. The familiar and slightly puzzling image—a young woman from Russian Poland who suddenly erupted on the German scene around 1900 and thereafter made a career as a brilliant publicist—is replaced by a far more complex and fascinating picture: that of a woman who was both a gifted theorist and a steel-willed conspirator, the central figure of a small but influential group of Polish revolutionaries who operated simultaneously in the Socialist movements of three countries—Russia, Austria-Hungary, and Germany; an organizer who covered her traces with such skill that even her closest Ger-

* *Rosa Luxemburg* (London, 1966).

man friends and associates had no real inkling of her true role in neighboring Poland and in the leadership of the conspiratorial Marxist group she had founded with her close personal and political associate Leo Jogiches. Though formally a German citizen (by way of a nominal marriage) since 1898, a prominent member of the German Social-Democratic Party, and a steady contributor to its journals, Rosa Luxemburg—almost down to the eve of war in 1914 when she partly relinquished her Polish ties— remained at heart what she had been since her student days in Zürich in the 1890s: the theorist of a self-appointed "peer group" of revolutionaries with a following among the Polish-speaking masses of the three Eastern Empires, whose simultaneous collapse in 1918 was to restore Poland as a nation, thereby paradoxically inflicting upon Rosa Luxemburg and her group (the SDKPIL—Social-Democracy of the Kingdom of Poland and Lithuania) the most shattering political defeat of her life.

The secret of Rosa Luxemburg's strange personality and career, one may now say with certainty, is to be found in the fact that for twenty years she was the principal link between the German Socialist movement and the totally different world of the conspiratorial and elitist Russo-Polish underground parties and sects. Manipulating her contacts on both sides with remarkable dexterity, she managed to appear in German eyes as an expert on the Russian situation, while representing the German Social-Democratic Party (the SPD) towards the Polish and Russian factions, including Lenin's Bolsheviks, with whom she alternately feuded and cooperated. So great was her operational skill (at least while she had the benefit of Leo Jogiches' advice) that she succeeded in getting her small Marxist group, whose following was limited to a few cities, accepted by the Germans as the official representation of the Polish workers in Germany, as against the more numerous Polish Socialist Party of her rivals, the PPS. This strange configuration in turn she exploited with relentless energy to impose herself on the cautious leadership of German Social-Democracy. To the veteran August Bebel and most of the other leaders she was primarily an ally against Polish nationalism: a growing force among the Polish masses in Silesia of which they stood in mortal terror (as did the Imperial German Government). As long as she was ready to battle the nationalists on their home ground, the SPD Executive forgave her almost anything, even her doctrinaire Marxism and her constant broadsides against their own somnolent passivity. It was for this that Bebel protected her against the South German "revisionists" and against her sworn enemies, the trade union leaders; for this that Kautsky (who liked her personally) opened the pages of his great theoretical organ, the *Neue Zeit*, to her and allowed her to lambaste his old opponent Eduard Bernstein to her heart's content. To the more cynical SPD bureaucrats, indeed, she was hardly more than an unconscious agent of Germanization among the Polish masses in Eastern Germany. The alliance collapsed only when in 1910 she tired of it and turned against Bebel and even against her old friend and protector Kautsky. Only then did she become the leader of the extreme Left in Germany. The whole of this deeply hidden labyrinth of Central and East European politics in the years before the First World War has been illuminated for the first time by Mr. Nettl's truly Herculean labors in the German and Polish archives.

That a degree of secretiveness, and even duplicity, should in consequence have been imposed upon a woman by nature candid, outspoken, and contemptuous of make-believe, must be laid to the peculiar world of Russo-Polish émigré politics from which in 1896 she suddenly emerged, to astound the Congress of the Socialist International with the spectacle of a fiery young woman of twenty-five informing the bearded veterans of a hundred battles that they knew nothing about the East European picture, and that moreover Marx and Engels had been wrong about it. To this point it will be necessary to return. What needs to be retained here is a biographical circumstance to which Mr. Nettl has lent some reluctant prominence: the fact that her deepest loyalties lay in an area which had little to do with her public life as a representative of German Socialism. As her biographer puts it:

Many of her German friends were totally unaware of the fact that on top of her full-time work in the SPD—and on the problem of Polish organization on German soil, in Pomerania and Silesia—she was simultaneously one of the main inspirers and leaders of a Polish party whose center of gravity lay in the Russian empire.

Not only were her relations with Jogiches, Marchlewski, and others of her circle more important to her than her German friends she actually disliked Germany and the Germans, though she lived there for twenty years and played a prominent role in the SPD. A self-conscious Easterner, she preferred Russian literature to German (admittedly a judgment shared by many discerning critics), described Russian as "the language of the future," and for the rest reserved her personal affection for the French, the Italians, and other Latins. It is a remarkable story, conceivable perhaps only in an age more liberal than ours, when disregard for national frontiers was thought respectable at least by Socialists. But in large measure it responded also to certain features of her background duly recorded by Mr. Nettl: her early involvement in the conspiratorial world of Polish émigré politics in Zürich and Paris, and her naïve assumption that the moral and intellectual standards of the Jewish intelligentsia in Eastern Europe were natural also to the labor movement, or at least could be implanted in it under the guise of "proletarian internationalism."

This is the key to the story. Mr. Nettl handles it gingerly, though from time to time he summons up courage to remind the reader that the intellectual leadership of Rosa Luxemburg's and Leo Jogiches' private creation, the SDKPIL, was largely (though not wholly) a Jewish affair. Today when this particular story has been played out to its dreadful finale, there is a natural reluctance to dwell upon these circumstances. Mr. Nettl wisely resists the temptation, though he is clearly unhappy with the notion that the emotional spring which fed Rosa Luxemburg's passionate loyalty to the International was a form of Jewish Messianism. He does not wholly repudiate the idea, but leaves it in the air. Her contemporaries were less inhibited. To the majority faction of Polish Socialism, the PPS, she was quite simply a Jewish intellectual who cared nothing for Poland; to the self-consciously Jewish leaders of the *Bund*, the mass movement of the Yiddish-speaking proletariat in Russian Poland, she was a traitor to her people. In her own eyes she was a true internationalist and the only consistent Marxist of the lot: this although her attitude on the Polish question was in flat contradiction to literally everything Marx (and even Engels) had said on the subject.

It is necessary to pause here. The subject is loaded with passion. It was the central issue of Rosa Luxemburg's political life —far more important to her than the boring quarrels within the German Socialist movement, or even the more fascinating disputations between Lenin and his Menshevik opponents (which she exploited with remarkable skill to promote her own group to a key position inside the *Russian* party). It was the one issue on which she stood ready to break with her closest associates and to fly in the face of every authority, including that of Marx. Poland was dead! It could never be revived! Talk of a Polish nation, of an independent Poland, was not only political and economic lunacy; it was a distraction from the class struggle, a betrayal of Socialism! If Marx had held a different view, then Marx had been mistaken. If the International solemnly went on record affirming the traditional Social-Democratic creed (Poland must be restored as a bastion against Tsarist Russia), then the International was misguided and must be told so, or its resolutions must be tortured to yield a different sense. Above all, the Polish Socialist majority party, the PPS, must be relentlessly pursued, up hill and down dale, and denounced as a nationalist organization falsely parading in Socialist clothing. If the very SDKPIL, her own brainchild, threatened to split and founder on this rock, so much the worse for it. One thing only counted: fidelity to proletarian internationalism as she understood it (and as Marx, poor man, had plainly not understood it). On this point, and on this alone, she was intractable. Even Jogiches at times thought she went too far, though he had originally helped her to evolve this attitude while they were both students in Zürich in the 1890s. Her other Polish associates put up with her fanaticism on the subject, though they did not share it. In the end, the allegedly impossible happened: Poland was restored in 1918, and her veteran friend and colleague Adolf Warszawski, with her reluctant consent, fused the remnant of their following with the left wing of the PPS to form the Polish Communist Party (the right wing under Pilsudski having split off). By then twenty years had been spent, or rather wasted, on one of the strangest aberrations ever to possess a major political intellect.

For the remarkable thing is that on the national question, and specifically on the issue of Poland, Rosa Luxemburg stood entirely alone. Not a single Marxist of her generation, outside her own immediate circle, agreed with her: not even Trotsky, in many respects her equal among the Russians (though they never took to each other); certainly not Lenin, who treated her views on the subject with the good-natured disdain he reserved for the handful of opponents for whom he had a personal liking. Elsewhere the damage was considerable. As time went on, her insanity—there is no other word for it—on the topic of nationalism developed into the gravest of her political handicaps. Her doctrinaire refusal to admit the legitimacy of *any* national movement in Europe was repudiated by Kautsky, by Plekhanov, by the Mensheviks, the Bolsheviks, and virtually every other Socialist group or personality. It angered the veteran leader of Austrian Social-Democracy, Victor Adler, who on this issue became and remained her personal enemy. It embarrassed her old friend and protector Kautsky. It undermined the position of her followers in Poland and her friends among the Russians. It maddened the Polish majority Socialists and drove their less reputable elements into paroxysms of anti-Semitic fury. It very nearly wrecked her own creation, the SDKPIL. It has remained to this day the greatest single obstacle to the revival of a "Luxemburgist" tradition of democratic Socialism in post-Stalinist Poland. And it was totally unnecessary. There never was the smallest justification for it, notwithstanding the pseudo-Marxist sophistries of her Zürich doctoral dissertation of 1898 on the industrial development of Poland: sophistries which her biographer treats with the gravity of a theologian expounding a particularly incomprehensible piece of ecclesiastical doctrine. It was, from start to finish, a display of sheer intellectual perversity, backed up and sustained by the strongest of her emotional commitments: the vision of a proletarian revolution which would institute a new world order. She went so far as to assert that while national self-determination was a farce under capitalism, it would be unnecessary under socialism. Why bother about it if the revolution was going to make all things new?

Her biographer, in general a wholehearted sympathizer with her person and her views, draws the line at this point, though unwillingly. On most other issues he tends to support her and to find fault with her opponents whenever possible, but her calamitous misjudgment of the national problem is too much even for him. He does indeed set out all possible mitigating circumstances at great length, but the effect is not the intended one; for the more earnestly, in his chosen role as counsel for the defense, he addresses the jury on behalf of his client, the clearer it becomes that the case is really hopeless. A more complete misjudgment of a political issue than Rosa Luxemburg's position on the national question was never seen or heard on land or sea. Yet strangely enough, it is this heroic persistence along the wrong track that lends pathos and distinction to her conception of socialism. For her, as for many other East European revolutionaries who had renounced all ties of class and nationality, the only loyalty was to the proletariat, the only true fatherland the International. When in August 1914 the sword broke in her hand, she seriously contemplated suicide.

It is this wholly abstract, totally unrealistic, yet unshakeable commitment to a vision transcending the circumstances of daily existence that sets Rosa Luxemburg apart and lends her the dignity of a tragic figure. As a theorist—*pace* her biographer—she does not take first rank. Her intervention in the German revisionist controversy around 1900 was limited to the political side, if only because she had no understanding of philosophy (a handicap shared by her biographer, to judge from his extremely odd notions about Kant). As an economist she was brilliant and suggestive rather than profound. *The Accumulation of Capital,* her major work, though a truly remarkable *tour de force* and shot through with extraordinary flashes of prophetic insight into the nature of imperialism, suffers from a fatal flaw: its central theoretical argument is based on a misreading of both Marx and mathematics. (As in the case of Poland she had tried to correct the Master, and predictably come a cropper, the usual fate of Marx's critics, even among Marxists.) Her other theoretical excursions remained fragmentary. She may have anticipated some of Trotsky's notions about the "permanent revolution," though her biographer denies it; but it was Parvus and Radek (both from Eastern Europe) who first developed what was later to become the specifically "Trotskyist" view of the world situation and the function of the coming Russian upheaval within it.

In the factional struggles among the Russian Marxists she wavered uncertainly between the Bolsheviks and their opponents, and in the end reluctantly underwrote the Bolshevik seizure of power in 1917, with qualifications which Lenin's followers have been busy repudiating ever since. She disliked Lenin's organizational concept, but had nothing to put in its place, except a vague faith in "the masses." In general, organizational questions bored her and she never bothered to equip either her Polish party or the German Spartakus League with the kind of effective leadership that might have placed either of them at the head of a mass movement. As a party leader she was effective only when steered by Leo Jogiches (who for years did the organizational work, while she wrote brilliant tracts demolishing their opponents) and promptly lost her bearings when their longstanding personal relationship broke up under the strain of the 1905 revolution and she had to navigate by herself. Her final throw, the Berlin rising of January 1919, led directly to her death, and thereby decapitated the nascent German Communist movement. Nor was this catastrophe accidental, for although the rising had been forced upon her (against her better judgment and that of her experienced Polish associates) by the unwisdom of Liebknecht and the *furor teutonicus* which had seized hold of the German Communists, her decision to participate in what she regarded as an act of madness was in tune with her mystical doctrine of loyalty to the proletariat. For the rest it was an almost literal application of the revolutionary lessons she had been preaching to the Germans since her own participation in the great Russo-Polish upheaval of 1905-1906. The only revolution she had ever wanted or believed in was a spontaneous uprising of the proletariat in the great cities of Central and Eastern Europe. When it came, she was ready for it, though she must have known that defeat was certain.

What then remains of Rosa Luxemburg? Strange to say, that which she least expected: a myth—that of the woman who embodied all the faith and hope of the old pre-1914 revolutionary Socialism, and who paid for it with her life. And something else: a kind of moral heroism. No one who reads her works or studies her career can fail to see that Rosa Luxemburg was above all a moralist. Though tone-deaf in philosophy (she seems never to have understood what the argument over Kantian ethics was about) she was totally serious, and totally committed, where political morality was concerned. For her, every political question had to be argued in ethical terms, though she would have been surprised to hear it said: was not Socialist humanism the most *obvious* thing in the world? Her moral rigorism on matters such as war, colonial exploitation, or the denial of freedom to opponents, lifted her beyond the confines of reformist opportunism and Bolshevist cynicism alike, into a region where she outdistanced her contemporaries. On moral issues her judgment was infallible. Just as in 1914 she saw at once that the International was dead and Social-Democracy, as she put it, "a stinking corpse," so in 1918 she coupled her reluctant acceptance of the October Revolution with an incisive critique of the Bolshevik dictatorship and the beginning of terrorism. Her posthumously published reflections on the Russian Revolution were brushed aside by Lenin. Even the exiled Trotsky refused to accept them. They have nonetheless become the testament of the old humanist Socialism which was shipwrecked in the First World War. In political terms her message was utopian, for a revolution which respects the liberty of *all* is the hardest thing in the world to achieve and perhaps impossible, unless backed from the start by the vast majority of the people. But then a truly democratic revolution was the only kind she had ever wanted. Minority dictatorship and terrorism did not appeal to her. What she stood for was lost in the bloodbath of 1914-1918, which in turn prepared the ground for the ultimate horrors of Stalinism and Fascism: both equally repugnant to the spirit of the woman over whose tormented body victors and vanquished in the first round of Europe's civil war marched into their inheritance.

Reflections on Trotsky[*]

I

• Revolutions give rise to myths, and these myths then help to shape the course of later revolutions. In the nineteenth century, revolutionaries everywhere saw analogies to what had been happening in France between 1789 and 1799 (or, if they were Bonapartists between 1799 and 1814). Every upheaval, however insignificant, was interpreted in terms of recent French history, usually misunderstood. Historians set the tone, and journalists caught the infection from them. When a rising took place, people spoke knowingly of tumbrils and barricades. (Actually there had been no barricades in the revolutionary Paris of 1789-1799, but it was assumed that there must have been because barricades figured in the insurrections of 1830 and 1848.) Radicals came to be known as Jacobins, or if they were somewhat less radical, as Girondins. The real nature of the dispute between these factions was ignored. Robespierre, according to taste, was a bloodthirsty tyrant, an incorruptible republican, or the leader of the middle class, intent on keeping the proletariat in its place. The fact that there was no proletariat, merely a mob of unemployed and casual laborers, of the sort that Marxists later came to call *lumpenproletarians*, was conveniently overlooked.

Above all, there was Thermidor. On the 27th of July 1794—the 9th of Thermidor, according to the short-lived republican calendar—Robespierre was overthrown by a hostile majority in the Convention, and the Reign of Terror cane to an end. Thermidor pleased the liberals, but it distressed the more radical democrats, for the Thermidorians did away with Equality and instead put Liberty first. Liberty of course was bourgeois liberty

[*] *Commentary* (January 1964).

—freedom to buy and sell. Thermidor was the triumph of the bourgeoisie, which on that day won control of the Revolution and held power for five years, until Bonaparte chased the lawyers out and established his personal dictatorship. But France remained bourgeois, and in 1830 the heirs of the Thermidorians once more returned to power, led by Louis Philippe and Guizot; only now they were called Liberals and wore sober frock coats instead of fanciful neo-classical dress. By 1840 the socialists had begun to see through all this, and eventually Marx came along and explained that the French Revolution had really been a bourgeois revolution, though draped in Roman costume, and that the "heroic illusions" of its chief actors were an unconscious means of promoting the drab reality of modern industrial-capitalist society.

This interpretation—which was in tune with Hegel's sardonic view of history as a procession of stages whose meaning is concealed from the participants (though plain to the philosopher) —had a sobering effect upon those who understood it. On others it acted as a tonic: if the secret of the bourgeois revolution had at last been pierced, it should now be possible to make a proletarian revolution, which would pass beyond the bourgeois stage and found Equality on the rule of the toilers. Hints that the toilers might be unfit to rule, and that the proletarian revolution might turn out to be just another historical masquerade leading to a new form of inequality, were dismissed as unworthy skepticism. There were some warning voices, but in general the Russian revolutionary intellectuals, who from about 1840 onward began to ponder these matters, refused to be deterred. Their business, as they saw it, was to make sure that next time there was no Thermidor, and that the Revolution went on *in permanence.*

The relevance of this theme to the life and work of the man who, more than any other, made of the Permanent Revolution a working concept and a political model, requires no emphasis in these days, when Communists the world over debate among themselves what went wrong in the Soviet Union after 1917 (or, once more according to taste, after 1921, when Lenin and Trotsky suppressed the Kronstadt rising and banned all factions within the ruling party). Any lingering doubts as to the central importance of the French example for the Bolsheviks—all of them, including Stalin—are stilled by the perusal of Mr. Isaac Deutscher's massive three-part biography of Trotsky. The literary merits of this work are considerable, but they alone do not account for the fascination of Mr. Deutscher's theme. Nor does the stature of his protagonist, though the final volume, which records Trotsky's eleven years in exile until his death in 1940, derives a tragic quality from the personality of the chief character.* Prometheus on his rock, Lear wandering about his blasted heath—these comparisons spring readily to a mind nurtured on literature, and Mr. Deutscher misses few opportunities to ram the point home. He is entitled to his hero worship, as others are entitled to their feeling that Trotsky—like other characters of tragedy ancient and modern—was largely instrumental in causing disasters to accumulate wherever he went, down to the personal tragedies which in his closing years struck within the inmost family circle. (His eldest son died mysteriously in Paris at the height of the Great Purge, a daughter from an earlier marriage committed suicide.) The harrowing tale unfolds to the last unbearable chapter in Mexico, where the assassin struck down an ailing, lonely, embittered man, whose creation lay in ruins, and who at the close of his life had begun to doubt his own inmost certainties. It is a story often told and destined one day to find its Buechner or its Brecht, for nothing is more inherently dramatic than this terrible finale to a life so crammed with triumphs and disasters; so paradigmatic too—as in a different key was Marx's stoical fortitude amid the grinding pressures of the Victorian era—of our turbulent and bloodstained epoch. Here one merely records that Trotsky has been fortunate in his biographer, for it would have been easy to sensationalize the subject or to drown it in learned scholasticism. Mr. Deutscher has avoided these pitfalls, and his readers have cause to be grateful.

* *The Prophet Outcast: Trotsky, 1929-1940* (London and New York, 1963).

They will be wise, however, not to regard this impassioned account of Trotsky's last years as the key to the historical lock which Trotsky himself failed to turn. Mr. Deutscher shares most of the illusions of his hero, and where he has discarded them, he substitutes others. In his concluding volume he has at last worked himself free from the doctrinaire strait-jacket imposed upon other writers by Trotsky's own interpretation of the "Soviet Thermidor" (in the first two volumes of his trilogy* this emancipation was only half complete). But while he now recognizes that most of these analogies were based on a misunderstanding, he himself goes on to promote new confusions. If Stalin is no longer the "grave-digger of the revolution," then he must be a combination of Robespierre and Napoleon incarnate, and his quasi-Bonapartist use of the Red Army to "export the revolution" from 1939 onward is obliquely defended by Mr. Deutscher as the only way out, and, all things considered, a "progressive" phenomenon. If Trotsky was wrong about the Soviet Union being on the road to a bourgeois restoration, and if his former adherents were also mistaken in calling its system "state capitalism," then it seems to follow for Mr. Deutscher that perhaps it is socialism after all, though to be sure the full socialist content still has to burst through the bureaucratic integument. These apologetics—an aspect of Mr. Deutscher's unwavering fidelity to Lenin and Leninism—occupy a not inconsiderable part of his third volume. He is generally fair-minded even in dealing with the *"literary Trotskisants"*—a number of names familiar to Americans are mentioned—who after 1940 broke away from Communism altogether; but his own essential orthodoxy is never left in doubt. Whatever the "literary intellectuals"—he is too polite to call them parlor Bolsheviks—may think about the matter, Mr. Deutscher's faith in the inherently progressive role of the U.S.S.R. has not been shaken even by the Stalinist experience. That chapter anyhow is closed. And does not history consist of a long series of such episodes, which for all their incidental horrors have brought mankind nearer to the promised land?

---

* *The Prophet Armed: Trotsky, 1879-1921; The Prophet Unarmed: Trotsky, 1921-1929* (London and New York, 1954, 1959).

Not that he is inclined to overlook the cost. There is in this third volume a blood-freezing account of the 1929-1930 "liquidation of the kulaks" which conveys some sense of the havoc wreaked upon the countryside by Stalin's war against the peasantry. And there are some grim pages on the slaughter of the Old Guard in 1936-1938, though otherwise the great purge—the *Yezhovshchina*—which swept away so many countless victims, appears only as the backdrop to what really interests him: the duel between his protagonist and the dictator in the Kremlin. Was it for this that so many thousands died and so many millions were packed off to Siberia? From Mr. Deutscher's account one might almost suppose that Stalin staged the great massacre merely in order to reaffirm his personal hold over his own deeply riven faction. No doubt the purge had a logic of its own: once set in motion the avalanche swept on, until millions not remotely connected with the power struggle found themselves in the camps. But surely at some stage a decision must have been taken to let the NKVD loose upon the whole terrorized country, until every vestige of opposition had been rooted out and every last individual in the whole of Russia battered into unthinking obedience. Mr. Deutscher half recognizes the probability of such a purpose. He points out that the purge prevented the bureaucracy—only the bureaucracy?—from settling down and developing a dangerous *esprit de corps*. But he is reluctant to confront the full logic of totalitarianism, and thus tends to remain within the confines of Trotsky's own interpretation: the purge was the major instrument of Stalinism, and Stalinism was the way in which backward Russia revenged itself upon the Revolution. Further than that he is not prepared to go.

This approach has its difficulties. Their nature is revealed in the densely packed chapter of Mr. Deutscher's third volume in which he comes to grips with Trotsky's critique of Stalinism, as set out notably in one of his last writings, *The Revolution Betrayed* (1936). This, as Mr. Deutscher points out, contains Trotsky's "classical indictment of bureaucracy." It also embodies Trotsky's tentative revision of his own earlier (and quite misleading) discussion of what he had called the "Soviet Ther-

midor." Here it is necessary to bear in mind that this particular
metaphor had already been employed in the savage factional in-
fighting of the late 1920s. In the second volume of his study
(published in 1959) Mr. Deutscher gave some examples of how
in 1926-1927 Trotsky and Zinoviev fell back on history when
they had run out of other arguments. Talk of "Thermidor" was
enough to make the strongest men blanch. In July 1927, five
months before his expulsion from the Party, Trotsky temporarily unnerved the Old Bolsheviks on the Central Control
Commission with a speech on the fall of Robespierre and the
destruction of the Jacobin regime. On an earlier occasion, Bukharin—the intellectual leader of the right wing—had reacted
with hysterical fury when charged with encouraging "Thermi-
dorian" tendencies. All the factions were in the grip of genuine
fear lest they unwittingly enact a repetition of that historic disaster. But it was a two-edged weapon. In 1929, when Stalin
turned against Bukharin and began his war upon the peasantry,
the exiled Trotskyists—then still living under a relatively liberal
regime, and even allowed to circulate their manifestoes—began
to wonder whether after all Stalin might not be in the "historic"
succession to Robespierre, in which case *they* were the Thermidorians! The thought alarmed them to such a degree that by
1932 most of them had made their peace with Stalin (not that it
saved them in the end). Unluckily for him, these were just the
years when Trotsky, from his exile in Turkey, was least able to
influence events. Left to brood in isolation, he readily convinced
himself that his supporters had sold the pass, and that he alone
saw matters in their true light. Stalin *could not* carry the Five
Year Plan through! Or if he did, it was not the plan that Trotsky
would have carried through: not a socialist plan, but a bureaucratic one! By 1936 this had become the new line imposed upon
the Trotskyist movement: the Soviet bureaucracy had "confis-
cated" the Revolution for its own benefit, though it was still the
ruling caste of a "workers' state." It was, to be sure, a tyrannical
and parasitic caste, which must be swept away to make "Soviet
democracy" possible; yet it was also the guardian of public property. As long as it defended the new "production relations"

against the world bourgeoisie, and against bourgeois tendencies at home, its historic role was "progressive," and Trotsky would go on supporting it, even though its leader slaughtered all the Trotskyists in the internment camps (Mr. Deutscher suggests that Trotsky was unaware of this) and in general did his best to imitate Ivan the Terrible. Caught in these insoluble contradictions, the Trotskyist movement—never more than a loose assemblage of small groups and individuals—destroyed itself in furious arguments, which in the end left Trotsky almost totally bereft of organized support.

In fact, the whole debate was unreal. A "workers' state" is no more conceivable than a "peasants' state," and the notion that the U.S.S.R. was at any time after 1917 close to becoming one belongs to the category of what Marx called "heroic illusions," along with the Rousseauist dreams of Robespierre. Trotsky could have solved his problem by conceding that "proletarian dictatorship" was a mere makeshift and the proletariat not fit to rule. In the closing months of his life he actually came near to confronting this truth, at any rate to the extent of suggesting that if the European working class did not seize power in the wake of the Second World War, the whole Marxist perspective might have to be written off. What really needed to be written off was not Marxism but the myth of the October Revolution; but then Trotsky had never drawn a distinction between the two. In his eyes the revolutionary message of Marxism had been validated by what Lenin had done in 1917. If by 1937 it looked as though the Revolution had been aborted, the disaster must be a temporary setback. Otherwise what would be left of the original message?

To these important problems Mr. Deutscher is not an altogether safe guide, since his own preconceptions incline him to believe that Trotsky's analysis "still offers the best clue to the subsequent social evolution": that is, to the post-Stalin regime's eclectic aim of eliminating the worst features of Stalinism, while preserving the new class relationships. He argues that Trotsky did not really envisage anything so utopian as the total elimination of the bureaucracy, merely a drastic curtailment of its privileges; and he suggests that this is currently being undertaken. On which the only possible comment is that in this case the Soviet "toilers" will have to go on being content with very little. It is all very well for Mr. Deutscher to write: "The problem of a bureaucracy in a workers' state is indeed so new and complex that it allows little or no certitude." However uncertain other things may be, it is undeniable that in what he is pleased to call a "workers' state," the workers are not the rulers but the ruled. This doubtless is inevitable; and moreover it is perfectly compatible with the usual definition of socialism (public ownership), though not with communism (common ownership). But it is not what the Bolsheviks set out to accomplish in 1917 and what Communists the world over are today still being promised, and promising others. Mr. Deutscher, a disillusioned ex-Trotskyist himself, is at pains to correct the misconceptions of his protagonist, but only in the interest of assuring his readers that the imperfect realization of the original purpose, in the present-day U.S.S.R. and the other Soviet-bloc regimes, is about all that can be expected in this world. He is clearly right; what may strike some readers as odd is his evident conviction that the original plan is still worth pursuing.

I I

The revolutionary in politics: this is not in actual fact the central theme of Mr. Deutscher's biography, but he might easily have organized his three volumes around it. Trotsky is the classic case of the revolutionary leader who is also an intellectual in the fullest sense of that much abused term: not one who makes use of other people's ideas, but one who *lives* his own thoughts, and whose commitment to an idea overrides all other loyalties. It is only when someone of Trotsky's stature appears that the full meaning of the phenomenon becomes evident. Here is the "union of theory and practice" incarnate in an orator who is also a statesman, a theorist who can move crowds, organize government departments, set armies on the march; a "professional revolutionary" with a matchless style and an educated taste for literature. No wonder he fascinated the youth of three continents. Is it possible, at our present distance from the scene, to find a niche for him, to bracket him with other major figures of recent history?

Not with Marx. Superficial resemblances to the contrary notwithstanding, the two men do not inhabit the same universe —a circumstance Trotsky, not otherwise given to modesty, was always ready to acknowledge. The difference does not lie merely in their respective intellectual endowments, though Trotsky was aware that abstract theorizing of the kind that was child's play to Marx was beyond his own capacity. There is also the difference in social circumstances and historical background. For all his radicalism and the revolutionary fling he enjoyed in his youth, Marx was profoundly integrated within the German and European culture of his age. At the deepest level he was at one with the social order whose doom he prophesied. There is something very revealing about his public status as a famous, learned, and somewhat irascible scholar of the late nineteenth century: a true Great Victorian, the contemporary (and admirer) of Darwin. One need only read his correspondence with Engels to see how profoundly both men were rooted in the conditions of their time and how much, for all their contemptuous indifference to the creeds upheld by majority opinion, they enjoyed being alive at that particular moment. No, Trotsky does not—except for certain inherited sensibilities of temper—relate back to Marx. Curiously enough he has more in common with Marx's arch-enemy, Mikhail Bakunin, and not only because Bakunin was a perpetual rebel who died in exile. He shares with the founder of Russian Anarchism a certain romantic conception of "the revolution" as a vast popular uprising against authority—all authority—which Marx (not to mention Engels) would have reproved. If the surviving Trotskyist sects in Europe, Asia, and Latin America have over the years become the successors of the vanished Anarchist and Anarcho-Syndicalist movements— one need only read their pamphlet literature to catch the essential similarity—they can find retrospective warrant for this curious "deviation" in Trotsky's personality and writings. With a vastly better intellectual equipment and far greater literary talent than Bakunin, Trotsky nonetheless had something of his romantic utopianism, his faith in "the people," his individualism, even his vanity: traits which Lenin sternly repressed in himself. Not surprisingly a good many people found Trotsky intolerable.

This is an aspect of his hero's personality which troubles his biographer. Not that Mr. Deutscher is inclined to minimize Trotsky's literary and intellectual gifts; if anything he makes too much of them, notably in the first of his three volumes, where even Trotsky's pre-revolutionary journalism is extolled in somewhat excessive terms. The awkward truth he has to face is that it is not easy to be both a profound thinker and an effective pamphleteer. Marx managed it, but then he was unique. In Trotsky's case it is possible to feel that the style of his pamphleteering was frequently superior to the thought-content that went into it. At times—e.g., in *The Revolution Betrayed*—form and content came together to make a whole. More often the rhetorician took over from the theorist and produced brilliant writing when what was required was hard thinking about unpalatable circumstances.

Mr. Deutscher, in his concluding volume, praises Trotsky's pamphlets on the German situation in the early 1930s, just before Hitler's rise to power. Having been among those who were privileged to read them as they came off the press, the reviewer is in a position to assure the student of Mr. Deutscher's volume that he is quite wrong about their influence, which was close to nil, and about their grasp of the German situation, which was vague in the extreme. They were indeed very brilliant, and of course vastly superior to the lunatic Comintern literature which treated Hitler as a minor nuisance compared to the real enemy, the Social-Democrats; but that is not saying a great deal. By any reasonable standard of political analysis, Trotsky's writings of the period must be judged a brilliant failure (though curiously he showed some grasp of the economic logic of Fascism in an article he published in, of all places, the quarterly *Foreign Affairs* in April 1934, a year *after* Hitler had come to power). It is not enough to say that in his pamphlets of 1931-1932 he made mincemeat of the Comintern line; of course he did. Anyone outside that madhouse in Moscow could see that Germany was heading straight for catastrophe. What he failed to do was to indicate an alternative to the official Communist line, which really amounted to letting Hitler seize power, in the expectation that he would shortly be overthrown by "the workers." Trotsky was almost as romantic about the capacity of "the workers" to resist a totalitarian dictatorship as were the German Communists, and as innocent as they of any understanding of the real nature of "capitalist crisis," to employ the term then much in vogue. Moreover, he had not the faintest notion of what National Socialism was really about, what were the emotional springs that fed it, and how far it could be expected to go. After the lapse of a generation one still recalls the amazement with which his own supporters greeted his confident announcement that the Storm Troopers—being of course "petty bourgeois"— were "human dust" which would evaporate at the first sight of a united working class. This was sad nonsense, though Mr. Deutscher treats it with dead seriousness, thereby giving at least one of his readers the impression that he has not learned much from the experience of the great catastrophe.

In reality the German debacle, and the simultaneous emergence of Stalinism in Russia as, so to speak, a going concern and a system of government, put the quietus upon the sort of revolutionary socialism that Trotsky believed in. His biographer has failed to grasp the connection between the Russian and the German catastrophes, because his gaze is too exclusively fixed on the bizarre dialectic of the Stalin-Trotsky duel for control of a totally disoriented world Communist movement. Moreover, his "realism" does not quite extend to a realization that Hitler, no less than Stalin, had something to teach the Communists. What he taught them (and what they subsequently applied in practice when their turn came after 1945) was the technique of the quasi-legal coup d'état and the subsequent reign of terror. The real answer to Hitler's seizure of power in Berlin in 1933 was the Communist seizure of power in Prague fifteen years later; using very similar methods, with the ailing Beneš substituted for Hindenburg. Since then there has scarcely been a Communist Party in the world that has not tried its hand at the game. In 1933 all this still lay in the future, and Trotsky was the last to perceive the lesson of events, which was that the age of *genuine,* spontaneous, popular revolutions was over, except in backward countries, from Cuba to Algeria. Even the October coup of 1917 had not been really spontaneous, but at least it was still backed by a genuine mass movement. Since then all successful seizures of power in industrial countries have had to be elaborately organized, with the masses no less than their "leading cadres" drilled beforehand. Backward countries, of course, are another matter, which may account for the fact that Trotskyist groups have had some successes in Bolivia, Ceylon, and even Algeria, but cannot boast any conquest, however minor, in the industrial centers of the world. It would not be quite true to say that in the 1930s no one had grasped this. Towards the end of the decade some people had, but they did not include Trotsky and his orthodox disciples. The point is connected with the wider subject of the intellectual's role in politics, which is why it is proper to note that Trotsky did not see what was obvious to some people who lacked both his mental powers and his background as leader of a victorious revolution. The explanation clearly is that he had been disoriented precisely by his and Lenin's triumph in 1917. Indeed he spent the remainder of his life in the blinding glare of this cataclysmic event. Whether Lenin—had he lived—would have done better, is questionable, though he had a marked streak of pragmatic adaptability lacking in both Trotsky and Stalin ("the two ablest men in the Central Committee," as he remarked on a famous occasion). Mr. Deutscher, who in general tends to see Stalin as the unconscious executant of Trotsky's ideas, is silent on this particular point, though articulate enough on others. He does have something to say, however, about a controversy which caused bitter dissension in Trotsky's entourage during his final years: the debate over what came to be known as the "managerial revolution," that is, the rise of a new ruling stratum.

It all began—as the reader of Mr. Deutscher's third volume can discover for himself in detail—with the Italian ex-Trotskyist Bruno Rizzi and his pamphlet *"La bureaucratisation du monde,"* published in Paris in 1939, not long after Trotsky in 1936 had given his own assessment of the "new class." Today, with the wisdom of hindsight and the accumulated experience of another quarter century, we are inured to the notion of "bureaucratic collectivism" as a new form of class rule, but in 1939-1940 Rizzi —and James Burnham, who largely based himself on Rizzi— sounded very shocking. What they proposed was of course unacceptable to Trotsky, for it amounted to saying that the Russian Revolution (like the French before it) had merely replaced one form of exploitation by another. If they were right, the Soviet bureaucracy, which Trotsky saw as a pernicious growth to be removed or at least cut down to size at the first opportunity, was really the essence of the whole matter. "Bureaucratic collectivism" had come to stay. The Bolsheviks had been utopians, just like the Jacobins before them (save for those like Stalin who had adapted themselves to the new trend). The classless society was an illusion, and the working class, so far from being the harbinger of a new order, was condemned to remain the "mass basis" of a system of inequality.

It is a tribute to Trotsky's intellectual integrity that while rejecting this thesis as unproved and improbable, he did not entirely exclude the likelihood that things might indeed go wrong. Writing in September 1939, shortly after the Second World War had broken out, he still maintained that the revolutionary potential of Europe was not exhausted; but for the first time he also envisaged the possibility that the working class might prove unable to throw up an adequate leadership and gain power for itself. In a pronouncement that startled his supporters, he declared that if at the close of the Second World War there was still no socialist revolution in the West, the Marxist-Leninist perspective would have to be written off: "We would then be compelled to acknowledge that the bureaucratic reaction was rooted not in the backwardness of the country, and not in the imperialist environment, but in the congenital incapacity of the proletariat to become a ruling class. Then it would be necessary to establish in retrospect that . . . the present U.S.S.R. was the precursor of a new and universal system of exploitation. . . . However onerous this . . . perspective may be, if the world proletariat should actually prove incapable of accomplishing the task placed upon it by the course of development, nothing would remain but to recognize that the socialist program . . . had petered out as a Utopia."

Thus at the close of his own life Trotsky stood on the threshold of a new epoch, and what he glimpsed was not the Promised Land, but an Egypt of perpetual bondage. With a stoicism that still evokes admiration he proceeded to outline the practical consequences to be drawn by those who, like himself, were determined to remain faithful to the cause—albeit hopeless—of the oppressed and the exploited: if Communism was an illusion "it is self-evident that a new 'minimum' program would be required—for the defense of the interests of the slaves of the totalitarian bureaucratic society." Coming from Trotsky, these are poignant words—among the most poignant ever uttered by a political leader in exile. They testify both to his intellectual candor and to his moral stature. Yet they also represent a devastating judgment upon his (and Lenin's) earlier certainties. If revolution and counter-revolution alike were about to issue in totalitarianism, the entire edifice of belief built upon the October Revolution lay in ruins.

That the dismantling of Utopia is by now complete, would be the judgment of most present-day Marxists, though not of Mr. Deutscher, who on this subject exudes a confident optimism of truly astounding proportions. The point would scarcely be worth pursuing were it not that it is frequently confused with a quite extraneous topic, namely the role of the revolutionary intellectual in the Socialist movement. It would seem that the confusion is at least in part semantic and has to do with the different uses to which the term "intellectual" can be put. Because Marx, Engels, Luxemburg, Lenin, Trotsky, Gramsci, Kautsky, the Webbs, Bernard Shaw, Léon Blum, and other notable figures in the history of Socialism were all intellectuals (what else should they have been?), and because in our own age the so-called "technical intelligentsia" is indisputably at the core of the various bureaucratic-collectivist regimes which currently occupy so large a part in everyone's thinking, it has become fashionable to argue from the first circumstance to the second, as though every nineteenth-century theorist at his desk had been a precursor of present-day industrial society. Because socialism stands for planning, and because planners have to work with scientists and technologists, the conclusion is drawn that the intelligentsia as such is responsible for totalitarianism! Even the most democratic and libertarian writers are saddled—a century or more after their passing—with responsibility for regimes which do their best to make the work of the critical intellect impossible!

In reality the equation "intellectuals=authoritarianism" won't hold up, if only because intellectuals are plainly at the core of all the liberalizing and "revisionist" tendencies in the Soviet orbit and elsewhere. It is true to say, however, that the relationship of the intelligentsia to the labor movement was not clearly worked out by the Marxists, while other Socialist schools (with the partial exception of the Fabians) never bothered their heads about it. What Lenin had to say was two-edged, and lent itself as easily to gross flattery of the supposedly faultless working class as to authoritarian whip-cracking over its head. Stalinism even managed to combine both features in a single system: on ceremonial occasions the "toiler" was solemnly upheld as a model, while in everyday matters his basic rights (such as the right to strike) were filched away. Trotsky for his part never wearied of belaboring his own supporters for being remote from the masses: quite oblivious to the fact that the masses preferred Stalin and that practically all his own adherents were intellectuals. This situation has persisted. The half dozen Trotskyist sects which in recent years have somehow managed to acquire a following were all started by intellectuals and largely staffed by them, while the workers showed little interest. A sociology of the Trotskyist movement, if it is ever undertaken, will doubtless disclose that the few working-class adherents it has acquired in Western countries were displaced Syndicalists who could find no other sect to attach themselves to. As an organization of the "revolutionary proletariat," Trotskyism has been as complete a failure as was Anarchism, and largely for the same reason: the industrial working class in advanced countries is not "revolutionary"—at any rate not in the sense that Trotsky (unconsciously following Bakunin rather than Marx in this matter) associated with the term. The final judgment on Trotsky as founder, leader, and almost sole existing theorist of the "Fourth International" must be that he launched it at the very moment when all the certainties it embodied had gone into the melting pot.

III

It has been necessary to dwell at some length on Trotsky's role in Communist history and on Trotskyism as a political phenomenon. But after all one is talking about the biography of a Russian revolutionary in the tradition of Herzen, Bakunin, and all those other "romantic exiles" to whom Mr. E. H. Carr many years ago devoted an enthralling study. The essential "Russianness" of Trotsky and his circle is well conveyed by Mr. Deutscher. It introduces an element of human warmth and even lends a note of charm to what is on the whole a very somber story. Trotsky possessed all the Russian gift for self-expression, combined with a very Jewish talent for constant intellectual ratiocination; and though it is tiresome to go on laboring the obvious, it must be evident that as a person he could have walked out of the pages of any of the great Russian novels. Mr. Deutscher is aware of the advantage this gives a biographer, and he rarely falters in his endeavor to bring the flavor of Trotsky's personality home to the reader. Sentimentality is kept in check, but there is no lack of graphic detail, and one or two minor surprises await the reader who has the patience to work his way through these three volumes (of which, incidentally, the third and last is the most revealing, as well as the most stylish). Inevitably, as the tale unfolds, from the almost halcyon stay on Prinkipo Island in 1929-1933, via the wretched wanderings around Europe in the middle 1930s, to the final agony in Mexico, the picture becomes progressively bleaker. But it is only near the close, with disaster crowding in from every side and the assassin lurking on the doorstep, that the reader begins to share the author's sense of reliving a tragedy of almost Shakespearean dimensions. Then Trotsky himself began to reflect upon his sufferings and upon the fate of those nearest to him—the son whom Stalin had exiled to Siberia, the other son who had died in Paris, the daughter who had taken her life, the burden borne by his wife, his faithful companion of so many misfortunes—and for the first time something like self-pity crept in. He had been reading the autobiography of a famed seventeenth-century heretic, the Archpriest Avakuum, banished as an "Old Believer" by the Orthodox Church to Siberia where his children died of disease and starvation, and later brought back to Moscow to be burnt at the stake. The thought crossed his mind that after all very little had changed in three centuries:

> Concerning the blows that have fallen to our lot, I reminded Natasha the other day of the life of the Archpriest Avakuum. They were stumbling on together to Siberia, the rebellious priest and his faithful spouse. Their feet sank in the snow, and the poor exhausted woman kept falling into snowdrifts. Avakuum relates: "And I came up, and she, poor soul, began to reproach me, saying: 'How long, archpriest, is the suffering to be?' And I said, 'Markovna, unto our very death.' And she, with a sigh, answered 'So be it, Petrovich, let us be getting on our way.' "

The quotation is from Trotsky's *Diary in Exile*, an account of his wanderings published in 1958 by Harvard, with a preface by Max Schachtman, one of the veterans of the Trotskyist movement, though currently (to Mr. Deutscher's evident disapproval) a Social-Democrat. It is a very moving document, rather more moving than Mr. Deutscher's biography, though perhaps that is an unfair remark. It also has the advantage of being short (not much more than 150 pages), and should be read by everyone interested in Trotsky's personality. It is a great pity that it came much too late for Mr. Edmund Wilson to incorporate in his book *To The Finland Station*, whose account of Trotsky in exile

is based on the 1930 *Autobiography*. In that year Trotsky was
still hopeful, for real disaster had not yet struck. By 1935, the
year of the *Diary*, he already had some cause to wonder about
his resemblance to the Archpriest Avakuum, for in that year he
was expelled from France, refused entry by most other countries, and finally allowed into Norway, only to be interned a year
later under humiliating conditions, due to Soviet pressure on the
rather philistinely fearful Norwegian Labor government. By
1940—when Mr. Deutscher perforce ends his tale—Trotsky still
had a few political illusions, but none about his own prospects.
While waiting for the assassin to strike he noted (in a brief
Testament appended to the *Diary*): "My high (and still rising)
blood pressure is deceiving those near me about my actual condition. I am active and able to work, but the end is evidently
near." It came exactly six months later, on August 20, 1940, in
an unexpected form, but under circumstances already pointing
to the early extinction of his physical no less than his political
life. The Testament closes (after some remarks about suicide)
with the words: "But whatever may be the circumstances of my
death, I shall die with unshaken faith in the Communist future.
This faith in man and his future gives me even now such power
of resistance as cannot be given by any religion." He was wrong,
of course: the faith he kept was very precisely of the religious
kind.

Over the whole scene of the *Diary*—as indeed over Mr.
Deutscher's final volume—there hangs the shadow of an approaching catastrophe. In December 1934, Sergei Kirov, the
Party boss of Leningrad, had been murdered—if one can believe
Khrushchev, at the instigation of none other than Stalin—and
the Kremlin reacted with a calculated ferocity that boded ill for
the future (though it did not daunt the Webbs, who were just
then about to compose their paean to the democratization of
Russia under Stalin). The *Diary* reflects the atmosphere on the
eve of the great bloodbath of 1936-1938. Early in 1935 Trotsky's
first wife and his younger son from a second marriage were de-
ported to Siberia, though neither had been politically active.
Soon more arrests and deportations followed, mostly of old

friends. The diarist recorded these calamities, and then mused idly over the fate of the Tsar's family—apparently without noticing the connection. On April 9-10, 1935, a lengthy entry records that the decision in 1918 to execute not merely the Tsar but his entire family was taken by the Politburo in Trotsky's absence, and that on hearing of it he voiced some mild surprise (his own preference had been for a public trial of Nicholas II alone). The note proceeds: "The Tsar's family fell victim to that principle which constitutes the axis of monarchy: dynastic succession." On the following page there is a brief, troubled, entry: "No news about Seryozha [his younger son], and perhaps there won't be any for a long time." There wasn't. Nor was there any hint that the author of these reflections had a premonition of destiny recoiling upon his head.

Trotsky's self-examination—notably in the *Diary*—is an impossibly difficult subject, because the view he took of himself and his role was at once so penetrating and so wrong-headed. Gifted with a capacious intellect and with great imaginative powers, he saw quite clearly that he represented a lost cause. At the same time he was convinced that history would vindicate him in the not very distant future. Every now and then he could claim to have been proved right. Thus when the Norwegian government in 1936 first interned him and then expelled him in distressing circumstances, he told the placid Labor Ministers (they included Mr. Trygve Lie who comes out very badly) in thundering tones that before long it would be *their* turn to seek refuge in exile. When the blow fell in 1940 and the Norwegian government did have to flee before the invading Germans, Trotsky might have had cause to feel that his prophecy had come true, the more so since he had told Trygve Lie to his face, in the presence of all his assembled officials, that the day was near when the Nazis would drive them out! (King Haakon, who led the sad procession into exile, is reported to have reminded his bedraggled Ministers of "Trotsky's curse.")

On other occasions he was less successful as a prophet, and the *Diary* as a whole is shot through with the sort of exasperated nagging that comes naturally to political exiles: all his enemies

must be cretins or criminals, and so, it turns out, were most of
his friends. If they were not cowardly traitors, they failed through
lack of imagination. All the Socialists without exception were useless, while the official Communists were slaves of the Kremlin—
that "historically doomed clique" of "degenerate and moronic
traitors," who unfortunately possessed power, while he had none.
Meanwhile Fascism was on the march, not merely in France
(this was 1935), but in England too(!), and "bourgeois democracy" clearly was about to give up the ghost. Indeed, imbecility
and corruption were spreading everywhere. "It is hard to imagine a more painful occupation than reading Léon Blum." "In
Belgium, Spaak has become a Minister. A miserable character!"
"Claude Farrère, whom I mentioned the other day, has been
elected to the Academy. What a revolting pack of old clowns!"
Western literature was mostly decadent; Soviet literature was
unreadable; only the classics were still tolerable. Politically there
was no ray of hope anywhere. France was rapidly going to pieces,
while England was merely "the last ward in the European lunatic asylum." The smaller countries were stupidly philistine, and
their leaders a collection of buffoons. Much of this unfortunately was true, but he missed all the factors in the situation
that did not fit his prepossessions: notably the underlying
strength of simple things like patriotism and democracy, which
later asserted themselves in the various Resistance movements.
Indeed on the assumptions made in the *Diary* and in his later
writings, the Resistance was incomprehensible, the more so
since it was predominantly non-Communist and actuated by
sentiments that had no place in his thinking.

   In fact the tide had begun to turn in the very month of his
death, August 1940. It is a pity that he did not live long enough
to take account of England's resistance under Churchill—a Tory
romantic with whom temperamentally (though not intellectually) he had something in common. About this time, too, his
erstwhile follower André Malraux attached himself to de
Gaulle. The Fascist challenge was beginning to produce its own
antidote, but the counter-movement was also a movement away
from Leninism and the myth of the October Revolution. Since

1945 the elites of Western Europe have been in possession of their own homemade myth: that of the Resistance. This is one reason—perhaps the major reason—why the whole tradition associated with Trotsky has now faded out.

It will not be revived by Mr. Deutscher's biography, and not only because on its political side his book is very largely a discreetly veiled apology for Stalin (and even more for Stalin's heirs). The fact is that Bolshevism is now as dead as Jacobinism, though there are still some regions of the world where the original tragedy is being re-enacted (in tragicomic form, to paraphrase Marx). Nothing can revive the illusions brought to birth and then destroyed by the October Revolution; not even the romantic halo which continues to surround the life and death of Leon Trotsky. Who in this day and age is going to believe in a proletarian revolution giving rise to a classless society, when the only revolutions actually under way are so clearly neither proletarian nor classless? For that matter, what Marxist is ever again going to invest his faith in the proletariat: a dwindling minority in the West and a passive object of manipulation in the East? Even Communists will have to do better if they want their cause to retain some relevance. (In practice they are increasingly coming to rely on the very "labor aristocracy" of technicians and skilled workers whom Lenin and Trotsky anathematized for so many years.) And behind the official façade of "Communism" in the Soviet orbit, there emerges with ever greater clarity the outline of a new society in which the planners hold control, while the technicians do their bidding and the workers are left to applaud. If this is socialism, it is certainly not classless. The last word lies with those erstwhile followers of Trotsky who broke away from him when they glimpsed the truth. Still it remains that by 1940 Trotsky had wrung from himself the admission that a long, dark, totalitarian night seemed about to precede the dawn, and that "the slaves" would need someone to defend them. Whatever honor Communism still retains was saved by its arch-heresiarch.

The European Civil War*

• Unlike its Communist rival, European Fascism has not hitherto been made the theme of notable philosophical investigations. There are some excellent historical studies of both the Italian and the German experience, but the philosophers have on the whole tended to subsume the topic under the more general heading of totalitarianism. The difficulty of dealing in rational terms with an irrationalist ideology may have something to do with it, but in the main this loss of interest must be due to the political misfortunes of the movement and the discredit which clings to its name. At its peak it did not lack defenders. The case of Heidegger—calling upon the students of Freiburg in 1933 to be loyal to *Volk* and *Führer*—is only the most notorious. There were others, equally "engaged" and even more pertinacious, notably Carl Schmitt, already known during the Weimar period for his championship of authoritarianism. A decade earlier the signal had been given in Italy by Giovanni Gentile, for many years Croce's rival in the exposition of neo-Hegelianism. Gentile had once represented the Italian version of liberalism (always a delicate plant), and he was still officially a liberal when in 1922 he entered Mussolini's first government as Minister of Education. He soon went over to Fascism, and his educational reform achieved the dual purpose of handing the elementary schools over to the Church, while reserving secondary teaching for the Party: a typically Italian compromise, much appreciated by the Vatican. It is odd to think that this destruction of the *risorgimento* tradition was accomplished by a liberal philosopher, but then it was an odd period altogether.

Since the philosophers have in recent years tumbled off the

* *The New York Review* (February 3, 1966).

bandwagon, one cannot blame the politicians for being coy. Who today wants to be known as a Fascist? There are at least a dozen regimes among the newly independent states of Asia and Africa which could in good conscience lay claim to the title, but their leaders would sooner be called Communists, even at the not very considerable risk of losing some of their American subsidies. The clearest case perhaps is that of Nasser. If anyone has the right to claim direct descent from the original fountainhead it is the Egyptian dictator, yet no one is more frantic in asserting the uniqueness and originality of his "Arab socialism." But then few aspiring politicians these days care to be associated with the memory of the Duce, let alone the Führer. Conversely, the Fascist label may be stuck on temporary dictatorships of the Consular, or "Roman," type, or on military autocracies which lack the essential support of a totalitarian party organization. Much depends on the actual circumstances of the case. An authoritarian regime which breaks down a primitive tribal structure may simply be doing the job of what used to be called the "bourgeois revolution," except that in this age it has to substitute itself for the bourgeoisie. But even Italian Fascism was not wholly reactionary: it made a small beginning towards the postwar industrialization drive. There were also some experiments with economic planning and state control which have been taken over (and expanded) by the various Italian governments since 1945. The present-day Spanish and Portuguese regimes are in an older tradition of Catholic authoritarianism. They lack the Fascist dynamic, although Franco tried, without success, to incorporate the few authentic Spanish Fascists in his regime. In the end he gave up and handed his administration over to the Opus Dei, an organization representing the Catholic *haute bourgeoisie*. Spain today is no longer Fascist, if it ever was. It is rather an old-fashioned police state which safeguards the privileges of the well-to-do.

The truth is that people have forgotten what Fascism was originally about. All they remember is Hitler and the extermination camps. But the bestiality of the Third Reich was rooted in circumstances peculiar to Germany, and the "intellectual" content of the Nazi cloaca cannot simply be equated with the heritage of European authoritarianism. As an ideology, Fascism antedated Hitler and has survived his fall. Its origins are complex, going back to the early nineteenth century, and in its modern form it includes at least one element which has retained its relevance for aspiring dictators: the attempt to fuse nationalism with socialism. It is true that the Communists have by now learned to play this particular game and indeed are proving quite adept at it—*vide* Castro's success in mobilizing Cuban nationalism, not to mention China and the various "liberation movements." But this is a late development—in the 1920s and 1930s they lagged far behind their rivals in this respect. Yet on the whole Fascism has been a failure, while Communism has become a world movement. Why?

The traditional Communist explanation—that Fascism was merely "the tool of the reactionary bourgeoisie"—is too silly to merit attention, quite apart from the fact that the Communists themselves no longer believe in it. Painful experience has taught them that the Fascist movement is quite autonomous and can be extremely dangerous to them. Pseudo-revolutionary it may be, but this does not make it "bourgeois." It is in fact anti-bourgeois, and this is just what gives it an appeal to people cast adrift by the disintegration of their customary way of life. The call for a "total" reorganization of society, which is the key element of every genuine Fascist movement, can be turned against the bourgeoisie as well as against the working class. All true Fascists are demagogues and modernizers; even Hitler fancied himself some sort of revolutionary. What distinguishes them from the Left is their irrationalism and their rejection of the entire corpus of liberal-democratic values.

Some, though not all, of these themes are explored, with great learning and considerable intellectual penetration, in Dr. Ernst Nolte's important study, now translated from the German.* A product of the postwar generation of German scholarship, Dr. Nolte is not weighed down by the bad conscience which afflicts

---

* *Three Faces of Fascism: Action Française, Italian Fascism, National Socialism* (New York, 1965).

so many of his senior colleagues. His treatment of the subject indeed displays a freedom from conventional preconceptions rare among German historians. That he is not quite unaffected by the spiritual climate of his native country appears from his inclination (understandable in the circumstances, but nonetheless regrettable) to demonize Hitler, instead of treating him as the residuary legatee of Pan-Germanism. There is too much about the *Führer's* private manias, and not enough about the collective obsessions of the German middle class. But no attempt is made to obscure the gulf which separated the monstrosities of the Third Reich from the comic-opera frenzy of Mussolini's New Rome. Dr. Nolte has no doubt at all what a German victory would have portended: the physical extermination not merely of the Jews, but of all East Europeans who could not be made to serve the purposes of the "master race." As he puts it (a trifle portentously perhaps, but then he is a philosopher as well as a historian): "The world was to be cured of the Jewish-Christian-Marxist doctrine of world redemption, and converted to that absolute sovereignty which was to bind the slaves forever to their slave fate." The leaders of the Third Reich (notably the SS, the core of the whole movement) really had taken Nietzsche seriously. So had large strata of the German educated class in general. For it is a myth that the Nazi movement represented only "the mob." It had conquered the universities before it triumphed over society. The SS leaders were for the most part academically trained, and at least one notorious concentration camp commander held a doctorate in philosophy.

How could a movement of this sort have gained power in a major European country? Dreadful though it is, the answer must be: largely by accident. For there can be little doubt that an early successful attempt on Hitler's person would have caused his party to collapse. Whether the Weimar Republic could have survived the economic and political crisis of the 1930s is a subsidiary question. Had it given way to a military dictatorship of the Conservative Light, as seems quite probable, there would at any rate have been no terrorism, no Second World War, no "final solution"—for Auschwitz was Hitler's personal idea. None of the other Nazi leaders (not to mention the Conservatives who helped him to power) were capable of conceiving such a project, let along carrying it through. The Third Reich was a one-man show. From start to finish Hitler alone exercised supreme authority, and when in April 1945 he pulled the pillars of Valhalla down upon his head, there was no one who could have entered a claim to the succession.

Yet there is also a sense in which Germany was ripe for Hitler, if not precisely for all his lunacies. Millions of Germans had not got over their longing for a return to the primitive racial community of the folk which would rid them at one blow of all the perplexities afflicting the modern world: capitalism, communism, liberalism, democracy, plutocracy, newspapers, elections, big-city life—the whole complex rigmarole of contemporary urban civilization. And there were national hatreds and racial animosities to be assuaged, military plans to be translated into reality, space to be conquered (at the expense of "inferior races"), ancient gods to be restored to their vacant thrones. This last was more than the crackpot idea of a few fanatics. It responded to ancestral longings in the German soul: the old pre-Christian gods were to be resurrected. This was truly a novel and startling idea. Neither Mussolini nor his French forerunners had ever dreamed of such a thing.

Dr. Nolte has organized his work around a comparative study of the two major European Fascisms—the Italian and the German—plus their unsuccessful French precursor, the Action française. In principle this approach is sound. If the execution does not quite come off, the reason is that he places too much weight on ideas as distinct from political circumstances and social pressures. This is a traditional German failing—the counterpart of the admirable German concern with the history of thought. Dr. Nolte has read Marx, but cannot quite bring himself to apply Marxian (or even Weberian) criteria to the study of the three movements he investigates; though in dealing with Mussolini he does bring out the peculiarity of the Italian situation in the 1920s, a situation characterized by crude middle-class hysteria about Communism, at a time when the CPI was a hopeless sect. (Thanks to Mussolini it has now become the largest Communist Party in Western Europe, and the second largest political force in its own country.) In general he is better on the filiation of ideas than on the interplay of social and political movements. His documentation is extremely good, but a little overweighted on the philosophical side. Moreover, he suffers from the modish neo-conservative disease of holding the Jacobins responsible for all our ills. He even sympathizes with Charles Maurras' rant about Rousseau and the tradition of "revolutionary romanticism." This is a theme made familiar by those eminent Anglo-American writers who in recent decades have entered a genteel plea for royalism, classicism, Anglo-Catholicism, and similar academic nostrums. But the true propagators of the faith beyond the borders of France were noisy vulgarizers such as Hilaire Belloc, Chesterton, and Pound. It was they who from 1900 onward tirelessly insisted that Dreyfus was guilty, that liberalism was a Jewish invention, and that Jewish bankers were conspiring to rule the world. In France and England they never got very far, but elsewhere the soil was less stony, and in the end a rich harvest was duly reaped.

It is this discontinuity between the abortive French proto-Fascism and its successful Italian and German offspring that presents Dr. Nolte with his most awkward problem. Since the Action française after 1920 was overtaken by more up-to-date versions of the creed, he is obliged to confine himself, so far as France is concerned, to the pre-1914 era. This makes it difficult for him to identify the cause of French democracy's relatively successful resistance to the disease, relatively, since in 1940 quite a number of Frenchmen showed themselves ready to mount the German bandwagon. The point he does not quite grasp (or as a German perhaps cannot quite see) is that national attitudes in the three countries were fundamentally different, and that the difference went back to the impact of the French Revolution. In France itself it was clearly impossible even for an indigenous Fascism to come to terms with the republican tradition. In the final analysis the ordinary Frenchman was not prepared to throw the principles of 1789 overboard. In Italy the impact of these principles had been considerably weaker, since the liberal *risorgimento* had not been a mass movement. (Dr. Nolte rather oddly contends that this was an advantage!) In Germany after 1870 liberalism counted for even less: by the later nineteenth century it was generally confused with Darwinism. That there were fundamental principles at stake, that to accept Fascism was to go back on the Enlightenment, was more easily perceived in an environment where popular attitudes had been molded by the struggle to impose or preserve the Rights of Man, a phrase which in German translation somehow has a faintly comic ring, redolent of pacifism, vegetarianism, and similar fads. There was no Clemenceau in Germany, but then there had been no Robespierre either. Kant indeed had admired the French Revolution, but German schoolbooks took care not to mention the fact. Their heroes were the nationalist ranters of the anti-Napoleonic struggle: Fichte, Arndt, and Jahn—the last a savage Teutomaniac whose ravings already prefigured much of the Third Reich and its frenzy.

If one happens to be a German academic of the conservative school, the contrast between French and German democracy is a trifle embarrassing. Dr. Nolte tries hard to be fair, but he is a stranger to the French republican tradition—a tradition exemplified by that archetypal Jacobin, Georges Clemenceau. He says all the proper things about the Dreyfus affair, but his heart is with the respectable conservatives who throughout the later nineteenth century carried on a rearguard action against democracy. He can even find excuses for the not-so-respectable, *e.g.*, the rabble-rouser Drumont whose *La France juive* set the tone for much of the later agitation against capitalism as "Jewish." A misconception, no doubt, but perpetrated in good faith, for "Was not Edouard Drumont, the originator of organized anti-Semitism in France, also a man of profound Christian feeling?" (p. 48). The answer probably depends upon one's notion of what constitutes Christianity. At any rate that fervent Catholic Charles Péguy had no doubt about it.

This is not the only bee in Dr. Nolte's capacious bonnet. There is indeed a whole swarm buzzing about, mostly of a familiarly ideological kind. He knows well enough that the conservative sociology of Le Play goes back to the anti-revolutionary doctrines of Bonald and de Maistre, but he seems to have no notion that there was also a Christian-Socialist tradition dating back to the Saint-Simonians, notably Pierre Leroux and Philippe Buchez; or that it was quite possible for Catholic democrats like Buchez and his progeny to be admirers of Robespierre. To read him one would imagine that all French Catholics accepted de Maistre's hysterical judgment on the Revolution as a "satanic" rebellion against the divine order. Nor is he on safer ground in referring obliquely to what he calls "the socialist conception that the revolution was a bourgeois undertaking to the detriment of the people" (p. 51). No socialist ever suggested anything of the sort. What they said was something quite different: that the bourgeoisie had become the principal beneficiary of the great upheaval.

Notwithstanding his tenderness for some of the intellectual ancestors of Fascism, Dr. Nolte has made an important contribution to the understanding of the phenomenon. The further away he gets from politics the more clearly he is helped by his philosophical equipment. Thus one learns a great deal from him about the curious intellectual ambience in which the original Fascist, or proto-Fascist, doctrine took shape on the eve of the First World War. Its central locus was the *cercle Proudhon* in Paris, where followers of Sorel met supporters of the Action française to debate the coming fusion of nationalist and socialist ideas: on an anti-liberal and anti-democratic basis, of course. Sorel's favorite student, Edouard Berth, later claimed that *"le fascisme avant la lettre"* was born in these encounters. Dr. Nolte disputes this, on the not very convincing grounds that the *cercle Proudhon* failed to convert Maurras and the Action française to its national-socialist doctrine. The fact itself is unquestionable: Maurras, an old-fashioned conservative, clung all his life to the paternalist doctrines subsequently endorsed by Pétain and the Vichy regime. But does it matter? Surely what counts is the theoretical breakthrough, not the question who eventually made practical use of it. For Maurras indeed the struggle against the Republic and its anti-clerical philosophy was the overriding issue. It made possible his tactical alliance with the Church, notwithstanding his own proclaimed atheism (by 1910 he had influential friends in the Vatican, including Pius X himself). But some of his followers were more alive to the situation, and when they failed to convert him to national-socialism, they broke away to form the first genuinely proto-Fascist splinter groups in France, where the attempt was made to convert the workers to nationalism by adopting an anti-capitalist platform. This really is the beginning and the end of the whole thing. It does not "explain" Fascism, but it describes it.

On the whole, Dr. Nolte's middle section on Italy is the best of the three. It deals succinctly with the complex of issues affecting Italian nationalism before and after the First World War, and manages to pull the political and the ideological strands together in a very satisfactory manner. One learns not only why Mussolini after 1914 gradually shifted from a primitive Marxism to an equally primitive anti-Marxism, but also how and why this personal evolution enabled him to synthesize the bellicose national-socialism of his original followers with the "pure" nationalism of conservative Fascists like Grandi, for whom the struggle against Bolshevism took precedence over everything else. (As late as 1919 Mussolini still saw himself as a rival of Lenin, and his recently founded Fascist Party as a revolutionary force, though opposed to Communism.) As for France, the connecting link, not surprisingly, turns out to have been the pervasive influence of Georges Sorel: already a factor in the evolution of the Action française (or at any rate its left wing) from straight conservative nationalism and anti-Semitism towards national-socialism. Sorel was probably a more important influence than Nietzsche, since the latter had no political doctrine, merely a generalized attitude towards life which was then quite popular among Socialists (Bernard Shaw among them). The savage, anti-human, "blond beast," aspect of Nietzscheanism, which later became so important in Germany and supplied the SS with whatever ideology it possessed, made no appeal in civilized Mediterranean lands.

What Sorel and Mussolini (and Lenin, too, according to Plekhanov, though Dr. Nolte appears unaware of it) got out of Nietzsche was the spirit of the Napoleonic dictum cited by Lenin in his last published piece of writing: "On s'engage et puis on voit:" hardly a Marxist precept. Dr. Nolte regards both Lenin and Mussolini before 1914 as orthodox Marxists, and then speculates on the reasons which led Mussolini to revolt against Marxist determinism, once he had left the Italian Socialist Party in 1914 on the issue of intervention in the war against the Central Powers. But Lenin was as much of an indeterminist as Mussolini (a fact noted by Plekhanov as early as 1905). Both men were temperamentally disposed towards a break with the Social-Democratic tradition, and for both the 1914-1918 war represented a crucial watershed. The difference (character and antecedents apart) lay in the fact that Lenin was a genuine theorist for whom Marxism remained important, while Mussolini was never more than a shallow publicist who could shift overnight from Marx to Sorel, and indeed did so when he found it convenient. The half-baked nonsense of Mussolini's journalism does not establish a critical counterpoint to Lenin's writings. The two men are simply not on the same level, any more than were Marx and Sorel. When Lenin discussed theoretical economics, or their practical application, he wrote with authority, while Mussolini knew no more about the subject than any other Italian journalist. This needs to be said as a corrective to the statement that both men departed in different directions from the same central tradition. Russian Communism in the 1920s had a genuine intellectual structure, whereas the windy nonsense of Italian Fascism rested upon an amateurish misappropriation of eclectic ideas concocted by second-raters like Mosca and Pareto. That both movements were totalitarian is hardly an excuse for neglecting these crucial distinctions. They tend to get overlooked by Dr. Nolte because he takes Mussolini too seriously. He even (p. 181) speaks of his "duel with Lenin" and describes the latter as "his great opponent." This, with all due respect, is nonsense. In Lenin's eyes an ignorant windbag like Mussolini could never rank as more than a squalid nuisance.

On the dialectic of the two great totalitarian movements, Dr. Nolte is eloquent and trenchant, though excessively inclined towards a species of apologetics fashionable among German conservatives. There is a rather alarming suggestion to the effect that Marx, Nietzsche, Maurras, and Mussolini were all somehow struggling with the same set of problems. Dr. Nolte is perhaps too close to the events he describes to perceive that what struck foreigners (and some Germans) about the Nazi movement was its cloacal aspect: the sheer indescribable swinishness of its representative figures, from its ideologists to its hangmen. It is literally true to say that no such bestial phenomenon had ever before appeared in European history (and one hopes never will again). But with this important qualification he is right to stress the metapolitical aspect of the European crisis between the wars. Where he goes wrong, again like so many Germans, is in overrating Nietzsche: not as an influence (his effect on two generations of Europeans was indeed very great) but as a systematic thinker. This is a wearisome topic, chiefly because it commits one to the investigation of a non-existent theme: Nietzsche's political thought. Instead of pursuing this red herring (very important to Dr. Nolte who indeed mistakes it for a whale), I am going to suggest that the true relationship between the two totalitarianisms is more clearly seen in the light of their common descent from a more important thinker, namely Hegel. There is a sense in which both Communism and Fascism have been trying, with varying success, to make sense of Hegel's ideas about history. The difference is that Fascism never produced a first-rate thinker, which is why it is nonsense to contrast its ideologists (Nietzsche included) with Marx. But it did produce something like a coherent attitude, and in the end it even gave rise to a political doctrine of sorts which could be made to rhyme with some of the realities of the modern age.

The point is best grasped by asking what either school made of the celebrated passage on the master-servant relationship in

Hegel's *Phenomenology*. So far as Marx is concerned we have the answer in his early writings, notably the *Paris Manuscripts* of 1844 (Dr. Nolte, needless to say, has a section on this theme: by now no German philosopher can afford to be without one). Briefly, the Marxian view can be summarized by saying that political conflict is a subordinate aspect of the historical process whereby man creates himself through his own labor, thereby "objectifying" and at the same time "alienating" his "nature." In picturing this situation, Marx, as it were, sides with the servant against the master (as a Jew, though an unbelieving one, he could hardly do anything else). For the conservative Hegelians and their Fascist successors, on the contrary, Hegel's Hobbesian pessimism about the role of force in history was important because it enabled them to side with the master. This is the philosophical core of the matter, but it also has a practical aspect, for on the Marxian assumption the political struggle, though real enough, was predestined to end in the attainment of "true freedom." This led to the notion that the state was somehow an epiphenomenon of the underlying socio-economic realm, that of the "servant." To the authoritarians and their Fascist disciples, on the other hand, war was everything and the state was eternal. Moreover, they wanted it to be a slave state, with themselves on top. In this respect they went all the way back to Plato, and their animus against the Jews in general and the Old Testament in particular was the counterpart of their excessive veneration for the Greeks, or at any rate for the authoritarian strand in Greek thinking which prefigured their own philosophy.

The political relevance of these seemingly abstract disputes became evident in the inter-war period, when Communist and Fascist movements struggled for mastery in Europe, on the commonly held assumption that democracy was finished (for a while indeed it looked as though it was). For it then turned out that each side to the dispute had got hold of one end of the stick and refused to let go: the Communists of the class struggle, the Fascists of the key role of political power. Since "politics" meant different things to them, there was no common ground until 1945, when the Stalinists—having meanwhile absorbed the

painful lesson Hitler had taught them—took over, without public acknowledgment, the Fascist idea of the state as the decisive
factor in terminating the class struggle and instituting a new
social order controlled from the top. The real theoretical discovery of Stalinism, after all, was not that one could lock up millions of prisoners in forced-labor camps and still retain the loyalty of some half-witted liberals, but that in our age the political
authority—the state—has become strong enough to reshape the
social order. This was something Marx—writing at the peak of
the liberal era—had not taken into account. Even Lenin,
though he finally took he plunge, was not quite sure it could be
done. The man who did it was Stalin. By now the conflict between the Communist and the Fascist doctrine of the state has
ceased to matter, though there remains a crucial difference in
orientation. After all even the Stalinists, to do them justice,
never thought the "lower races" should be exterminated and the
workers held in permanent subjection, whereas most Fascists
thought (and think) just that. In the end it is a question of
Weltanschauung. In other respects the two sides are now
equipped with pretty much the same set of political concepts.

It is a tribute to Dr. Nolte's book that it raises these issues,
though to the reviewer's mind they are not dealt with in an entirely satisfactory manner. In any case this is an important work,
marred by a few minor flaws, such as an overestimation of the
purely intellectual content of Fascism. It is also a very learned
work, and its appearance in a more than adequate translation is
to be welcomed. We shall not soon have a better account of the
political and spiritual factors that went into the European catastrophe between the wars. Since the destruction of Germany as a
nation was the principal outcome of this upheaval, it is fitting
that a major study on the topic should have been written by a
German.

The German Ideology*

• Germany, home of lost causes and battleground of rival creeds, has never lacked thinkers able to rise above the clash of parties and the collapse of empires. One may say that the country's unfortunate history has had its compensation in the national genius for abstraction. What was lacking on earth was recovered in the metaphysical heavens. After the Reformation had split it apart, the nation's fragmented unity was restored in the realm of spirit. From Leibniz and Lessing to Schopenhauer and Nietzsche, by way of Goethe and Hegel, the poets and thinkers (most of them Protestants: the Catholic contribution was principally made in the domains of architecture and music) labored to construct an ideal Germany in the clouds. Even the Bismarckian unification of 1870 did not really close the gap, and anyhow it lasted only until 1945. Based on Prussia and the Protestant North, it was too narrow to encompass the whole of Germany. In 1933 the Catholic South had its revenge. Since then the country has once more been partitioned—this time along an East-West axis, with a caricature of Russian Communism installed in a fragmented remnant of the old Prussia, and the remainder organized around the wealthy and philistine Rhineland, perhaps the only part of Germany which ever became thoroughly bourgeois and today consequently rivals Belgium and Switzerland in the complacent mediocrity of its politics.

Professor Loewith's important work *From Hegel to Nietzsche*†
—now at long last translated almost a quarter century after its first appearance—treats the subject in a manner which accords well with the traditional German genius for *ex post facto*

* *New Statesman* (April 23, 1965).
† (London, New York, and Chicago, 1964).

rationalization of historic misfortune. Massive and scholarly, though carrying its vast load of learning with remarkable elegance, it deals with the latest and most catastrophic chapter in the long and lamentable story of a nation which for centuries filled with a semblance of life the moldering carcass of the Holy Roman Empire. His theme is circumscribed by the events marking the rise and fall of German nationalism in the modern age: the French Revolution and the twentieth-century crisis of Western society.

Quite properly, he begins with Goethe and Hegel, on both of whom the storm of the Revolution broke in the most palpable fashion. Hegel finished his first and greatest work, the *Phenomenology of Mind*, the day before Napoleon, on October 14, 1806, finished the ghost of the Holy Roman Empire at the battle of Jena. From the window of his study the philosopher watched the conqueror riding through the town. Not many weeks later, Goethe (in his official capacity as head of the Weimar administration) met the Emperor at close quarters. Neither Goethe nor Hegel had any illusions as to what all this portended. They knew that for Germany too the Middle Ages were over, and tried to communicate this thought to their countrymen. Hegel had earlier dreamed of a "Caesar" who would unify the Germans, by force, from above, though he prudently confided this thought to an unpublished essay (lately included in a collection of his political writings). He was more realistic than Goethe to whom nationalism remained antipathetic. But for Hegel too it was the state that mattered, not the nation: a factor in his relative unpopularity during the Third Reich, whose ideologists preferred the declamatory pathos of Fichte to Hegel's dispassionate concern with *raison d'état*.

The checkered political history of modern Germany, however, is somewhat marginal to Professor Loewith's work whose central theme is rather the dissolution of Protestant Christianity and its replacement by the secular faith in History. Himself in the tradition of Jacob Burckhardt (Heidelberg, to which he returned after years of exile largely spent in the United States, is not far from Burckhardt's cherished Basle), he views the nineteenth

THE CONCEPT OF IDEOLOGY : 240

century as a curtain-raiser for the disasters of our own age. *From Hegel to Nietzsche* is first and foremost a study in disintegration. Its spirit is conservative in the proper meaning of that much abused term. One hesitates to describe it as "Christian conservative," for there are indications that the author shares the pessimism of his favorite writers concerning the possibility of a Christian civilization. His faith—if it can be called such—is that of Kierkegaard and of Nietzsche's friend Overbeck who regarded as inherently paradoxical the attempt to reconcile Christianity and culture, though he also believed that neither Christianity nor European civilization could exist without one another. The dialectic of this relationship has furnished a theme for German thinkers since the days when Hegel first set the European mind on the road towards that uniquely Western achievement, the "philosophy of history." Nietzsche, though not a dialectical thinker, belongs to this tradition, whence the title of Loewith's work. In its own way his book is a distinguished contribution to a discussion in progress among educated Germans ever since they began to lose their inherited faith.

This part of Loewith's analysis should appeal to theologians. Those among them who are familiar with his brief 1949 study titled *Meaning in History* will not be surprised to find him resolutely on the side of thinkers who refuse to lend an eschatological meaning to political revolutions (whether Communist or Fascist). Loewith, who was driven from Hitler's Germany and has said harsh things about Heidegger, is in a Protestant tradition (though himself of partly Jewish descent). What this tradition implies in practice may be inferred from a passage in his 1949 essay where he described the transformation of medieval spiritualism into a revolutionary faith, incorporated in

> a philosophical priesthood which interpreted the process of secularism in terms of a "spiritual" realization of the Kingdom of God on earth. As an attempt at realization, the spiritual pattern of Lessing, Fichte, Schelling and Hegel could be transposed into the positivistic and materialistic schemes of Comte and Marx.

From there Loewith went on to draw a rather strained and unconvincing analogy between the Third International and the

Third Reich. The topic has in recent years been rendered familiar by his German and American pupils and plagiarists. In Loewith's own writings it preserves a dignity which is inevitably lost
when the critique of utopianism is turned into an apologia of
the status quo: possibly a fate which in the end awaits every
thinker who takes his stand on the conservative side. In Loewith's interpretation of the nineteenth century, this theme is
crossed by another one to which he has chosen to give the rather
infelicitous subtitle "Studies in the History of the Bourgeois-
Christian World," infelicitous because a writer who judges history from a theological standpoint surely ought not to take the
"Bourgeois World" quite so seriously. It is of course a fact that
Goethe and Hegel belonged to that world, as did Marx, to
whom Loewith devotes a carefully balanced (though fundamentally hostile) chapter. And it is arguable—at any rate it is argued
by Loewith—that Kierkegaard is to be understood as a critic of
"bourgeois Christianity," rather than as a rebel against Christendom *tout court*. In this manner one obtains a perspective on
what Loewith calls "the revolution in nineteenth-century
thought." That revolution is thought by him to have been accomplished mainly by three thinkers: Marx, Kierkegaard, and
Nietzsche; and what they revolted against was either bourgeois
society or bourgeois Christianity. Since societies are transitory,
this leaves Christianity as such intact. Hence Loewith feels able
to conclude his work on a note of resigned confidence:

> Since Hegel, and particularly through the work of Marx and
> Kierkegaard, the Christianity of this bourgeois-Christian world
> has come to an end. This does not mean that a faith which once
> conquered the world perishes with its last secular manifestations.
> For how should the Christian pilgrimage *in hoc saeculo* ever be-
> come homeless in the land where it has never been at home?

This question is plainly addressed to theologians (or anti-
theologians). To a reader who does not share Loewith's presuppositions, the purely historical aspect of his theme presents itself
somewhat differently. At the risk of unfairness it may be summarized in some such terms as these: Germany having wrecked
both itself and Europe, it was incumbent upon German writers

—even upon a writer like Loewith whom the Third Reich had exiled and who was contemptuous of its ideologists—to discover a metaphysical referent for the national disaster. The referent turned out to be the crisis of modern life, and at a remove the secularization of religious faith. Since the catastrophic outcome had been dimly foreshadowed in some of Nietzsche's utterances, it did not matter that the masters of the Third Reich thought of themselves as Nietzscheans. Neither apparently did it matter that the peculiar "German Ideology" which culminated in the frenzy of 1933-1945 had arisen as a reaction to the French Revolution and *its* secularization of faith. In brief, the traditional conservative understanding of German history could be retained. As for the rival liberal and Marxist interpretations, they were presumably discredited: the first by its shallowness, the second by the outcome of the Russian Revolution, which had revealed itself as a mere repetition—on a larger scale, and attended by even more dreadful holocausts—of the French.

The thesis is plausible, and Loewith presents it in a manner which raises the debate above the level where it had been left by the ideologists of Fascism and Stalinism, from Oswald Spengler to Georg Lukács. (Anyone who imagines that Loewith can be met with the kind of argument that Lukács deploys in *The Destruction of Reason* is in for a disagreeable surprise.) Yet the case is far from watertight. For all Loewith's profound learning and scholarly fairness, he writes as an apologist of the conservative school, and that school has never faced what to radicals must seem the central feature of the whole story: the circumstance that the catastrophe of European civilization occurred in conservative Germany, not in liberal Britain or in republican, post-revolutionary France.

The basic fact about German history since the eighteenth century has been the failure of the Enlightenment to strike root. Conceived too narrowly from the start as a mere critique of religion (and even then largely confined to the Protestant middle class), this early liberalism lost whatever political relevance it had once possessed in the panic wave set going among conservatives by the French Revolution. By the time the nationalist move-

ment began to form, between 1810 and 1820, the dominant
ideology among educated Germans had become that of Roman-
ticism, and the movement's edge was from the start turned |
against Western rationalism. Germany thus entered the industrial age with a mental makeup that was still predominantly medieval. The political defeat of liberalism between 1848 and 1871
did the rest. Once Bismarck had done his work, the country was
basically estranged from the West, and its representative
thinkers thereafter spent their energy on ambitious intellectual
syntheses designed to show that what looked to outsiders like
retrogression was really evidence of spiritual profundity. This
"German Ideology," which in all essentials was already formed
in the 1840s, came to full efflorescence during and after the
1914-1918 war. Its literary documents include—in addition to
Spengler's work—Thomas Mann's *Unpolitical Reflections,* a
manifesto from which its author was at pains in later years to
dissociate himself.

The relevance of these familiar facts for Loewith's theme
arises from a circumstance to which he gives no attention, but
which is crucial to an understanding of the historical dialectic
between the French Revolution and the German Counter-Revolution: the gradual abandonment by the Germans in the later
nineteenth century of that faith in Reason which the Encyclopedists had in common with Kant and which was briefly en-
throned during the French Revolution. It has been a matter of
critical importance for the whole subsequent history of Europe
that German nationalism took shape in a mental climate hostile /
to the universalism of the advanced Western nations. Where
the French believed in Man, writers like Fichte taught their
countrymen to believe in the destiny of the German. This narrowing of perspective went hand in hand with a refurbishing of
illusions centered upon the country's past. The very democrats
who met at Frankfurt in 1848 had their heads stuffed with nonsense about restoring the Holy Roman Empire in its ancient
boundaries. Then as later any attempt to drag the country out of
its obsession with the Middle Ages was denounced as un-
feeling, rationalistic, and subversive of "German Christendom."

It is the fundamental weakness of the conservative school—represented at its highest level by serious and responsible writers like Loewith, at its worst by men like Spengler and Heidegger —that it has never come to terms with this aspect of Germany's national catastrophe. Even for Loewith there appears to be a *hiatus irrationalis* between the Romantic nostalgia fashionable in late-nineteenth-century Germany and the monstrous apparition of the Third Reich. The escape route, for him as for lesser conservative thinkers, lies through an amalgamation of all the specifically modern trends into a single phenomenon variously described as "the revolution," "the modern age," or "the end of the bourgeois-Christian world." The latter term, with its unhappy conjunction of religious and political terms, discloses the Achilles heel of conservatism: the failure to incorporate sociological realism within a philosophy of history whose tacit assumptions have remained obstinately theological, *i.e.*, medieval. If European history is the history of Christendom, there is no sense in lamenting the catastrophe of bourgeois society: surely a minor episode which need not disturb the composure of the theologian. Yet it is a curious fact that already in 1848 loud cries of distress came from Protestant writers like Kierkegaard and from Catholic orators like Donoso Cortes. What alarmed these traditionalists were the first (and at that ineffective) rumblings of what has since come to be known as democracy. As for Tocqueville, he saw ruin threatening France if the socialists, with their crazy notions about equality, ever got the upper hand.

If today these alarums are apt to strike one as tedious and a little childish, one may be tempted to suspect that their authors were dismayed by something other than the decay of traditional religion. This is not to deny that the decline of faith did in fact occur, and that—in Germany at any rate—it has been attended by terrible consequences. It is merely to point out that the consequences were most catastrophic precisely in those parts of Europe where the message of the Revolution had been defeated or had never penetrated.

An Intellectual Disaster[*]

• Georg Lukács has long been a puzzle to a considerable number of sympathizers for whom Marxism in its Sovietized form has become an embarrassment and who look for a return to the Hegelian, *i.e.*, German-idealist, sources of their faith. In principle his philosophic origins in the pre-1914 age, and his checkered political career since 1918, seemed to mark him out as the spokesman of a "Western" form of Marxism, the more so since orthodox attacks on his real or supposed heresies have erupted at intervals over the past four decades.

Yet a truthful account of his numberless deviations and recantations during this period must add to the embarrassment which his putative followers experience when contemplating the ravages of the Stalin era. From the first passive acceptance of official discipline in 1923-1924, via the abject repudiation of his earlier views in 1934, to the abortive rebellion of 1956 and the subsequent reversion to semi-orthodoxy, Lukács' habitual style of accommodation to the changing requirements of the Party line has baffled both friends and detractors. Like Ehrenburg—a comparatively minor figure, but in some respects his opposite in the journalistic field—he has survived the terrors of the Stalin era, to emerge at last into the comparatively tolerant, but distinctly philistine, atmosphere of the 1960s. It is as though Condorcet had lived to witness the triumph of Louis Philippe and Guizot. The irony is heightened by the fact that Lukács, to judge from his public pronouncements, is quite unaware of the radical discontinuity between his own system of values and that of the society which has arisen from the revolutionary cauldron of the past half century.

[*] *Encounter* (May 1963).

The somewhat spectral quality of Lukács' survival in an East European environment which has outgrown, or repudiated, his original hopes and anticipations is reflected in the tone of the preface to the lengthy essay on modern literature he composed in 1955-1956.[1] Dated "Budapest, May 1962," this foreword employs the post-Stalin terminology officialized since 1961, while retaining the essentially Stalinist characterization of the Soviet orbit as a realm of "socialism" opposed to a Western capitalist-imperialist bloc. At the same time, Lukács has taken advantage of the new climate to stress the perils of "dogmatic sectarianism," whereas the original German preface (written in April 1957, i.e., six months after the abortive Hungarian rising in which he had briefly come out on the "revisionist" side) not only dwelt explicitly on "Stalin's positive achievements," but made the dutiful affirmation that revisionism was to be regarded as "the greatest present danger for Marxism." Confronted with such a record of pliability, the critical spectator may be forgiven for wondering whether Lukács' current strictures on dogmatism are anything but further evidence of an unbroken determination to remain in the swim.

Yet paradoxically it is just this fanatical attachment to the Party line—whatever it may be at any moment—that rescues Lukács from the imputation of mere opportunism. He has often changed his mind about this or that aspect of Soviet reality, but he has never—since the crisis of 1923-1924 which resulted in his silent capitulation to the hierarchy—wavered in his conviction that in the long run the Party cannot err. Moreover, internal evidence suggests that his submission to Marxism-Leninism has long been total. This, incidentally, is the prime reason why for the past decade he has disappointed his "revisionist" would-be followers. They were waiting to hear him say some of the things that since 1956 have publicly been said in Poland (and latterly even in Czechoslovakia, not to mention Yugoslavia). But though in 1962 he felt able to affirm that "the disastrous legacy of Stalinism" must be got rid of, this was capped by a reminder

[1] *The Meaning of Contemporary Realism*, translated from the German by John and Necke Mander (London, 1963).

that the task was "to rediscover the creative core of the teaching
of Marx, Engels, and Lenin"—as though Lenin were not the
principal obstacle to the "Westernization" of Marxism! So far
from this being mere lip-service, a consideration of Lukács'
present-day views on contemporary literature shows him to be
indeed a good Leninist—hence incapable of making those critical distinctions which have enabled Marxist writers in Western
Europe (and the genuine "revisionists" in Poland) to say something sensible about the quite real problems of intellectual sterility and pointless literary artifice which confront European and
American literature at the present time.

Ideally it ought to be the critic's task to demonstrate all this
in detail, taking as one's text both the essay on *Contemporary
Realism* and the earlier volume entitled *The Historical Novel*.[2]
Although (or because) twenty years lie between their writing,
the two books complement each other. *The Historical Novel*
was composed in the winter of 1936-1937, at the very height of
the Great Purge, and some two years after Lukács—in an address to the philosophical section of the Communist Academy
in Moscow—had performed the first of a long sequence of public acts of self-abasement by denouncing his own pre-Leninist
writings (notably the famous *History and Class-Consciousness* of
1923) as "idealist" and "objectively" counter-revolutionary.

> The front of idealism is the front of Fascist counter-revolution
> and its accomplices, the Social-Fascists. Every concession to ideal-
> ism, however insignificant, spells danger to the proletarian revolu-
> tion.[3]

Though less frenzied in tone, Lukács' critical writings during
this period, including *The Historical Novel*, faithfully reflect the
temper of this remarkable pronouncement, notably in their determination to rewrite the history of contemporary literature in
terms of Fascism and anti-Fascism. To this end "the historical

[2] London, 1962.
[3] "The Significance of *Materialism and Empirio-Criticism* for the
Bolshevization of Communist Parties," *Pod Znamenem Marksisma* (July-
August 1934), pp. 143-148. See Morris Watnick's essay on Lukács in
Revisionism, ed. L. Labedz (New York, 1962), in which this episode is
analyzed at some length.

novel of anti-Fascist humanism" (as represented by some worthy, but distinctly second-rate, German émigré authors of unimpeachably bourgeois-democratic outlook: it was after all the Popular Front period) had to be provided with a genealogical tree reaching back to Walter Scott: not a democrat, but a realist, hence to Lukács a forerunner of his real heroes: Balzac and Tolstoy.

This approach presumably accounts for the fact that when *The Historical Novel* was published in translation in 1962, it was well received by a number of British reviewers who did not greatly care for the author's Marxism, but liked his fondness for Scott. One wonders, though, what they made of a passage like the following (p. 64):

> Scott had only one worthy follower in the English language who took over and even extended certain of the principles underlying his choice of theme and manner of portrayal, namely the American, Cooper. In his immortal novel cycle, *The Leather Stocking Saga* [*sic*], Cooper sets an important theme of Scott, the downfall of gentile [*i.e.*, tribal] society, at the center of his portrayal. Corresponding to the historical development of North America, this theme acquires an entirely new complexion. In Scott it is a case of a centuries-long, conflict-ridden development, of the various ways in which the survivals of gentile society are accommodated to the feudal system and later to rising capitalism. . . . In America the contrast was posed far more brutally and directly by history itself; the colonizing capitalism of France and England destroys physically and morally the gentile society of the Indians which had flourished almost unchanged for thousands of years.

This might be described as orthodox Leninism, both as to sentiment and style. (Lukács' insensitivity to the German language, in which he has composed nearly all his writings, and his indifference to style in general, would require separate treatment: it seems to have been part of his self-imposed Bolshevization, for prior to the 1924 catastrophe he affected an elegant, even somewhat precious, manner.) Its relevance to literary criticism is debatable. In any case, 350 pages of this sort of thing, unrelieved by a single gleam of humor, might seem rather a burden upon the reader. Yet even this turgid monograph is not

without merit, once account is taken of the fact that the author
is concerned with long-run changes in the cultural pattern. Since
for Lukács (as for every Hegelian) form and content make a
whole, he occasionally succeeds in relating formal changes—*e.g.*,
the Romantic "poetization" of the historical novel—to conflicting tendencies in society. Thus, to take one of the many examples he offers, in discussing the Romantic upsurge in French
literature after 1815 he is able—with the help of Marx admittedly—to discern the survival in Chateaubriand of that part of
the Enlightenment tradition which had its original locus in the
courtly aristocracy, and to contrast both his and Vigny's "ahis-
toricism" with the continuation of the eighteenth-century tradition in Stendhal and Mérimée. This sort of historical-sociologi-
cal cross reference can be illuminating when backed by wide
reading, and in the more strictly literary parts of *The Historical
Novel* the method does come to life: notably in the section contrasting the novel and the drama. Indeed when he is analyzing
the formal (and historical) differences between the epic and the
drama, Lukács here and there almost recovers the intellectual
level of his youthful work, culminating in his fragmentary but
magnificent *Theorie des Romans* (1916). This may be no more
than a way of saying that he has always lived on his early insights, but that is a common enough fate. The tragedy is that
these insights have been progressively buried under a monstrous
load of sociological jargon, self-conscious popularization, and polemical journalism.

It is true that so far as subjection to the official line on "Socialist Realism" is concerned, the worst now seems to be over.
In the 1960 preface to the English edition of *The Historical
Novel*, dutiful praise of Halldor Laxness (an Icelandic novelist
and Party member) was balanced by an appreciative reference
to Lampedusa's *Leopard*, a fairly safe choice in view of Lampedusa's unmistakable descent from the realist Stendhal, but still
a gesture in the Western direction which Lukács would not
have permitted himself a few years earlier. Similarly, the essay
on *Contemporary Realism* (written in 1955-1956, *i.e.*, during
the first uncertain "thaw") marked a considerable departure

from the rigid posture of the immediate postwar years, when Lukács "conformed" to the extent of denouncing practically all important Western writers as reactionary warmongers.[4] By comparison with the frenetic nonsense Lukács produced during the closing years of the Stalin era—he was of course under considerable pressure to demonstrate his orthodoxy, but writers have traditionally been required to show some concern for intellectual standards, as well as for their skins—his later manner is fairly detached and at times almost mellow. Thus, in *The Meaning of Contemporary Realism,* not only is there a somewhat grudging attempt to make sense of Kafka, but the criticism of modern music in general, and Schönberg in particular, is backed by a quotation from the Western "modernist" Adorno (though objectivity is not carried to the point of informing the reader that Adorno is a Hegelian and a Marxist).

For all these welcome changes in tone and manner, Lukács' current assessment of modernism effects no real departure from his previous position. Perhaps that was not to be expected. What is remarkable is that he has not advanced beyond the simple-minded antithesis realism-decadence which was his theme in *The Destruction of Reason.* Indeed at one point (*Contemporary Realism,* p. 62) he reverts to that monstrous work for the purpose of acquainting the reader once again with his obsessive notion that the departure from "bourgeois realism" paved the way for a progressive collapse whose stations were marked by the names Dostoyevsky-Nietzsche-Hitler; with Joyce and Kafka relegated to the margin among those writers who—whatever their political views—"connive at that modern nihilism from which both Fascism and Cold War ideology draw their strength." At this level, not only is there no meeting place for different viewpoints, but the temptation to repay the writer in his own coin becomes overwhelming. After all, we now have it on the best of authorities that Stalin's *univers concentrationnaire* differed from Hitler's chiefly in that the number of his

---

[4] Cf. his seven-hundred-page diatribe against modern philosophy, *Die Zerstörung der Vernunft* (1952-1953), where *inter alia* Bertrand Russell is introduced as an accomplice of both the Pope and the Pentagon.

251 :   *An Intellectual Disaster*

victims was possibly even larger. This may seem irrelevant, but a
critic who politicizes every topic—to the point of solemnly treating Kafka's nightmares as evidence of "the diabolical character
of the world of modern capitalism"—is asking for trouble. The
more so when he affects to regard Freud, the greatest representative of the Enlightenment tradition in modern times, as an
obscurantist and contrasts him unfavorably with the simpleton
Pavlov. If Lukács really believes this sort of nonsense—it is
never quite certain how much of what he says represents actual
convictions—one can only conclude that twenty years of Zhdan-
ovism, plus an endless series of accommodations, have permanently impaired his critical faculties.

Two separate aspects of this intellectual disaster must be distinguished. In the first place, Lukács manifestly has failed to do
for East European Marxism what writers like Sartre, Lefebvre,
Ernst Bloch, T. W. Adorno, Walter Benjamin, and the Italian
Marxists of Gramsci's school have done for the sociology of culture in Western Europe. He nowhere reaches their level, and
this failure is due not to his Marxism but to his involvement
with Soviet orthodoxy: an orthodoxy rooted in Chernyshevsky
and the other founders of the nineteenth-century Russian Populist school. Moreover, his obstinate refusal to see that "modernism" is a truly international phenomenon compels him to side
with Eastern officialdom in opposing the genuinely creative, lib-
erating, and *truly realist* tendencies at work in Soviet and East
European life and literature since the "thaw." If he were really
what his admirers mistakenly imagine him to be, he would by
now have become the patron saint of "revisionism." Actually
there is good reason to believe that he is an isolated figure even
in his native Hungary: not because the regime wills it (he is in
fact quite free to write and publish), but because the younger
generation has turned its back upon him. And no wonder: his
attitude to modernism is really no different from that of officialdom, though nowadays expressed in more temperate language.
What are young people in Budapest, Prague, or Warsaw to
make of a critic who treats "socialist realism" as the only legitimate successor to "bourgeois critical realism"?

There is, of course, a case to be made for the proposition that the socialist movement has inherited the realist strain in nineteenth-century literature, although Lukács' persistent denigration of Zola—not a true realist, merely a "naturalist"—makes one wonder whether he is not secretly wedded to Victorian notions of propriety. But a critic who dismisses the whole of modernism as "decadent" shows that he is simply unaware of what is going on around him. If anything is certain, it is that the younger generation in the Soviet orbit is tired of "socialist realism" and as instinctively "modernist" as its "alienated" counterparts in the West. And what are Western readers to make of Lukács' curiously old-fashioned insistence that "the contemporary bourgeois writer will have to choose" between Kafka and Thomas Mann? The fact is that neither the writers themselves nor their readers are any longer "bourgeois." They are intellectuals living in an industrial society whose tensions necessarily give rise to problems which modernism undertakes to solve: problems no different from those experienced by people in the Soviet orbit, except that in the West political freedom makes life rather less intolerable. If Lukács were really trying to bring Marxist sociology to bear upon this situation, he would realize soon enough that where art is concerned the problem is pretty much the same in East and West. He could then still give vent to his dislike of modernism, but at least he would be relieved of the pseudo-problem he has created for himself by treating it as "bourgeois," when in fact it is one of numerous signs that bourgeois culture (the only culture he really understands) is coming to an end.

It may seem odd that the principal intellectual exponent of "socialist realism" should be so obstinately wedded to the tradition of what he himself calls "bourgeois critical realism," but Lukács has always entertained an anti-naturalist bias and looked to art—specifically literature—for a manifestation of "objective reality." As a youthful neo-Kantian before 1914 he backed this choice with different arguments, some of them bordering on Platonism.[5] His objection to naturalism was that it tended

[5] Cf. *Die Seele und die Formen* (Berlin, 1911).

to destroy the form-creating, and therefore life-sustaining, values
of the tragic drama. . . . The drama is bound to be trivial
when that which is close to life conceals what is dramatically real.
. . . The inner style of the drama is realistic in the medieval,
scholastic sense, and this excludes every modern realism.

Almost forty years later, in prefacing the essay collection published in English under the title *Studies in European Realism*
(1950), he was still pursuing the search for the same form-creating and life-sustaining values; only now they had been located in
history, and Marxism had become the philosophy that enables
the writer to understand the meaning of history.

So far, so good—at least as regards consistency. After all,
Marxism *did* emerge from German Idealism, and "respect for
the classical heritage of humanity in aesthetics" is something
Lukács has in common with other Marxists. So is the conviction
that "this classical heritage consists in the great arts which de-
pict man as a whole in the whole of society." Again it is legitimate—if perhaps a trifle utopian—for a critic to look to socialism as the means of restoring those aesthetic values to which
bourgeois society appears to be hostile. This choice, too, was
rooted in the specific experiences of Lukács' pre-1914 phase
when—like other aestheticists—he deplored the prevailing naturalist style which appeared to represent a pseudo-critical accommodation to an ugly environment. From this romantic and
aristocratic aestheticism—Lukács' writings of the period have
distinctly Nietzschean overtones—the *salto mortale* into revolutionary Marxism after 1917 was at once difficult and easy:
difficult because it required a leap to the other extreme of the
anti-bourgeois spectrum; relatively easy because the underlying
attitudes did not have to be altered. Bourgeois society was still
the enemy, with the difference that Marxism now provided the
means of defining both its decomposition and the persistence of
certain progressive features ("bourgeois critical realism" from
Goethe and Balzac to Thomas Mann) which could be treated as
allies in the increasingly violent struggle against philosophical
idealism, subjectivism, nihilism, and their artistic correlative:
decadent modernism.

THE CONCEPT OF IDEOLOGY

Here then, for all the temporary accommodations to the vagaries of the Party line, there is something like consistency. But there is also tragedy, for in the one respect in which Lukács has remained true to himself—rejection of naturalism and adherence to the classical heritage—he has failed to establish a position which transcends the usual sectarian quarrels. To do this he would have had to see the modern situation as it really is, and for that his critical apparatus was inadequate. By now, thirty years of apologetics have taken their toll, and the disciples who claim for him the status of "the Marx of aesthetics" merely disclose their own inability to measure the extent of his failure.

Failure on an enormous (though rather anti-heroic) scale, for Lukács had it in him to apply Marxism to aesthetics at a level adequate to the subject matter. Though lacking true originality —the notion that in his own sphere he rivals Marx can be entertained only by people who have not read either—he possessed a theoretical equipment superior to that of most Central European scholars of his time. His range was extraordinary, and his youthful exposure to German intellectualism in its pre-1914 peak period provided an immensely hopeful starting point, the more so since he was an instinctive cosmopolitan and quite free from the specifically German narrowness. With this background, and equipped with an intellect not indeed very powerful (abstract reasoning was never his forte), but subtle, flexible, far-ranging, and genuinely critical, he might have achieved something comparable to the attainment of Dilthey and the other great neo-Kantians in the pursuit of what the Germans call *Geistesgeschichte*: a major body of work in the Hegelian-Marxist tradition which could by now have enabled the intelligentsia of East-Central Europe to emancipate itself both from its own provincialism and from the pseudo-universalism of Soviet ideology.

The true outcome—however impressive the sheer bulk of his critical work, and very occasionally the quality of insight into certain predicaments of nineteenth-century European society— must be counted among the major debacles of the Hitler-Stalin era: an intellectual catastrophe no less real because its effects are impalpable, and because it relates to a dimension which society has increasingly relegated to the margin of existence. Instead of a genuine critique of modernity in all its forms, he has produced a vast corpus of dogmatic writing attuned to a simplified dualism which eludes the pressing problems of industrial civilization in East and West alike; instead of authentic dialectical Marxism, there is blind commitment to the simplified Leninist version; instead of genuine controversy, the stereotyped language of the Cold War. At the close of sixty years of intensive and far-ranging activity, Lukács has not merely failed to effect the synthesis his readers had the right to expect from him: he has lent the weight of his authority to a system of political and cultural retrogression. It is one of the worst intellectual disasters of this disastrous age.

part four

SURVIVALS AND NEW ARRIVALS

Beyond the Fringe*

• Anarchism, like Anabaptism, has become respectable. In its heyday the movement had a uniformly bad press, aside from being treated as dangerous by governments and police authorities. Now that it no longer exists—for in its pure form it died with the Spanish Civil War of the 1930s—its legendary founders benefit from the indulgence commonly extended to the defeated. This is an old story. If there were any Albigensians around today, one may be sure the Pope would be polite to them—he might even invite them to attend future sessions of the Vatican Council. It is too bad they were all exterminated in that thirteenth-century Crusade (the only one to achieve its aim —all the others were military failures). Anabaptism too no longer terrifies. The spiritual descendants of Thomas Muenzer and John of Leyden are today's liberal Protestants. Who can imagine anyone calling for their blood? Luther thought Muenzer a child of Satan, and Muenzer repaid the compliment. Nowadays Lutherans and Unitarians are more likely to invite each other to tea than to fling excommunications around.

Anarchism too is rapidly approaching the stage where it will be socially smart to profess at least a sympathetic interest in it. In Britain it has long been acceptable, at any rate in its nonviolent form. No one worries about Bertrand Russell, who may be described as a distinguished fellow traveler. Sir Herbert Read, a paid-up member, has accepted a knighthood from the Queen. What would Proudhon have thought of that? It would probably have confirmed him in his morose dislike of the English. Marx perhaps would not have been surprised, but then he had always taken a poor view of the anarchist fraternity. His ghost must

* _The New York Review_ (March 25, 1965).

have chuckled when in 1922 the Bolsheviks published Bakunin's abject *Confession to the Tsar*, penned in jail seventy years earlier: a document that might have come straight out of Dostoyevsky. In those days confessions were still genuine, and Bakunin was doubtless sincere when he painted himself as "a prodigal, estranged and perverted son before an indulgent father," as well as a Pan-Slav patriot and hater of all things German. The episode—it was no more than that—has been an embarrassment to his biographers, and Mr. Joll, in his new work on the subject,* hurries away from it as soon as he decently can. People who are congenitally out of tune with the Dostoyevskyan temperament will be inclined to treat the incident as evidence of a basic instability in Bakunin's character. In later years, when he was safely abroad hatching conspiracies (most of them never got beyond the talking stage), there was also the little matter of his association with the murderous Nechayev, who crops up as one of the characters in *The Possessed*. But this topic has been exhaustively discussed by the historians, and Mr. Joll does well to dismiss it briefly.

The Anarchists, as was to be expected from the distinguished author of *Intellectuals in Politics*, is both scholarly and readable: a tribute to the traditions of the Oxford historical school. Mr. Joll has a firm hold on the European background, though it is possible to feel that he might have made more of the 1871 Paris Commune. This after all was the real test of Proudhonism, and what is more, the surviving Proudhonists came out of it with their personal prestige intact, though only at the cost of jettisoning some of their master's more eccentric teachings. Perhaps this is why Mr. Joll does not say much about the matter. He has a weakness for Proudhon and is reluctant to be harsh about his failings, which were considerable. The fact is that Proudhon, with his tolerance for Louis Bonaparte, his Anglophobia and anti-Semitism, his defense of Negro slavery (he publicly sided with the South during the American Civil War), his contempt for national liberation movements, and his patriarchal notions about women and family life, does not make a suitable model

* James Joll, *The Anarchists* (Boston and Toronto, 1965).

for present-day libertarians. Marx paid him a compliment when
he called him a *petit bourgeois*. He was in fact a peasant, or to
be precise, he was half peasant-half-workman, at a time when
the French working class had not yet emancipated itself from its
rural origins. This accounts for the popularity his doctrines
enjoyed in his lifetime; it also explains why his influence
faded when France became an industrial country.

The valuable side of Proudhon's teaching—his emphasis on
self-help and his distrust of centralized authority—was taken up
a generation later by the men who founded the Syndicalist
movement in France. Syndicalism—unlike pure Anarchism,
which established itself in the *Quartier Latin* and eventually
merged with the literary fad known as Surrealism—made a permanent contribution to French public life, and it did so with the
help of the Proudhonist heritage: at any rate in the form in
which it entered the labor movement of the 1890s. Proudhon's
numerous crotchets included a conviction that abstention from
politics was mandatory if the movement was not to be corrupted. Fortunately, his latter-day disciples ignored his advice,
and eventually they absorbed just enough of Marx's teaching to
enable them to come to grips with industrial society. The up-
shot was Syndicalism, which may be described as a fusion of
Proudhonism and Marxism. Mr. Joll pays a generous and overdue tribute to its real animator, Fernand Pelloutier, who died of
tuberculosis at the age of thirty-four, having spent himself in the
service of the movement. It is typical that for the general public
(but not for the French working class) he should have been
overshadowed by that irresponsible chatterbox Georges Sorel,
who took up the Proudhonist legacy and gave it a twist which
led some of his pupils to Fascism, via Charles Maurras and the
Action française; not to mention Nietzsche, who was also much
admired by the bomb-throwing kind of Anarchist. Mr. Joll is
extremely patient with all these aberrations: a little too patient
at times. But he is right to stress the filiation which runs from
Proudhon and the Commune to modern Syndicalism. In France,
and subsequently in Spain, the Anarchists did make contact with the workers' movement, and what came out of this

fusion was valuable. The pity is that it took them so long, and that so much energy was devoted to the pursuit of absurdities, such as Bakunin's characteristic vision of armed risings by the *Lumpenproletariat* of Southern Italy: an interesting anticipation of some present-day rebellions, in Latin America and elsewhere, which by now have virtually cut their connection with the traditional labor movement.

Anarchism indeed was both a throwback to the radical revolts of the pre-industrial age, and a prefiguration of trouble to come in certain regions of the globe which have only recently begun to feel the pangs of industrialization. For the most part these are non-European regions in which the industrial revolution has impinged upon cultures still wedded to their agrarian origins. Peasant unrest is a typical reaction to this situation. In the 1870s, when Bakunin and Malatesta spun dreams of armed risings all over Italy, the stage had already been passed when power could be seized by these means in any European country. Armed bands might indeed—as one of Malatesta's associates put it in 1881—"move about in the countryside as long as possible, preaching war, inciting to social brigandage, occupying the small communes, and then leaving them after having performed there those revolutionary acts that were possible, and advancing to those localities where our presence would be manifested most usefully." These tactics failed to work in Sicily and Spain, but they made some sense in Latin America, where many Anarchists emigrated, and they are currently being tried on a larger scale in Southeast Asia. Insofar as it was an agrarian movement, Anarchism still had a future, but not in Europe. Not even in Russia, where the Anarchist utopia petered out with Makhno's rising in the Ukraine during the Civil War: a rising directed impartially against the Whites and the Bolsheviks. Perhaps the movement's formal death occurred in February 1921, when for the last time the black flag of anarchy was carried through the streets of Moscow behind the coffin of Peter Kropotkin. A fortnight later the sailors at Kronstadt rose against the Soviet government with the cry "Freedom of speech and press for workers and peasants," and it took a prolonged artillery bombardment (and thousands of executions after the fighting) to put them down. "At last the Soviet government with an iron broom has rid Russia of Anarchism," Trotsky remarked on that occasion: clearly not foreseeing that a few years later his principal support would come from a handful of Syndicalists, in France and elsewhere, who had decided to overlook his share in the Kronstadt massacre.

What remained in Western Europe after the agrarian utopia had faded, and after the more practical spirits had hived off to found trade unions, was the practice of throwing bombs, alternating with the explosion of literary manifestoes. On occasion both went off simultaneously, as when the Parisian writer Laurent Tailhade, who had glorified the exploits of his friends (*"Qu'importe les vagues humanités pourvu que le geste soit beau"*), lost an eye when a bomb exploded while he was having dinner in his favorite restaurant. More commonly the bomb came first, to be followed by lengthy speeches in court and wordy appeals on the part of literary sympathizers. These included distinguished scholars like Kropotkin and Elisée Reclus, as well as artists like Pissarro and Signac. When in 1894, following the assassination of President Carnot, the police seized the subscription list of the Anarchist journal *La Révolte*, which had once been edited by Kropotkin, they were embarrassed to find Alphonse Daudet, Anatole France, Stéphane Mallarmé, and Leconte de Lisle among the paper's subscribers. None of them had ever condoned violence, and the case was thrown out of court. But assassinations continued, and the movement's intellectual sponsors frequently found themselves in an awkward position. Kropotkin and Reclus took the sensible line of condemning terrorism while refusing to sit in judgment on the individuals concerned. Some of their associates were more reckless. In the end, the whole terrorist phase petered out in isolated acts of desperation which merely served to give the movement a bad name and confirmed the Socialists of the period in their refusal to heed anarchist criticism (some of which they might with advantage have taken to heart).

But what finally killed Anarchism was the Russian Revolution, followed two decades later by its epilogue: the Spanish Civil

War. Spain was the one country where the Anarchists (or more precisely the Anarcho-Syndicalists) had assembled a mass movement. When their leaders in 1936 swallowed their principles and joined the Republican government in its fight against Franco, they made nonsense of their own doctrine; and when they failed to instill discipline in their supporters, they as good as admitted that Anarchism did not work. The final act in Barcelona, in May 1937 (when the GPU helped the Spanish Communists out of their embarrassment by arranging to have the Anarchist and Trotskyist leaders quietly murdered in jail) merely wrote the epitaph of the whole movement.

Mr. Joll's sympathetic study will help to give the reader a better perspective of the libertarian tradition. He is temperate and fairminded, though rather too inclined to rehash Proudhon's and Bakunin's tiresome complaints against Marx. The simple fact is that until Marx came along the socialist movement was very largely run by self-educated cranks, of the kind who go about in every age endlessly repeating a few stock phrases. Marx took hold of the movement, made something out of it, and incidentally got rid of the cranks. Naturally they resented him. Bakunin complained loudly that he was a German Jew whose only merit was to have written *Capital* (which Bakunin tried in vain to translate—it was too tough for him, and anyhow he never finished anything). Things had been easier in the good old days when a slogan like "Property is Theft" did duty as a political platform. After Marx one had to do some thinking, and the true anarchists were never very strong in that department. There is a case for saying that what really did them in was their incapacity for sustained thought. It was only afer they had absorbed Marx that the Syndicalists were able to make some headway, and by then classical anarchism was on the way out.

Mr. Max Nomad's reminiscences* furnish a suitable counterpoint to Mr. Joll's learned study. Sixty years in the anarchist movement have given him the necessary perspective, and after a long life spent wandering about in two continents he is able to sit back and take a tolerant view of his old comrades. The ac-

* *Dreamers, Dynamiters and Demagogues* (New York, 1965).

count of his perambulations is a bit disjointed, but there are some lively anecdotes and he does present his heroes in the round. He has got them all—the crackpot philosophers, the failed politicians, the artists, the vagabonds, the holdup men. There is an interesting comment on Machajski—that incongruous libertarian with his scheme for "emancipating the working class through a world conspiracy of professional revolutionists, who naturally would have to be either intellectuals—that is, members of the rising new class—or self-educated ex-workers, which amounted to the same thing." One seems to catch in this disillusioned, and disillusioning, remark a hint of some latent discovery about the nature of revolution. Can it be that Trotsky and Machajski were really not so very far apart?

What puzzles me, though, is Mr. Nomad's dedication. The list includes, in addition to Louise Michel and Errico Malatesta, who properly belong in it, such incongruous figures as Spartacus, John Brown(!), and Karl Liebknecht, who was not remotely an anarchist; plus a group of philosophical skeptics, from Zeno to Anatole France. I have a strong suspicion that France would have declined the honor, preferring dinner with the Duchesse de Guermantes, while Zeno most likely would have doubted Mr. Nomad's existence. Or does he mean the later Zeno, the founder of Stoicism? However that may be, Mr. Nomad has brought his old friends back to life, if only for a moment. It is an enjoyable book, but for the real thing one must go to the source of it all, Proudhon's tirade against authority, as rendered by Mr. Joll:

> To be governed is to be watched over, inspected, spied on, directed, legislated, regulated, docketed, indoctrinated, preached at, controlled, assessed, weighed, censored, ordered about . . . noted, registered, taxed, stamped, measured, valued, assessed, patented, licensed, authorized, endorsed, admonished, hampered, reformed, rebuked, arrested. It is to be, on the pretext of the general interest, taxed, drilled, held to ransom, exploited, monopolized, extorted, hoaxed, squeezed, robbed; then at the least resistance, at the first word of complaint, repressed, fined, abused, annoyed, followed, bullied, beaten, disarmed, garrotted, imprisoned, judged, condemned, deported, flayed, sold, betrayed, and

finally mocked, ridiculed, insulted, dishonored. That's government, that's its justice, that's its morality!

Who can resist such rhetoric? I for one cannot. At the next opportunity I shall refuse to pay income tax.

The Revolution of 1848 *

• French universities are notoriously short of space. If there is ever a student uprising similar to the one at Berkeley, it will be directed not against bans on political activity but against lack of classroom facilities. There are a hundred thousand students in Paris alone (four times as many in the country as a whole), and although new buildings are being rushed up as fast as possible, many thousands still have to cram into the Sorbonne: the aged and wheezing *mater et magistra* founded in 1215 by Philip Augustus to commemorate his victory over the English at Bouvines. Now that France once more has a monarch (though an elective one) capable of routing the Anglo-Saxons, better days may dawn for students and lecturers, but some of the extra space will be needed to accommodate the growing audience which for years has followed M. Raymond Aron's lecture course "Les grandes doctrines de sociologie historique." It was time this was made available to foreigners, and the text of the lectures (substantially unaltered, so far as one can judge) has now been published in a handsomely edited English translation.†

As an expositor of other men's doctrines, M. Aron has few rivals. He is marvelously clear, invariably fairminded, and very rarely inaccurate. Now and then he slips up, and his translators, who have stuck closely to the text, duly reproduce his mistakes. Thus he makes the odd statement that "at the end of his life" Marx acknowledged having discovered the doctrine of class struggle in contemporary French historians. Actually Marx

---

* *The New York Review* (May 20, 1965).
† *Main Currents in Sociological Thought:* Volume I, *Montesquieu-Comte-Marx-Tocqueville. The Sociologists and the Revolution of 1848* (New York, 1965).

made a remark to this effect when he was quite a young man. This cannot have surprised anyone, since it was generally understood that the notion of class conflict had been suggested by Augustin Thierry, who had begun his career as a youthful assistant to Saint-Simon. In general, however, M. Aron avoids the more obvious mistakes which generations of teachers have transmitted to their pupils. He is not as learned a Marxologist as the late Georges Gurvitch, but he knows the subject well enough. He knows and understands Comte even better, but his real concern is with the two other thinkers he has chosen to interpret: Montesquieu and Tocqueville. They were liberals, and M. Aron, though always fair to socialists, is in the liberal tradition. His work, therefore, may be described as a critical analysis of French history since about 1750, from the standpoint of a sociologist who asks himself why the liberal tradition has not, on the whole, been as influential as the socialist one.

How does Marx fit into this theme? M. Aron in his lectures treats him as an honorary Frenchman, and this for two good reasons: first, Marx derived his socialist doctrines from France and constructed a political model on the analogy of the French Revolution. Secondly, the theory of industrial society is the common property of Comte and Marx, though Comte was not concerned with capitalism or the class struggle. Moreover, both men were indebted to Saint-Simon, the founder of French socialism, who was also the originator of the first, still somewhat hazy, notions about scientific industrialism as the wave of the future. It is true that Marx had a poor opinion of Comte, but it is now believed that some of Saint-Simon's later writings had been drafted in part by Comte, who was then his secretary. It may therefore be argued that there is a filiation by way of Comte of which Marx was unaware. M. Aron does not go into this matter (which was discussed at length some years ago by Dr. Hayek in his *Counter-Revolution in Science*) and what is perhaps more regrettable, he says almost nothing about Saint-Simon. The present reviewer would have welcomed an introductory chapter on Saint-Simon, instead of M. Aron's account of Montesquieu's political doctrines, which had very little to do with

269 : *The Revolution of 1848*

sociology, and even less with industrial society. But M. Aron's
real concern is with the theory of liberal democracy, and for
this purpose Saint-Simon clearly is not very relevant, since he
was neither a liberal nor a democrat. All the same, it is a pity he
has not followed Dr. Hayek's example and discussed the relationship between the Saint-Simonian school and the *École Po-
lytechnique*, where since Napoleon's days a large part of the
French intellectual elite has undergone its training. Most of the
early Saint-Simonians were *Polytechniciens*, and they developed
a "technocratic" doctrine of socialism long before people had
heard of the managerial revolution. Now that Europe has almost completed the journey from utopia to technocracy, this
topic merits attention.

What M. Aron offers instead is an essay in what he himself
calls "historical sociology." To the distinction between this type
of approach and ordinary political history it will be necessary to
return. Meanwhile one may note that Aron has set himself two
distinct themes: the Montesquieu-Tocqueville view of French
political history since the eighteenth century, and the sociology
of the Industrial Revolution, as interpreted by Comte and Marx.
Put schematically, one may say that he gives the reader a critical
interpretation of both the bourgeois revolution and the Industrial Revolution. Their conjunction underlay some of the most
dramatic episodes of French history in the nineteenth century,
notably in 1848, when the Republic was proclaimed, and a civil
war between bourgeoisie and proletariat fought in the streets of
Paris, while the rest of Europe stood appalled. Since this upheaval involved both Marx (who had just written the *Manifesto*) and Tocqueville (who in January 1848 predicted the
coming upheaval from the rostrum of the French Parliament),
M. Aron is able to pull the strands of his argument together
in his final chapter, where he contrasts Marx with Tocqueville,
and goes into some detail about the Industrial Revolution and
its impact on the nascent bourgeois democracy.

Is this an acceptable procedure? I think it is, on the understanding that M. Aron is dealing with what is really the history
of a particular kind of revolution. There was no corresponding

THE CONCEPT OF IDEOLOGY

phenomenon in Britain—there the Industrial Revolution, curiously enough, was not accompanied by a political one—and the British thus missed the formative experience of an armed conflict between the classes. This explains why British socialism remained reformist, and the labor movement respectably liberal-radical. It also accounts for the prevailing mood among British historians. Since they lived in a stable environment—and moreover in a country which dominated the world—they were able to go on treating history as the record of more or less successful political manipulations. The assumption was that every sound political organism has a capacity for adapting peacefully to social change. Departures from this rule counted as evidence of abnormality or unsoundness. The absence of such a consensus in France was much deplored in the nineteenth and twentieth centuries by writers of the liberal school: that founded by Montesquieu and continued by Tocqueville. It is also deplored by M. Aron. He acknowledges somewhat reluctantly that so far as industrial society was concerned, the theoretical breakthrough was made by the socialists and by the followers of Comte, but his heart is with Montesquieu and Tocqueville.

He even attempts—unsuccessfully, in the reviewer's opinion —to establish Montesquieu as an important forerunner of modern sociology. This is the least plausible part of his work. He has an easier time with Montesquieu's rather Whiggish writings on constitutional history, which may be said to have pioneered the pro-British tradition among aristocratic liberals in France. French liberalism has indeed suffered from the taint of Anglophilia. The constitutional Royalists of 1789 were fervent Anglophiles, and this duly counted against them. It was only after the fall of Napoleon that they were able to make themselves heard, but then this kind of liberalism is a post-revolutionary phenomenon. It is odd that M. Aron does not recognize this. It is even odder that he fails to stress the connection between Montesquieu's writings and the late-eighteenth-century aristocratic resurgence against the Bourbon Monarchy which preceded the Revolution and in a sense made it inevitable. There is a kind of amiable perversity about this blindness. Unquestionably both

Montesquieu and M. Aron would have been guillotined under
Robespierre, but this must not be allowed to count in their
favor. People may be guillotined for all sorts of reasons, good,
bad, or indifferent. In the case of Montesquieu, and of M. Aron,
one can think of sound reasons why in 1793 it would have been
expedient to do away with them, or at least to make them emi-
grate. To be fair, M. Aron recognizes this himself and indeed
says so with the greatest candor.

A different, though related, problem arises in connection with
M. Aron's treatment of Tocqueville: not the Tocqueville whom
Americans know and admire, but the pessimistic conservative
who watched the fall of Louis Philippe in 1848, and in the following year served for some months as Louis Bonaparte's Foreign Minister. The upheaval had thrown a heavy strain on his
aristocratic liberalism. In particular he was appalled by the san-
guinary "June days" of 1848, when the Paris proletariat was
butchered by the Army, under the auspices of a Republican government which was distinctly too radical for Tocqueville, though
it did its level best to protect property and reassure the bourgeoisie. Tocqueville, as was to be expected, sided firmly with the
party of "Order." In his *Recollections* (written years later and
not published in his lifetime) he still cast the blame for the
disaster on the socialists, who in his opinion had terrified the
bourgeoisie (in point of fact their leaders had made themselves
ridiculous by joining a bourgeois government they were powerless to control). Tocqueville drew no distinction between genuine revolutionaries like Blanqui, and moderates like Louis Blanc,
who stood for peaceful social reform. He noted that the Industrial Revolution had created a proletariat, and that the masses
had been permeated by "economic and political theories which
were beginning to make their way and which strove to prove
that human misery was the work of laws and not of Providence,
and that poverty could be suppressed by changing the conditions
of society."

This is a side of Tocqueville about which his admirers tend to
be silent, but M. Aron is too candid to suppress the evidence. He
interpolates an embarrassed passage on "the deeply conservative

liberal who thinks that social inequalities are part of the eternal order of providence" and then goes on to suggest that Tocqueville and Marx took pretty much the same view of the social causes underlying the civil war of 1848: they just happened to be on different sides of the barricade. Tocqueville, he accurately notes, "belonged to the bourgeois party of order and during the June days was prepared to fight against the insurgent workers." Later on he sided with the more conservative Republicans who opposed Louis Bonaparte. "He was defeated, but he was not surprised at his defeat, for from the first day of the Revolution of 1848 he believed that free institutions were temporarily doomed. . . . He fought against the solution that seemed to him at once most probable and least desirable—which is characteristic of a sociologist of the school of Montesquieu."

It is also characteristic of M. Aron. Of course there is this difference: in contemporary France the proletariat is no longer a menace to the established order. On the contrary, it is the foundation of the new industrial society. Social conflicts now relate to wages and are on the whole conducted peacefully. In short, the class struggle is over. What nowadays passes for "class conflict" would not have terrified Tocqueville, and it does not terrify M. Aron. His liberalism is thoroughly democratic and leaves room for a modest degree of socialist planning. His favorite statesman is M. Mendès-France. This needs stressing, so as not to give the impression that M. Aron is in any way to be identified with the bloody-mindedness of his hero. He admires Tocqueville, but has no illusions about him. This attitude is to be recommended. In particular it is worth recommending to those writers who in recent years have popularized Tocqueville while staying silent on his involvement in the conflicts which tore French society apart. One understands him a great deal better if one knows that in 1848-1849 he belonged to the "party of Order," and that this party believed liberty to be incompatible with democracy (not to mention socialism). Liberals in Britain held the same view, but they were spared the ordeal of their French colleagues, and so were able to preserve a good conscience. The British counterpart of the "June days" was the waterlogged fiasco on Kennington Common in April 1848, when the Chartists presented a petition to Parliament and then trudged home in the rain without so much as firing a shot. But then Britain was already an industrial country, and the industrial working class is not given to violence. It prefers strikes to barricades. By now this is generally recognized, even by Communists (except in Peking and Havana), and talk of "red revolution" no longer frightens anyone.

The implications of this change are worked out in the more sociological parts of M. Aron's analysis, notably in his discussion of Comte's theory of society and Marx's doctrine of economics. On these subjects he is, as might be expected, knowledgeable and fairminded, though not very original. His discussion of Marx is conventional, though competently done. He has a rather summary chapter on the Hegelian heritage and a few passages on the currently fashionable topic of Marx's early writings. Possibly by way of reaction to the Marx-baiting industry of the 1950s, there has in recent years been a tendency to treat these writings as central to the understanding of Marxism as a philosophy. At the other extreme there are those who deny that concepts such as "alienation" have any relevance to Marx's work as an economist. M. Aron steers a sensible middle course and in the end leaves undecided the question whether *Capital* could have been written by anyone who did not hold the particular beliefs to which Marx had committed himself before he became an economist. The nearest he comes to a conclusion is to say that Marx's critique of capitalism "was at the same time a philosophical and moral critique of the situation imposed on man by capitalism." This leaves unexplored the link between Marx's philosophy and his economics. The link was in fact sociological: it rested on the idea that bourgeois society is just that particular kind of society in which individuals are dependent on an economic process which has got away from them and taken on the fantastic appearance of a self-sufficient realm of "economic laws." As long as people consider themselves subject to "laws" which are really objectifications of their own uncomprehended activities, they are "alienated." It follows that "alienation" still persists even under so-called socialism, as long as commodities are exchanged, or salaries paid, in accordance with the "law of value." This doctrine is subversive of Soviet "socialism," and the Communists have done their best to obscure it, but it has recently begun to emerge in the shape of "revisionist" literature and deserves every encouragement. Unfortunately it is also subversive of capitalism. This may be the reason why Western writers are almost as nervous about it as their Eastern colleagues, though unlike the latter they cannot suppress it, and indeed have no such intention.

As one would expect, M. Aron is more sympathetic to Comte than to Marx, but his sympathy stops short of accepting Comte's notion that political phenomena are best understood in terms of an underlying social process tending to bring about a universally valid type of society—modern industrialism. M. Aron objects to this (as he does to Marx's related, though more complex, approach) that insufficient regard is paid to the autonomy of the political realm. He sees Comte as the ancestor of a tradition culminating, via Durkheim and his school, in contemporary sociology; and he holds that this tradition has failed to show adequate regard for the stuff of political conflict and decision-making. This is surely to confuse the proper business of the political historian with the rather different problems that present themselves to any theorist of social change, whatever his standpoint. The (real or fancied) uniqueness of any particular political conflict is not questioned when the larger historical process is itself examined with a view to establishing some general theory of social change. It is of the essence of such theories that they seek to classify historical events in accordance with abstract types or models of social organization. Marc Bloch's classic analysis of feudal society is a case in point. Yet Bloch was a historian—perhaps the greatest of his generation. His work could not have been done by a sociologist, but neither could it have been done by the kind of writer who treats the political process in isolation from the social system. In what has been

called "Bloch's insistent references to the *ambiance sociale to-*
tale,"* the category of totality raises its head.

It is not a category to which the reader of Aron's work will
gain an easy introduction. His concern is with the uniqueness of
the historical event, and at a remove with the social constraints
exerted upon political systems by cultural and economic factors.
Nowhere does he come to grips with the notion that the political process itself may be seen as a social phenomenon—that the
way in which a society alters its political institutions is analyzable in social terms. Yet it is along these lines that the sociology
of politics may be expected to develop, now that the impact of
positivism and Marxism has been absorbed, and historians have
come to see that their traditional concern with purely political
history was itself an ideological phenomenon.

* See the Foreword to the English translation of his work and Bloch's
own introductory remarks.

From Pascal to Marx[*]

• Is there a sense in which both Existentialism and Marxism can be described as reactions against the rationalist world-view inaugurated by Descartes? Those familiar with postwar French literature will be aware that this question has troubled the adherents of both schools and given rise to controversies from which political overtones have not been absent. In the public disputations which over the past decade have involved Sartre and his disciples on the one hand, and orthodox Marxists like Roger Garaudy on the other (with Henri Lefebvre perhaps occupying an intermediate position), there has been a tendency for both sides to dissociate themselves from the Cartesian heritage. Catholic philosophers likewise, in their effort to comprehend the Marxian critique of religion, have on occasion fallen back upon an "existential" approach already exemplified by Pascal, and subsequently restated, two centuries later, in Kierkegaard's rebellion against Hegel. In this perspective, Descartes and Kant appear as the twin pinnacles of European rationalism, while the dissolution of their respective systems is seen as the precondition of a "dialectical" structure of thought: religious pessimism on the one hand, humanist optimism on the other. A good deal of recent Catholic writing in France turns on such considerations, while from the Communist standpoint M. Garaudy, in his *Perspectives de L'Homme*, has rung the changes on the same theme, and done so with an evident desire to accommodate what from his standpoint appears as the heritage of religious irrationalism.

In this exegetical ebb and flow, a minor but not unimportant point was marked by the appearance in 1955 of M. Lucien

[*] *New Statesman* (September 4, 1964).

Goldmann's study *Le Dieu caché*, now available in an English translation.* A scholar of Rumanian origin who underwent his philosophical training in the Vienna of the 1930s, then still the home of Austro-Marxism, M. Goldmann made up for the natural handicap of the foreigner by a greater familiarity with Kantian and Hegelian philosophy. His dissertation on Pascal and Racine impressed the learned world sufficiently to win him a chair at the Centre des Hautes Etudes in Paris. It also gave renewed stimulus to a debate already in progress, though the participants seem on the whole to have remained unaffected by personal oddities such as M. Goldmann's excessive veneration for Lukács, whom he has occasionally classed with Hegel. Again, they appear not to have been unduly impressed by his attempt to dethrone Kierkegaard in favor of Kant as the outstanding modern exponent of "tragic" thought, or by his insistence that the familiar parallel between Pascal and Kierkegaard is due to a misconception. Educated Frenchmen have since 1945 grown familiar with Central European philosophy, and eccentric *obiter dicta* on the subject no longer claim attention merely because they emanate from a foreigner.

What then is the common theme running through the discussion? One relevant topic may be indicated by citing M. Goldmann's dictum that "Marxism begins with a wager." The term has evidently been chosen with a full realization of what it connotes in the context of this particular debate. True, M. Goldmann rejects what he describes as the attempt "to Christianize Marxism or to introduce transcendental values into it." Marxism is this-worldly, and its "wager" is simply on the ability of man to make his future. "The transcendental element present in this faith is not supernatural and does not take us outside or beyond history; it merely takes us beyond the individual." Still, the term "wager," and the even more evocative "transcendental," knocks rather a large hole into the traditional understanding of dialectical materialism. To make the point even plainer, M. Goldmann goes on to affirm that Marxist thought

---

* *The Hidden God* (London and New York, 1964).

THE CONCEPT OF IDEOLOGY

leaps over six centuries of Thomist and Cartesian rationalism and renews the Augustinian tradition. It does not, of course, do this by reintroducing the same idea of transcendence, but by affirming two things: that values are founded in an objective reality which can be relatively if not absolutely known (God for Saint Augustine, history for Marx); and that the most objective knowledge which man can obtain of any historical fact presupposes his recognition of the existence of this reality as the supreme value.

Without going into the difficulties of this position, its originality may be appreciated—especially in the light of M. Goldmann's further affirmation that

if we are to arrive at a scientific knowledge of man, we must begin by the wager, or assumption, that history has a meaning. We must therefore set out from an act of faith, and the phrase *Credo ut intelligam* provides a common basis for Augustinian, Pascalian and Marxist epistemology. . . .

Now there are two things to be said about this. In the first place, Mr. Philip Thody's translation takes considerable liberties with the text. Thus where M. Goldmann differentiates Marxism from Augustinianism "sur le point de la transcendance où leur différence reste radicale," his translator gives the impression that the quarrel is merely over a particular "idea of transcendence." (He also for some reason translates "connaissance positive de l'homme" as "scientific knowledge of man"—hardly fair to M. Goldmann, who is not a positivist in the usual meaning of the term.) Secondly, however, M. Goldmann is himself responsible for some of the resulting obscurities, since his terminological usage wobbles dangerously between neo-Kantianism, Marxism, and "religious atheism," so that he is able, in one and the same breath, to disclaim any theological attachments and yet to describe both "tragic" and "dialectical" forms of thought as "philosophies of incarnation." "Il s'agit de l'incarnation des valeurs et des significations dans le monde réel," he adds in a footnote. Mr. Thody translates "both demand that values should become reality in the real world," which again is slightly off the point, but then it has to be admitted that with M. Goldmann one never quite knows how far he is prepared to go in the direction of idealism. I read him to mean that values *are* incarnate in the real world, which is what Hegel and Marx believed; but since he regards Kant as both a "tragic" and a "dialectical" thinker (this will come as a surprise to many, but Lukács in 1923 suggested something of the sort, and for M. Goldmann this is enough to override all other considerations), a different interpretation can perhaps be justified.

It may be asked what all this has to do with Jansenism, which is the ostensible subject of M. Goldmann's work. The answer is that he regards Pascal and Racine as the key figures in the politico-theological crisis which convulsed mid-seventeenth-century France: a crisis involving (a) the disintegration of the traditional social order, (b) the dissolution of the Thomist worldview, and (c) certain mundane conflicts between the Court and the social stratum to which Pascal and Racine belonged, the *noblesse de robe*, this last a uniquely French phenomenon of uncertain origin. His treatment of this admittedly very complex theme apparently struck French readers in 1955 as a particularly enlightening example of the Marxian approach to the problem of historical "totality." Jansenism as the ideology of the *noblesse de robe* is indeed an excellent subject for a Marxist. This was shown as early as 1934, when the late Dr. Franz Borkenau published his unfairly neglected work on the philosophy of the seventeenth century, *Der Übergang vom feudalen zum bürgerlichen Weltbild.* The thesis that Pascal (without being aware of it) acted as the spokesman of a stratum of society whose tacit support lay behind the Jansenist heresy was there set out at some length: along with a number of highly original and pertinent reflections on the social role of theology in an age of crisis. M. Goldmann (without ever so much as mentioning Borkenau) goes over the same ground in rather more pedestrian fashion, and in the end comes up with the identical conclusion: Jansenism is to be understood as the ideology of the *noblesse de robe* in its struggle against the Court and the Jesuits.

This may well be the case. But his discussion of the topic raises an awkward problem to which he does not seem to have quite found the answer: if the theological dilemma was rooted in a particular political situation—the inability of the *noblesse*

de robe to make sense of its intermediate position between the
Court and the Third Estate—then where precisely does one
draw the line between mundane and metaphysical preoccupations? For M. Goldmann the "paradoxical situation" in which
the *noblesse de robe* found itself in France around 1660—hostile to the emerging Royal absolutism, yet unable and indeed
unwilling to destroy it, as the Puritans had recently done in
neighboring England—is not simply an accidental background
to the work of Pascal and Racine: it provides, he says, "the infrastructure for the tragic paradox of *Phèdre* and of the *Pensées.*" Now infrastructure is a dangerous word: it leads to superstructure, and once one begins to think in such terms it is not
easy to escape the conclusion that Jansenism was "mere ideology." Marx never made this mistake, but some of his followers
did, and even M. Goldmann, for all his sophistication, once or
twice goes very near the edge.

The basic argument appears to be this: the crisis of the seventeenth century involved both a new system of government and a
new picture of man and society. It did so because medieval doctrine was no longer adequate, and this inadequacy came out
both in the Cartesian demolition of the traditional world-view,
and in the subterfuges to which the Jesuits (enemies both of the
Jansenists and of Descartes) were driven in their attempt to salvage the Aristotelian-Thomist heritage. As opponents of the
Court, the Jansenists were obliged to evolve a "paradoxical" or
"tragic" outlook, while it was left for the Enlightenment of the
following century to step into the Cartesian inheritance. Descartes was too much of a rationalist, and too much of an opti-
mist, to satisfy the religious craving which found expression in
Jansenism. The Jesuits distrusted him, but the Jansenists—with
their minds fixed upon the Augustinian paradox of a *Deus absconditus* presiding over an evil world and a hopelessly corrupted human nature—were even less inclined to follow him.
They correctly sensed that his rationalism left no room for the
living God whom they sought. Pascal and Racine reflected the
Jansenist predicament at the ultimate—metaphysical or poetic
—level. They were in some sense the precursors of Kant, Hegel,

and Marx, in that they intuitively sensed the "dialectical" character of reality: a reality from which "God is absent," *i.e.*, the meaning of which cannot be grasped by the intellect because, in plain terms, it has no meaning. As committed Christians they fell back upon an irrational faith where their modern successors have gone forward to a rational one. What then connects them with Hegel and Marx? Primarily the fact that they felt obliged to undertake a desperate "wager" on the reality of the *Deus absconditus*, where the modern Hegelian wagers on the future of man and the rationality of the historical process.

It will now, I hope, have become clear why M. Goldmann's exegesis of Pascal and Racine made an impression upon French scholars who might have been supposed to know the subject by heart. If Borkenau's pioneering work is set aside (unfortunately it was never translated), he may be said to have introduced his readers to a novel interpretation of an important chapter in their own intellectual history. This is sufficient claim to eminence. Without going so far as to say that he has botched an important theme, it is permissible to feel that he has not made the most of his opportunity. Ingenious rather than profound, scholarly in a crotchety fashion, yet unable to submerge his personal eccentricities, he is weakest where Borkenau was strongest: he conveys no sense of what it must have been like to live in an age of deep mental distress. The reason, one surmises, is that for all his talk of "crisis" and "wager," he is at heart untroubled by the metaphysical anguish of his heroes. There is a certain complacency about his tone which does not sit well with his assumption of the prophetic role. Yet *The Hidden God* is a work of genuine distinction and, for all its repetitiveness and turgidity, well worth reading (especially in the French original). It is not, I think, the revelation for which the New Left has been waiting; but it tries to deal with fundamentals, and even its failure is a kind of triumph.

Philosopher in Revolt*

• In 1961 M. Jean-Paul Sartre paid a brief visit to Cuba and had a conversation with Castro, in the course of which there occurred the following memorable exchange (reported by Sartre in the account he wrote of his trip, and now preserved for posterity by Mr. Wilfrid Desan in a new book on Sartre's philosophy):†

"Man's need is his fundamental right over all others," said Castro.
"And if they ask you for the moon?" asked Sartre.
". . . it would be because someone needed it," was Castro's reply.

Mr. Desan's comment on this is, "Sartre had found a friend, one who understood that the one humanism that is possible is founded 'neither on work nor on culture . . . but on need!'"
My own, somewhat more jaundiced, exegesis of the above passage is that Castro had sized Sartre up correctly as someone who would stick to generalities and avoid painful topics, such as the (temporary) suppression of liberty. The two men of course also have other points in common, notably their joint descent from Jacobinism, but that is another matter.

It has to be reported that much of Mr. Desan's work is at the level of the passage just cited: verbose, rhetorical, and awe-struck. This is a pity, for it is plain that he could have written a better book had he allowed his critical sense more play. His own background is French, and his earlier work includes an interpretation of *L'Être et le néant*, that great, inflated, word-intoxicated monstrosity of a book in which Sartre—writing in Paris

* The New York Review (January 28, 1965).
† The Marxism of Jean-Paul Sartre (New York, 1965).

during the German Occupation—introduced his countrymen to
the mysteries of German metaphysics. Mr. Desan knows enough
about France, and about philosophy, to do justice to Sartre's
intellectual accomplishment, and if *The Marxism of Jean-Paul
Sartre* is on the whole a disappointing book, the reason is not to
be found in any lack of technical accomplishment on the author's part. It is quite simply that he has been unduly impressed
by Sartre's public status as the central figure of postwar French
intellectual life.

Of the importance attributed to Sartre even by his opponents
there can be no doubt. By near unanimous consent he is the
Callas of French literature: a star whose bravura performances
make up for the frequent lack of an adequate libretto. *"Sartre,
c'est aussi la France,"* de Gaulle is said to have remarked on an
occasion when there was some inconclusive talk of legal action
against him for calling upon conscripts to refuse service in Algeria. These two great egotists concur in believing that were it not
for their presence, France would sink to the level of mediocrity
so manifest elsewhere in contemporary Europe. As one who
happens to share this view (or something like it) I am nonetheless skeptical about the claims made for Sartre, by Mr. Desan
and others, in the domain of philosophy properly so called. It
may be the fault of my Central European upbringing, but I find
it difficult to take Sartre seriously as an expositor of either Hegel
or Husserl. In any case it is notorious—and Mr. Desan candidly
makes the point—that both Sartre and Merleau-Ponty learned
all they knew about Hegel from Alexandre Kojève's celebrated
lecture course at the Ecole des Hautes Etudes between 1933 and
1939, years notable in European history for other reasons as
well. As Mr. Desan says quite rightly, it was only then that "the
introduction to Hegel, and with this a genuine Marxist intellectualism" occurred in France. Previously Marx had been known
to most Frenchmen only as an economist, and as for Hegel, the
academic world had only the vaguest notion of what he was
about. Kojève's lectures (published in book form in 1947) were
an eye-opener, the more so since they drew attention to those
passages in the *Phenomenology of Mind* where Hegel, in his

customary crabbed and hermetic fashion, recommended the French Revolution and Napoleon to his German contemporaries as the current manifestation of the World Spirit.

In recent years then the French intellectual elite has been in possession of a key to Hegel which, by a singularly fortunate coincidence, also made possible an interpretation of Marx at a level far above the crudities of the Leninist school. The postwar "discovery" of the young Marx could be popularized (by Sartre among others) on the basis of what he and others had previously learned from Kojève, who for his part tended to treat politics as unimportant; it was one of his favorite notions that the entire European civil war between Communists and Fascists was nothing but a squabble between left-wing and right-wing Hegelians.

Had Mr. Desan taken the trouble to pursue this theme, he might have written an interesting book. Unluckily for himself and for the reader, his aim is more ambitious: a critical exposition of Sartre's views on Marxism, notably as formulated in the *Critique de la raison dialectique* (1960). In addition, the reader of Mr. Desan's study will find him busily at work explaining and (as a rule) defending his hero's views on related topics, though some minor parts of the canon—such as Sartre's six-hundred-page investigation of Saint Genet's posterior—are prudently ignored. Learned enough in its way, the book nonetheless strikes at least one reader as fundamentally unsatisfactory. The tone is too deferential, the difficulties are too systematically eluded, and above all the paradoxical nature of Sartre's relationship to Communism (as distinct from Marxism) is not properly brought out.

For this last it would indeed be unfair to blame only Mr. Desan. Others too have been baffled by Sartre's intellectual gyrations: from the despairing cynicism of *Les mains sales* (1948) to the frenzied fellow-traveling of *Les Communistes et la paix* (1952), and onward via the rebuke to the Russians for interfering in Hungary (1956), to his championship of Castro (1961) and the rejection of the Nobel Prize (1964), this last in a manifesto which absurdly mingled perfectly sound arguments with disingenuous rubbish about Pasternak. Unlike Merleau-Ponty, who around 1950 decided once and for all to have done with Stalinism, Sartre has kept up a love-hate relationship both with Moscow and with the French Communist Party, seemingly undeterred by its one-sided character. For while he has largely absorbed the Communists' style of reasoning, there is little evidence that he has had any reciprocal effect upon *them*. Indeed his latest Communist critic, M. Jacques Houbart, in a recently published essay (*"Un Père dénaturé"* [Paris, 1964]), bluntly denounces Sartre as a typical bourgeois intellectual: harsh words, considering the effort Sartre has made to turn himself into a Marxist; yet not, I fear, entirely unjustified.[1]

M. Houbart's tract has come too late for Mr. Desan's study. I am not sure what he would have made of it, but in all probability his comment would have been sorrowful rather than angry. For Mr. Desan shares with Sartre a desire to get beyond the current controversies in France, and in particular to get beyond the Communist version of Marxism. At the same time he is acute enough to perceive that Sartre himself has failed to accomplish this aim. As he puts it in his summing-up, Sartre has never really stopped being a Cartesian, which for practical purposes means that he has never stopped being an individualist. Now it is arguable that at the personal level this does no harm: after all, Marx and Engels were a great deal more bourgeois than Sartre, and Marxism itself may be described as a creation of the bourgeois mind. The real trouble is that one cannot extract the Marxian view of history from the Cartesian vision of the Self as sovereign. "Descartes did not beget Marx," as Mr. Desan correctly puts it. But Descartes did beget Sartre (with a little help

[1] More recently there has been further evidence that the French Communist Party is able to dispense with Sartre. Its intellectual life currently (in 1967) turns on the conflict between M. Roger Garaudy and M. Louis Althusser. The debate between them, whatever its merits or demerits, is at any rate unrelated to Sartre's highly personal brand of existentialized Marxism. M. Garaudy perhaps is no more than a competent popularizer. M. Althusser for his part may be described as a grave and learned, if somewhat scholastic, exegete of Marxism-Leninism. But here is the point: neither man is concerned to argue about Sartre; he is of no interest to them. And indeed there is no reason why he should be.

from Edmund Husserl), and in consequence Sartre's followers have been saddled with a method which does not help them in their efforts to get beyond Marx. Let me hasten to add that this in no way excuses the nonsense talked by Stalinists (Lukács among them) some years ago about Existentialism as a "petit bourgeois" deviation. These tedious diatribes, which understandably aroused Sartre's irritation, were as irrelevant as they were foolish, and have been quietly abandoned in recent years by the more civilized Communist spokesmen in France. Yet it remains true that one cannot employ Sartre's method, as developed in the *Critique*, for the purpose of saying anything very useful about history. Cartesianism apart, there is Sartre's reliance on the phenomenological method developed by Husserl and his disciples. Now phenomenology, in one of its aspects, is really a species of Platonism. In Santayana's phrase, it is "intuition of essence." This may be useful to writers concerned with aesthetics, but it is of no earthly use in trying to make sense of historical *processes*; and this (not to mention his obsession with problems of personal morality) is the root cause of Sartre's failure.

In a way this appears to be Mr. Desan's own regretful conclusion. But before he reaches it, the conscientious reader has to make his way through some pretty arid stretches of interpretation. The *Critique* itself is largely unreadable, and Mr. Desan's exposition, though commendably brief, is almost as abstract as the original. It is also almost wholly uncritical. Mr. Desan has a few reservations about Sartre's political record, but hardly any about the preposterous concepts developed at wearisome length in the *Critique*: notably Sartre's treatment of "scarcity," his weird notions about human "serialization," and his obsessive stress upon the importance of "terror" as the real stuff of political organization. He seems not to have noticed that Sartre's view of history is the counterpart of his readiness to put up with totalitarianism in its Soviet form, or that his qualified apologies for Stalin are in harmony with his belief that "terrorism" is at the base of *every* political organization. It is all very wearisome, and one must, I think, conclude that the political sociology lengthily expounded in the *Critique* has proved sterile. It is really no more than a complicated way of talking *about* phenomena with which historians and sociologists are perfectly familiar.

What then does Sartre's critical examination of Marxism finally amount to? On the positive side, he has carried further the destruction of the simplified materialist ontology which serves the Communist movement as an *ersatz* religion. In this way he has compelled the more literate Communist theorists to bring their writings up to a more respectable level. Hence there is now in progress a perfectly genuine three-cornered debate a- mong Marxists, Catholics, and Existentialists in France. For this welcome change in the intellectual climate Sartre can take some credit, though much of it is due to the late Merleau-Ponty. Negatively, Sartre has dazzled and confused an entire generation by a species of intellectual sleight-of-hand, by libertarian postur- ing in the service of totalitarianism, and by a combination of po- litical fellow-traveling with respectable Cartesian metaphysics. He has thus made it possible for his followers to declare them- selves in sympathy with "the revolution," without being Com- munists. And he has done so in a country where no "revolution" was or is possible, and where the Communist Party is becoming an anachronism.

This last point is central to an understanding of the effect Sartre's dialectics have had upon an intelligentsia brought up on revolutionary rhetoric, in a society where these slogans were los- ing their power over men's minds. Before Communism had be- come just another political party it was an eschatological move- ment, in a situation where eschatology was out of place. The net effect was to equip an entire generation of Frenchmen with a "false consciousness." Because it was so easy to see 1917 as the fulfillment of 1789, Leninist rhetoric could be grafted upon a sectional Labor movement which was never remotely within sight of gaining power, and would not have known what to do with it if power had somehow fallen into its lap. French Com- munism was and remains a substitute for an event destined never to take place. The early Christians awaited the coming of the Saviour, and what they got instead was the Church. The

French intellectuals expected the coming of the Revolution, and what they got was the Communist Party. This observation is not to be found in Sartre's writings, but it is the sort of thing he *might* have said, and I hereby make his followers a free gift of it. Mr. Desan, in an otherwise learned and useful book, regrettably comes nowhere near making the point.

Sartre, Marxism, and History*

I

• In postwar France the philosophers were resolved not to interpret the world but to change it. For a few years it looked as though the forces let loose at the liberation might transform society and bridge the gap between the intellectual elite and the masses. But history refused to be rewritten, the revolution did not take place, and the philosophers returned to their studies. Sartre is the inheritor of this failure. The formal peculiarities of his work are not accidental. They are imposed upon him by his commitment to a goal which he shares with the Communists, but interprets in a spirit incompatible with their rigid doctrine. To understand his position in present-day France one must relate his attempt to forge a new intellectual synthesis to the antecedent loss of his earlier political hopes. It is not the first example of an aborted revolution having produced, as a side effect, a philosophical sanctuary wherein the unrealized aims of men are preserved against the day when thought and action shall once more be made to coincide.

The *Critique de la raison dialectique* is Sartre's most ambitious work to date. Moreover, unlike *L'Être et le néant*, whose appearance in 1943 inevitably partook of the nature of a clandestine operation, it is among the best-advertised philosophical productions to have seen the light in recent years. In de Gaulle's France, Sartre is very much a public figure—the unofficial philosopher of the non-Communist Left—and his pronouncements are treated with respectful attention by a public not averse in its own fashion to a modest degree of hero-worship. These external circumstances are interiorized (to employ a favorite Sartrean

* *History and Theory*, II (1963).

concept) in the structure and tonality of his work, whose goal is nothing less than the completion of Marxist philosophy: itself deemed by the author to be unsurpassable in the present epoch of history. The first volume of the *Critique*—a massive tome, the principal part of which bears the subtitle *Théorie des ensembles pratiques*—outlines the general scheme. We are promised a successor which will, one may suppose, spell out some of the detailed implications of Sartre's theory of history. But even at the current preparatory stage it is evident that this is to be the fulfillment of a program sketched out more briefly in earlier days, when Sartre was still the exponent of German philosophy on French soil. By its very title the *Critique* reveals both its inspiration and the ambition to pass beyond Kant and his successors. At the same time the original commitment to practice (*engagement*) remains in force. Sartre's *magnum opus* is no mere investigation of other men's ideas, let alone a sketch for a new and improved academic philosophy. As a thinker he is concerned with changing the world: in this respect at least he remains a Marxist. Yet his Marxism is not that of the Communists, not even that of a former Communist like Henri Lefebvre, whose polite but implacable criticism of Sartre[1] has drawn the line between traditional Marxism and Sartre's own highly individual synthesis of Hegel, Marx, and Heidegger. It is not the least intriguing aspect of this situation that Lefebvre—though pardonably a less original and fertile mind—is quite obviously superior to Sartre in his understanding of Marx. Indeed his criticism, for all its urbanity, has the remorseless tone one associates with painfully acquired professionalism. It is as though a veteran practitioner were patiently explaining to a gifted novice what all these technical terms are about. Yet Sartre can claim to have spent many years in the arduous task of penetrating the mysteries of Hegelian and Marxian dialectics. If he can still be faulted by a writer inferior to him in general ability, the cause must lie in some radical incongruity of his subject matter with the cast of mind he brings to it. In fact, as we shall see, the original tension

[1] "Critique de la critique non-critique," *Nouvelle Revue Marxiste* (July 1961).

between Marxism and Existentialism, which lies at the root of
Sartre's political and literary activity over the past two decades,
has not been resolved, though in his latest work he has made a
truly monumental effort to effect a synthesis of these two modes
of thought. But before considering the implications of this failure—perhaps the most interesting in contemporary French literature, and certainly the one most pregnant with consequences
of a political order—we must take the plunge into Sartre's philosophy as spelled out in his earlier writings, and then inquire
how far he has remained true to his original standpoint.[2]

I I

To be aware is to be aware of something, and at a second remove to be aware of myself as a reflecting being. I am conscious
of an object, and of other objects forming a world, but I am not
conscious of my own consciousness, as though I could watch
myself from an imagined outside. Yet I know that I exist, and
this awareness sets me off from objects which are "simply
there." In transcending my contingent existence I remain a
being which is incomplete and, because it is incomplete, strives
after union with that which is given in thought. This union is
unattainable for man, but the urge to attain it determines man's
being. Consciousness separates me from that which merely sub-
sists, and propels me towards that which is imagined. This pro-
pulsion is freedom, which is not *a* human property, but *the*
human property, or rather the particular mode of human existence in the world. In consciousness I am aware of myself as a
being whose aim is to overcome the contingency of mere existence. But the aim is unattainable, for the mind is eternally sepa-

---

[2] For details concerning Sartre's "deviations" from Marxian orthodoxy
the reader must be referred to Lefebvre's essay. In what follows his critical
points are taken for granted. They are valid against Sartre, whether or not
one accepts Lefebvre's own standpoint (which is not that of the present
writer). Their validity is quite simply due to the fact that Sartre has
evolved an all-embracing system of his own whose internal logic is at
variance with the Marxism he professes. For a rather more rigidly Leninist
criticism of Sartre than that offered by Lefebvre, see Jacques Houbart, *Un
Père dénaturé* (Paris, 1964), where Sartre's philosophy is described, un-
kindly but not inaccurately, as "une idéologie parasitaire" (p. 141).

rated from that with which it is trying to unite. Having thus chased the dialectic of *en-soi*, and *pour-soi*, being and consciousness, through seven hundred pages in *L'Être et le néant*, Sartre concludes that the urge to become *causa sui* is doomed to failure. "*L'homme est une passion inutile*."

In the *Critique*, Sartre returns to the charge, though this time from a different standpoint. *L'Être et le néant* was fundamentally a treatise on individual existence, and only at a second remove concerned with human society. The *Critique* is meant to bridge the gap (and to meet the charge that Existentialism is simply a variant of individualism). At the same time Sartre intends to show that his philosophical approach is superior to what he describes as "contemporary Marxism," although "I consider Marxism the ultimate philosophy of our age." Present-day Marxism, in Sartre's view, has shed its philosophical dimension and moreover has become the tool of short-range political purposes. It has thus lost the capacity (if it ever possessed it) to grasp the complex mediations which link the individual to the social whole. These mediations relate back to the dialectic of being and consciousness which Sartre had described in *L'Être et le néant*. Thus although he has now become critical of Existentialism, and even describes it as a parasite on the major philosophies, Sartre still believes that the analysis of Being he undertook in his earlier work is a step towards his mature synthesis. His theory of society is intended as an advance beyond Marxism. Formally, however, the *Critique* presents itself as an attempt to outline the logic of a Marxist anthropology. The "profound significance of History and of dialectical rationality" is to disclose itself through an analysis of human nature, but of human nature correctly understood, that is, in its concrete historical setting. Such an analysis will both illuminate history and "reconquer man inside Marxism" through a proper understanding of the Marxian notion of *praxis*.

The manner in which Sartre goes about his task has exposed him to the charge of not really understanding the dialectic, while on the other hand his obsessive concern with the totality of history has laid him open to the damaging suggestion that his thinking has been shaped by recent political experiences. Yet even at the peak of his frenetic fellow-traveling, Sartre was never a theoretical Leninist; and today, when he has recovered his poise, he remains estranged from the conventional rationalism which for over a century has shaped the outlook of the Left in France.

The fact is that all these correlations do not really help one to grasp the peculiarity of Sartre's position in a France which has not undergone a Communist revolution, and consequently has not adopted Marxism as its official philosophy. In a country which in some respects has remained both bourgeois and Cartesian, he—at bottom a Cartesian of bourgeois origin—has to struggle hard against the traditional pull which tends to reintegrate every thinker of the "Left" within the confines of traditional bourgeois radicalism. Hence his determination not to be mistaken for just another rationalist. Hence too his emphasis on German thinkers—from Hegel to Heidegger—and his unflagging (and occasionally ludicrous) attempts to impose himself upon the Communists as one who understands their aims better than they do themselves. To the intellectuals, Marxism is a philosophy, and since Sartre treats it as such, he is apparently closer to the "real" Marx than the Party theorists, who are obliged to operate at a level not too remote from the understanding of their followers. At the same time they are in no position to retort that Marxism is not really a philosophy at all, but rather a radical critique of philosophy, since this would mean going back on the whole bizarre systematization undertaken (in France as elsewhere) by the Communists in response to the petrifaction of Marxism in the Soviet Union.[3]

[3] Since the above was written, there has been a change in this respect, a change associated with name of M. Louis Althusser. Here at last there is a professional philosopher who is also a prominent Party member without being committed to the official eclecticism. For Althusser, a complete Marxist philosophy remains an unfulfilled desideratum. (See his *Pour Marx* [Paris, 1966], *passim*.) Only the cornerstone of the building has been laid: the structure remains to be erected (*ibid.*, p. 21). For all its apparent modesty, this approach discloses a resolute determination to build a total system. Is it an accident that Althusser (like Antonio Gramsci a generation earlier) operates within a Catholic culture, as the theorist of a movement which for its adherents has become a substitute for the Church? At any

But enough of Sartre's role as the philosopher of a nonexistent revolutionary movement. What is he actually saying that has not been said before by either Marxists or Existentialists? Here one must differentiate between the opening section of the *Critique*, subtitled *Question de méthode*, and the much bulkier part titled *Théorie des ensembles pratiques*. The introductory section—hardly more than a lengthy essay, and published as such originally in *Temps Modernes* in the autumn of 1957—contains both Sartre's critique of traditional Marxism and his reaffirmation of the general position set out in *l'Être et le néant*. As such it outlines an aim and indicates the methodological principles to be followed in the main work. The latter—the real *Critique*, for which *Question de méthode* serves merely as an appetizer—is a very different matter indeed. Here Sartre expounds, at tremendous length and with a formidable display of logical ingenuity, his conception of how society operates, once individual practice has been effectively socialized into group behavior. Here then is the test of the method. Does it in fact contribute something new? In order to simplify matters I shall treat the opening essay as the key to Sartre's performance, and the bulk of the *Critique* as the more or less successful application of his peculiar methodical principle. By way of anticipation it may be observed that the relative dimensions of these two sections are inversely proportionate to their real value: most of the genuinely novel and fruitful ideas are to be found in the introduction, while the enormously inflated second part revolves around the exposition of a few not very startling notions about the socialization of human behavior. This may be an illustration of the familiar rule that criticism is easier than construction, or it may be due to Sartre's greater expertise in philosophy and literature compared with the subjects he tackles in the main work. Whatever the reason, it imparts an extra grimness to the *Critique* and renders its study far from pleasurable. This, however, is unimportant. Hegel's *Phenomenology* was not easy reading

---

rate the effective completion of his project points in the direction of an all-encompassing synthesis. Impressive in its way, there is nonetheless something scholastic about it. One wonders what Marx would have thought of it.

either, and Sartre's evident conviction that the time has come for a successor to that seminal work deserves careful consideration. The execution of so ambitious a project would clearly be worth a great effort; the question is whether he has brought it off.

III

The argument of the introductory section (*Question de méthode*) is fairly straightforward, though the reasoning behind it is complex. Sartre begins by reasserting the Hegelian principle that History discloses the Truth about Man and his place in the world. This disclosure he describes as Reason: once more a concept derived from Hegel, but given a polemical edge by Sartre's stress on the contrast between his own philosophical anthropology and that of positivism, with its casual acceptance of many truths and many histories. What Sartre calls the "totalizing" character of his enterprise amounts to saying that he aims at the intellectual perception of the world insofar as it can be understood. This understanding is historical (because Reality is Process) and dialectical (because there is interaction between Being and Consciousness). "No one, not even the empiricists, has ever described as Reason the simple arrangement—whatever it may be—of our thoughts. 'Rationalism' requires that this arrangement should reproduce or constitute the order of being. Hence Reason is a certain relationship of consciousness and being." [4] If this relationship is a "twofold movement within consciousness and being," such a *relation mouvante* can legitimately be termed Reason. The question then arises whether the *Raison positiviste des Sciences naturelles* is that which we actually encounter in anthropology, or whether a true understanding of man does not imply a different kind of Reason. Sartre's reply to this preliminary question is affirmative: the understanding which permits us to grasp the process of history is the dialectical Reason of Hegel and Marx.

So far we seem to be on familiar ground, but Sartre's invocation of Hegel, and his employment of concepts previously elabo-

[4] *Critique de la raison dialectique*, p. 10.

rated in *L'Être et le néant,* already points in the direction of his subsequent repudiation of "orthodox Marxism," as formulated not by Marx himself but by Engels, Plekhanov, and Lenin. The dialectic of being and consciousness is the common property of Hegel, Marx, and the Existentialists, but it does not fit the categories of "dialectical materialism" as understood since Engels. In consequence Sartre feels obliged to expel Engels from the Marxist pantheon, but while this purge makes his task easier, it also sharpens the contrast between his existentialized Marxism and that of the orthodox and semi-orthodox, including Lukács. In fact Sartre has several brushes with Lukács, whom in one place he rebukes, with good reason, for having presented a caricature of Existentialism during the early post-war discussion.[5] Behind these disputations lies the fact that Sartre —like the early Lukács of *History and Class Consciousness* (1923), but unlike the later Lukács, for all his much publicized heresies—has no use for the simple-minded epistemological realism of Engels and Lenin. In intellectual terms this is a considerable gain, but it makes it difficult for him to stake out a claim for the Marxist succession. In fact he is obliged to state that "Marxism has come to a stop" (*s'est arrêté*), and this not only for external reasons, but because the central truth revealed to the Existentialists was never, after the death of Marx, adequately perceived by his followers. This truth is the absolutely irreducible character of the historical event, taken in its concreteness. Instead of trying to grasp the individual manifold as it presents itself in history, Marx's followers have typically tried to subsume its manifestations under a few general concepts which were invested with a spurious super-sensible reality. Thus we now have, on the one hand, the conservative sterility of academic positivism, and on the other, the frozen apparatus of orthodox Marxism. "In the face of this twofold ignorance, Existentialism was able to revive and maintain itself because it reaffirmed the reality of man, as Kierkegaard affirmed his own

[5] *Ibid.,* pp. 24, 34. The reference is to Lukács' polemical work *Existentialisme ou Marxisme* (Paris, 1948; second ed., 1961).

reality against Hegel." [6] But Existentialism is merely a signpost. The true task of dialectical Reason consists in bringing the whole of history within the compass of understanding, and to this end the Marxian categories are indispensable. Moreover, the Marxian union of theory and practice remains *"une évidence indépassable"* until there is genuine freedom *for all* beyond the mere production of material life. When this stage has been reached, Marxism will disappear. "A philosophy of liberty will take its place. But we possess no means, no intellectual instrument, no concrete experience, which permits us to conceive either that liberty or that philosophy." [7]

The problem which Marxism, in its contemporary guise, has failed to solve, or even to take seriously, is that of mediation. It treats personalities and events abstractly because it subordinates them to a preconceived schematization. Thus in studying the history of the French Revolution, the Marxist historians—Sartre makes a point of citing the Trotskyist sympathizer Daniel Guérin, but his criticism applies to French Marxists in general—lose sight of the particularity of events, and even misinterpret their meaning, because they start from fixed premises which have acquired the force of dogma: for example, that the struggle between Girondists and Montagnards represented a class conflict, whereas in actual fact it was an upheaval within a fairly homogeneous stratum of politicians and intellectuals. [8] Most Marxists likewise presume to know what is basic and what is merely accidental, so that for example they dismiss Napoleon's

[6] *Ibid.*, p. 28.
[7] *Ibid.*, p. 32.
[8] *Ibid.*, pp. 33 ff. Reflections on the French Revolution recur at length throughout Parts I and II, sometimes where they are least expected. By contrast, there are only the briefest references to Russian events since 1917. This may be due to Sartre's greater familiarity with French history, but it also seems to reflect an underlying awareness that it is easier for Marxists to make sense of Jacobinism than of Bolshevism. At any rate Sartre has nothing very illuminating to say about either Lenin or Stalin, whereas he is extremely knowledgeable and informative about Robespierre. In the same way, his literary analyses are concerned with Flaubert and Valéry, not with Tolstoy and Gorky, let alone "Socialist Realism," which he treats with contemptuous silence.

career as a mere episode, though they might have learned from Marx's own analysis of the 1848 revolution and its aftermath, the Bonapartist coup d'état, that history is always the history of *this* particular event and *those* particular actors, whose appearance at *this* particular moment must be understood in all its concreteness.[9]

Plainly, Sartre's criticism of the usual run-of-the-mill Marxist historiography is sound. It is less clear what he proposes to put in its place. The general principle, namely that the sense of an epoch is to be understood through an imaginative grasp of its central events and personalities in all their concreteness, is unobjectionable; but it remains a mere aspiration as long as we are not given some instances of how it is to be done. A related difficulty arises from Sartre's insistence that the imaginative understanding of the single event is the *raison d'être* of Existentialism. This leaves it uncertain whether his own kind of analysis is to be included within the Marxist canon, or merged with it to form a higher synthesis. On balance Sartre seems to favor the latter procedure, but his remarks are open to varying interpretations. The point where he comes closest to a confrontation with Marx himself, and not merely with his bumbling acolytes, is marked by an interesting reflection on the materialist conception of history:[10] if men are molded by anterior circumstances, how can they develop the spontaneity required to inaugurate a radical break with the past? In reply, Sartre introduces a familiar solution: if history is not simply a *vis a tergo*, it is because consciousness represents the element of freedom which enables the participants to educate themselves through what Marx called *praxis*. The contradiction is lived by the whole society, but in particular by the exploited class which is at once the passive object of external determinations and the active agent of a transformation which will make Man the master of his fate. Men anticipate the future by shaping their circumstances in accordance with their desires. The element of freedom is embedded in the time sequence, inasmuch as men relate themselves consciously

[9] *Question de méthode*, pp. 56 ff.
[10] *Critique*, pp. 60 ff.

to their future as well as to their past. "The dialectic as a movement of reality collapses if time is not dialectical, that is, if one
refuses a certain action of the future as such." [11] This line of
thought permits Sartre to integrate his version of the dialectic
with his analysis of consciousness, for the notion that "man defines himself by his project" acquires a practical content if it can
be shown that the historical process is kept going by a dialectic
of ends and means which is both *imposed* (by material pressure) and *willed* (by the human agents of what from one particular angle looks like necessity). And this in fact is what Sartre
proposes to demonstrate. [12]

Before trying to decide how far his own project has in fact
been executed, let us note in passing that Sartre treats Marxism
as a system of thought which can be brought up to date by graft-
ing a different philosophy—Existentialism—upon the main
stem. This seems reasonable enough until one recalls that the
youthful Marx saw in the revolutionary "union of theory and
practice" the means of *overcoming* philosophy, while the mature Marx got rid of the dualism of thought and reality by investing his faith in *science* (though he left it to Engels to complete the circle with the construction of a materialist ontology
which reads the dialectic back into nature). In contrast, the *Critique of Dialectical Reason* is intended as the legitimate successor of the *Critique of Pure Reason;* not because Sartre means to
remain in the Kantian tradition, but because Kant's (and Descartes') manner of posing the problem is also his own. Like
them he is out to elaborate a unified world-view by way of deduction from a few self-evident propositions. The main difference is that instead of asking: "How is experience possible?" or
"How are synthetic judgments possible?" he asks: "How is history possible?" "How is the dialectic possible?" And since this
problem is tied up for him with the question of man's nature,
the answer quite naturally leads back to the traditional themes

[11] *Ibid.*, pp. 63-64n.
[12] *Ibid.*, p. 95: "Donc l'homme se définit par son projet. Cet être
matériel dépasse perpétuellement la condition qui lui est faite; il dévoile
et détermine sa situation en la transcendant pour s'objectiver, par le travail,
l'action ou le geste."

of ontology: existence, essence, freedom, immortality. While this metaphysical concern represents Sartre's claim to being taken seriously as a philosopher, it evidently constitutes an additional hazard to his search for an empirical basis on which to rest his thinking. For if the foundations are laid by philosophical reflection on the nature of man, the subsequent empirical investigations into the actual workings of society must be largely predetermined. There is of course no way of approaching the subject in abstraction from some kind of philosophy, but Sartre goes very far in prejudging the outcome of his findings. In fact his empirical excursions largely boil down to a kind of self-questioning about the reliability of the principles from which he proceeds.

The truth is, however, that Sartre has no choice. For it is one of his root assumptions that the inherent problems of dialectical reasoning are ultimately ontological. He makes this clear in a passage towards the beginning of Part II [13] where he refers briefly to "the fundamental difficulty of dialectical materialism" as being due to the fact that Marx, by inverting Hegel's philosophy, "laid bare the true contradictions of realism." Hegel's system was self-consistent because, granted its metaphysical starting point, the unhampered process of reasoning could only result in the discovery of the essential reasonableness of the world, thus enabling the mind to identify itself with its object; whereas Marx established once and for all that there is no such circularity and that reality remains irreducible to speculative thinking. Yet Marx wanted to retain the dialectic, and Sartre is obliged to note that this raises a difficulty, especially if Engels' solution of a "materialist dialectic" embracing the physical universe is rejected. For if Hegel's idealist system is untenable, and if there is no materialist dialectic in the sense postulated by Engels (and by the "orthodox Marxists" who followed his lead), how can we be sure that the logical concepts in our heads correspond to something in the structure of reality? One cannot elude this question by taking refuge in the scientific study of real or supposed interconnections in nature, for this is to sink to the

13 *Ibid.*, pp. 120-127.

level of empiricism. Alternatively, for a materialism which treats
the world as "given," history becomes a special case of natural
evolution. But Sartre is persuaded that the meaning of history
can never be approached by this route. It must be discovered in
the historical process itself, through an investigation of man's
activity, his *praxis*. The Marxian antinomies of being and consciousness, which came to light when the Hegelian synthesis collapsed, must be overcome through an effort to lay bare the ontological structure of historical reality. The elucidation of this
structure will demonstrate that Man does not simply submit to
the dialectic, but that he *makes* it.[14] This demonstration is the
subject of what Sartre calls his theory of the *ensembles
pratiques*.

I V

With the foregoing in mind we seem to have secured a vantage
point from which to proceed straight to the goal of rendering
plain the dialectical character of human action. Nothing of the
kind. Instead of plunging into history we are made to embark
upon an enormous and very wearisome detour into anthropology, in which the few stable landmarks are submerged under an
endless and largely irrelevant conceptualization of a few supposedly typical human activities and character traits. Instead of
the promised land we are offered the purgatory of Sartre's logical treadmill.

The trouble begins with his notion of the *"pratico-inerte,"* by
which he designates the unrelated practice of human beings
caught up in the immediacy of their daily toil. This is done
through a process to whose analysis Sartre devotes over two hundred pages of hairsplitting ingenuity. The "inert practicality" of
society—that is, its failure to comprehend itself *as* society—is
traced back to its anthropological ground in the blind activity of
isolated beings, each of whom takes itself as the sole center of
reference. The only bond that unites them is *need* in an environment of *scarcity*, the latter designating at once a social milieu

[14] *Ibid.*, p. 131.

and a time sequence from the primitive tribe to present-day society. Within this universe of toil, scarcity, material pressure, and constant danger of famine, the primitive individuals originally come together for purposes of food gathering, production, and other economic activities which gradually form a bond between them. One might suppose that they do this by cooperating, but in the nightmare universe of which Sartre is the creator, and which he controls and operates, cooperation plays a very minor role. Men are from the start pitted against each other, in such a fashion as to make violence and mutual slaughter not simply a daily occurrence—that would scarcely be news to anthropologists—but *the* constitutive element of their lives and consequently of their "natures." Everyone sees in his fellow man the Other who threatens to deprive him of his own meager food supply. This constant exercise of distrust, enmity, and violence is rooted in the "world of scarcity." In Sartre's opinion, Marx and Engels did not give sufficient attention to "scarcity as the negative unity (imposed) by matter via labor and the conflicts of men." [15] "The historical process is not to be understood without a permanent element of negativity, at once exterior and interior to man, namely the perpetual possibility *within his own existence* of being the one who causes the Others to die, or whom the Others cause to die, in other words scarcity." [16] Sartre rejects the theological notion of a fixed and permanent human nature, but insists that, although violence is not to be regarded as an inborn trait, "it is the constant inhumanity of human conduct as interiorized scarcity, in brief, that which causes everyone to see everyone else as Other and as the principle of Evil." [17] This relationship governs not merely primitive society, but the whole of history down to our days. It is therefore not the case that class society represents the disturbance of an original primitive concord, as Engels tries to make out in his *Origin of the Family,* and as the Marxists have continued to maintain. On the contrary, enmity to one's fellow man has always been the un-

[15] *Ibid.,* p. 221.
[16] *Ibid.*
[17] *Ibid.*

written law of human history. The argument must be cited at
some length:

> This means that scarcity, as the negation within man of man by
> matter, is an intelligible dialectical principle. It is not my purpose
> here to give an interpretation of prehistory or to revert to the no-
> tion of classes and to show, after so many others, how they came
> to be founded. . . . I only want to show that the disintegration
> of the agricultural commune (where it has existed) and the ap-
> pearance of classes (even admitting with Engels that they arise
> from a differentiation of functions), whatever may be the actual
> conditions, is intelligible only within the original negation. Mate-
> rially in effect, if the laborers produce *a little more* than is strictly
> necessary for the society, and if they are administered by a group
> freed from productive labor which . . . can divide the surplus
> among itself, one does not see why the situation . . . should
> change; it seems to me on the contrary that we seize the mecha-
> nism of transformation and its intelligibility if we admit . . .
> that the differentiation occurs in a society whose members pro-
> duce always *a little less* than is necessary for the whole, so that the
> constitution of an unproductive group has for its condition the
> undernourishment of all, and that one of its functions is to select
> those who are to be eliminated. . . . It is within a humanity of
> which even today millions literally die of starvation that History
> has developed through the differentiation of functions and sub-
> groups. . . . Inversely, the unproductive groups, always in dan-
> ger of being liquidated because they are the absolutely Other
> (those who live upon the labor of others) internalize this ambiva-
> lent otherness and comport themselves vis-à-vis the individuals
> either as though they were Other than man (but positively, like
> gods), or as though they were the only men in the midst of an-
> other species (reduced to subhumanity). As for the group which
> is sacrificed, one can truly speak of struggle in characterizing its
> relations with the Others. . . . We shall see later how these
> . . . attitudes transform themselves. . . . What mattered was
> to show the first conditioning of men by internalized matter.
> . . . It is this which even today furnishes an intelligible founda-
> tion to that accursed aspect of human history where man at every
> instance sees his action stolen from him and totally deformed by
> the milieu in which he inscribes it. It is this tension which . . .
> by the possibility for everyone to see his closest friend coming
> towards him like a strange and ferocious beast, lends to every
> *praxis*, at the most elementary level, a perpetual statute of ex-
> treme urgency and turns it . . . into an act of hostility against

others individuals or groups. . . . One must look for the negation *at the start*. And we have stated [*nous venons de constater*]
that under the regime of scarcity the negation of man by man
was taken up and internalized by *praxis*, the negation of man by
matter insofar as [matter represents] the organization of his being outside him in Nature." [18]

Thus human nature is shown to have been conditioned by a
state of affairs which bears a marked resemblance to a concentration camp. And let it not be objected that Sartre at first refused to believe the evidence when around 1948 it began to be
rumored that Stalin's *univers concentrationnaire* was based on
the twin principles of forced labor and no food for those who
fell short of the target. Philosophers are entitled to take some
time before they assimilate the common stock of factual information at the disposal of their fellow men. At most one might
observe that Sartre has fallen from one extreme into the other,
and projected his discoveries backwards into prehistory. But
readers of his novels and plays will realize that this too would
not be quite fair. The author of *La Nausée* and *Huis clos* has
always taken a dim view of the capacity of human beings to
overcome their ingrained destructiveness. And who shall blame
him? Are we not all the beneficiaries of an experience which has
made Freud's disillusioned view of humanity seem mere common sense? If there is ground for skepticism it concerns not so
much Sartre's anthropology as the use he makes of it in linking
individual praxis with the collective *pratico-inerte*. The starting
point of his analysis is the assertion that man from the outset
sees his fellow man as the Other, to be exploited or liquidated,
and that it is this "negativity" which has kept history going.
This may be a useful antidote to idyllic notions, but Sartre relies
rather too much on the category of Otherness (*altérité*). He
attempts, for example, to deduce the nature of political authority from it. I have not so far quoted the key sentences from the
lengthy passage already referred to:

Thus we grasp immediately that the groups concerned with administration, management, and direction are at once *the same* as

[18] *Ibid.*, pp. 221-223; trans. from the original.

those whom they administer (insofar as the latter accept them)
and *other than they*. For they are at once those charged with
determining *the Others* within the group, that is to say, with
choosing the victims of the next redistribution [of the exiguous
food supply], and those who are themselves *the Others*, in the
sense that they are totally superfluous [*excédentaires*], consume
without producing, and constitute for everyone a pure menace. In
the milieu of scarcity, the differentiation of function (however it
may have come about, for Engels takes a very simplistic view of
it) implies *necessarily* the constitution of an excessive (but accepted) group, and the constitution through the latter, via the
complicity of many Others, of a group of undernourished producers.[19]

It is probably no accident that Sartre wrote this during the
years of the Algerian conflict, to which he and other Frenchmen
gave much anguished thought, and which clearly inspired his
lengthy analyses of colonialism in the later sections of the *Critique*. As a description of a certain type of primitive exploitation
it may pass muster. As a theory of the state—even an imperial
slave state such as the Roman Empire—it is inadequate. But
Sartre is not content to put his blood-chilling picture forward as
an account of certain historically conditioned relationships. He
will have it that it discloses a universal typology of human behavior, which at one and the same time illustrates the dialectic
of history and the psychology of the individual "in the milieu of
scarcity." In fact his whole theory hinges on this conjunction of
altérité and *aliénation*: it is only because everyone sees in his
neighbor primarily the Other that history has developed as it
has.

Compared with this framework, the concrete examples Sartre
brings forward to illustrate what he calls the *pratico-inerte*—that
is, the blind operation of social forces uncontrolled by critical
insight into the outcome of their activities—are not very startling; nor do they throw a great deal of light on his favorite
category, Otherness (*altérité*), unless its meaning is stretched to
include the failure to perceive what one's actions mean to
others. This may be simply a consequence of not knowing what

19 *Ibid.*, p. 222.

other people are doing, which is scarcely blameworthy, though it
is likely to have disagreeable consequences. Sartre cites two familiar instances which historians and economists had noticed
before: the progressive deforestation of China through the uncoordinated activities of millions of peasants over thousands of
years; and the self-defeating attempts of European governments
in the sixteenth and seventeenth centuries to import gold from
America without causing a price rise. The case of deforestation
had already occurred to Engels (though with reference not to
China but to the Mediterranean lands); the other example was
cited by Marx (and before him by Adam Smith) without reference to philosophy. There is of course no reason why Sartre
should not illustrate the concept of "inert practicality" by seiz-
ing upon these well-known instances of human imbecility, but
by themselves they do not establish his claim to have evolved a
new method of investigation, though he is doubtless right in
complaining that "the simpletons of Marxism have calmly suppressed the moment of individual *praxis* as an original experience of the dialectic, or in other words, as the dialectic which
realizes itself in practical experience. They failed to see that one
must conserve the basic reality of this moment or suppress the
truth of alienation." [20]

Perhaps the whole matter comes down to the point that
Sartre is concerned primarily with the descriptive analysis of individual and collective patterns of behavior. He certainly shows
a tendency to confuse such description with the discovery of a
dynamic principle that "totalizes" uncoordinated behavior into
"wholes." Hence Book II (pp. 381-755) is given over in its en-
tirety to an intricate analysis of group and class structures as
social wholes whose functioning is supposed to lay bare the peculiar mechanism whereby history comes into operation (this
part of the work bears the title *Du groupe à l'histoire*). It is here
that the category of "totalization" finally comes into its own.
Previously one had only caught glimpses of it. On page 18 of the
opening section, Hegel's thought was described as "the most
ample philosophic totalization" yet achieved, which seemed to

[20] *Ibid.*, p. 373.

suggest that the totalizing faculty is located in the consciousness of the philosopher. But that would be Hegelianism pure and simple. Sartre (in this respect following Marx) believes that the meaning of the historical process can be grasped from the inside, as it were, only by those who are actively engaged in promoting its forward movement. At the same time he is clearly fascinated by the Hegelian notion of a dialectical process which "comes to itself" in the consciousness of the beholder. Thus on page 154 he speaks of a constitutive dialectic that "grasps itself . . . via the individual *praxis*," which rather sounds as though the dialectic were an independent motive force; and in Book II he expounds at length a methodological principle best described by saying that he identifies "totality" with structure. Although he makes the point that the "ontological structure of the group" (p. 438) is constituted by human *praxis* (instead of being "organic" as with the Romantics) the *praxis* that constitutes the group is precisely the "inert practicality" of Book I, which in its turn exemplified no more than a certain community of destiny imposed by uncomprehended material necessity. Sartre's humans do not cooperate: they are thrown together, or as he puts it, "serialized," by danger, by hunger, by external pressure, by group hostility, by machinery, or simply by having to wait for the bus. Insofar as they rise above this primitive level (that of the "*groupe de survivance*") to form a more active and conscious unit, they define themselves once more by the presence of an external enemy, while in relation to longer stretches of time Sartre seems to believe that the archetypal group is the sworn confederacy.

It would be wrong to give the impression that Sartre's approach is wholly abstract. Where he has at his disposal historical or sociological material which happens to fit his preconceptions —such as studies of the French Revolution or of modern syndicalism—his analyses are often instructive and even brilliant. Unfortunately such excursions into genuine history are rare. For the most part the reader has to make do with the rotation of Sartre's logical steam engine.

Sartre in fact is at his best when he deals not with history but with individuals, and this is perhaps the central weakness of his ambitious synthesis. The point has been made by his critics that for all his employment of the terms "dialectic" and "totality," he remains schematic in his description of how the "dialectical totality" articulates itself into its components. This, however, is not due to any weakness in his analysis of human motivation: he has the dramatist's eye for "character" and for the dense opacity of individual behavior. The trouble seems rather to stem from his obsessive concern with "structures" inside which the individuals are encased like flies in amber. This is related to what appears to be an ingrained peculiarity of his mode of viewing the world. As a former Cartesian who by an effort of will has turned himself into a thinker of the modern post-Hegelian kind, Sartre remains haunted by the Cartesian problem of relating the outside world to the solitary individual, while at the same time his intellectual conscience tells him that he ought to be thinking about the ongoing historical process. The result, as often as not, is an uncertain compromise between ontology and empiricism. It may seem a trifle harsh to say, as Lefebvre does, that "precisely because he pursues speculatively the search for the foundation, he does not attain anything fundamental," but one sees what his critic has in mind. Notwithstanding some brilliant excursions into applied sociology, Sartre on the whole remains "abstract" in that he rarely succeeds in grasping the historical moment in its uniqueness. "Matter" and "consciousness," when brought face to face, turn out to be linked only by the tenuous bond of his own speculative construction; the transition from one stage to the next is managed only with the greatest difficulty, whereas hundreds of pages are devoted to the analysis of static relationships; and finally the dialectic, from being an intelligible principle of historical existence, becomes an independent motive force. None of this is surprising to the student of his earlier work, or indeed of the literary and philosophical tradition in which he grew up. Sartre would not be the important figure he is were he not profoundly steeped in the French philosophical tradition. It is his indebtedness to the cast of thought established by his ancestors which causes his peculiar synthesis of Marxism and Existentialism to have so strange a flavor of Port-Royal about it.

V

An adequate critique of the *Critique* would take up too much space, but something must be said about Sartre's theory of the state. This topic, which occurs towards the end of this work (pp. 586 ff.), is rooted in his concept of "the whole," and at the same time it concerns politics properly so called. It can therefore be treated as the link between his anthropology and his political commitments.

To start from the non-metaphysical end, Sartre's political philosophy is substantially that of Hobbes, though his language is that of Heidegger. The essence of the state is sovereignty; the latter is defined as the particular way in which institutions emerge by taking up into themselves the "reified" life of their members. As the "inert persistence of a reified organization" in the midst of a social grouping, the institution establishes itself "as the elementary and abstract permanence of the social past *as Being*. . . ." The institution in turn, "as the exteriority of inertia," gives rise to *authority* as power over the subordinate functions which keep the system in balance. The root of authority is the position of the mediator between conflicting individuals and subgroups, and we have seen that for Sartre social life is a *bellum omnium contra omnes* which can be held in check only by the constant exercise of a factor whose extreme manifestation is *terrorism*. "Thus the *chief* is produced at the same time as the group itself, and produces the group which produces him, so much so that in this elementary moment of experience the chief can be anyone. Or if one prefers it, the quasi-sovereignty of each is one of the constitutive bonds of the group." [21] Authority is an institutionalization of the personal power which arises spontaneously from the fact that conflicts must be settled by "regula-

[21] *Ibid.*, p. 586.

tors" who lend themselves to this role. Demagogues, terrorists, organizers, and military chiefs all have their root in the primitive nexus which is "the diffused power of life and death over the traitor, or if one prefers it, the fraternity-terror, as the basic determinant of sociality. This permanent and living structure of coercion is a necessary determinant of sovereignty as authority." [22] The mediator (*"tiers régulateur"*) originally embodies and concentrates "the internal violence of the group as the power to impose his regulation," [23] and this is the source of all later sovereignty. Authority is constituted power to impose the death sentence. It never loses its original character, however much it may be mediated and watered down by subsequent social developments. At a higher level the atomized ("serialized") community discovers its spurious unity in the chief or ruler it has projected from its inert midst, and the ruler then enters into a dialectical relationship with the other social institutions, while appearing (or pretending) to be their original fountainhead. The ultimate source of sovereignty is thus not a social contract, but quite simply the praxis whereby an individual organizes and reorganizes his personal field of reference with a view to goals of his own choosing. Man is, so to speak, sovereign by nature, and historical sovereignty is the extension of this primary relationship to other persons whose activities are unified, the only limit being the sovereignty of rivals. At the historical level the ruler mediates between institutions which have themselves arisen from the reification of relationships among men rendered passive. "And this institution need not in the least be accompanied by a group consensus, since on the contrary it establishes itself on the impotence of its members." [24] If the *ultima ratio* of the state is violence, this is because the ruler draws his authority from this source. "Produit par la terreur, le souverain doit devenir l'agent responsable de la terreur." [25]

All this is rather Hobbesian, and in retrospect one sees why Sartre had little difficulty in accommodating himself to Stalin-

[22] *Ibid.*, p. 587.
[23] *Ibid.*
[24] *Ibid.*, p. 595.
[25] *Ibid.*, p. 600.

311 : Sartre, Marxism, and History

ism, as long as he felt reasonably certain that the ultimate aims of the regime were more or less his own. Even in the *Critique* although he now dismisses "proletarian dictatorship" as a mystification and remarks quite accurately that "the real dictatorship was that of a group which reproduced itself and exercised its power in the name of a delegation which the proletariat had not given to it," [26] he insists that this was inevitable and "from the viewpoint of the masses neither legitimate nor illegitimate. . . . Historical experience has undeniably revealed that the first moment of socialist society in process of construction could only be . . . the indissoluble aggregation of the bureaucracy, the Terror, and the cult of personality." [27] In short, Sartre's attitude to the Russian Revolution and Stalin is more or less that of Hegel to the French Revolution and Napoleon. In both cases, too, the philosopher who sums up the sense of the epoch is obliged to acknowledge that Minerva's owl had to wait until it got dark enough to fly out. The chief hope he offers for the future is that this inability to get beyond the terroristic relationship of the "regulator" to the group is not necessarily final. Other forms of reciprocity may become possible, and already one can perceive—that is to say, Sartre can perceive it, now that Stalin's successors have spelled it out for him—that "the sovereign must gradually abandon the monopoly of the group." For a change we have Montesquieu instead of Hobbes: enlightened despotism is expected to reform itself, peacefully and from above. But not, it seems, to the extent of bringing about the "withering away of the state." This may be a realistic perspective, but it rules out the centerpiece of the original vision, for if the state remains in being *after* the Revolution, genuine freedom is as far off as ever.

Like the French Army advancing to Waterloo, "without fear and without hope," Sartre thus approaches the future with a strong dose of stoicism. To some extent his political philosophy represents a tacit acknowledgment that the particular type of human self-estrangement embodied in the relationship of domi-

[26] *Ibid.*, p. 629.
[27] *Ibid.*, p. 630.

nation and subjection can at most change its form. The reverse side of this coin is his tendency to take for granted the permanence of alienation, in particular the disjunction of particular wills and the "general will" which has been one of the perennial themes of political thought. Sartre is in a dilemma here, for which of course he is not personally responsible: history has not borne out the hope that this cleavage can be overcome. To a Marxist this might suggest the probability that the proletariat may fail to accomplish what was supposed to be its historic mission. In that case, alienation will persist and so will philosophy: either as a repository of unfulfilled human aspirations (its traditional role), or as an assemblage of scientific techniques enabling the new ruling elites to manipulate the societies they control. There are some signs that Sartre is not altogether blind to this prospect. It might, however, have been better if he had spelled it out, instead of leaving the reader in an uncertain twilight of doubt concerning Leviathan's future.

As matters stand, Sartre's philosophy of history presents itself as a speculative system which transforms the concepts of Marxian analysis—history, *praxis*, class conflict—into ontological notions and then sets up a dialectic between them. At the same time he clearly regards his own theorizing as a guide to action— as though it were not in the nature of philosophy to come *after* the event! This contradiction is something Sartre refuses to acknowledge. He therefore remains at the Hegelian level, though his purpose is to complete the critique of Hegel. This is perhaps only another way of saying that he may have misconceived his current role, for in actual fact the revolution to which he still looks forward is already completed and lies in the past. Moreover, it is just this which makes it possible for him to take a synoptic view of it. Subjectively, however, Sartre's commitment to the idea of "changing the world" is unquestionable, as is his belief that the last battle has not yet been fought.

This commitment comes out in his concern with history as "totalization," and here he is able to play off the Hegelian theme to some effect. Traditional philosophy assumed that the totality of the world is an ordered Whole whose essence can be grasped by the intellect. Now to say that "the Whole" is intelligible is tantamount to saying that it has an identifiable structure.[28] It also presupposes, if not an "absolute moment" in time, at any rate a critical moment. Time need not stand still to oblige the philosopher, but there have to be privileged moments when the process discloses its meaning. In their different ways both Hegel and Marx thought they had lived through and perceived such a moment. This sets the dialectic off from historical relativism with which it is sometimes confused: a thinker who believes he knows what Man is and what History does, has no need to concern himself with the argument that all our knowledge is subject to the flux of time and circumstance. If there are moments when history discloses its own secret, we are relieved of the pseudo-problems with which positivists and skeptical relativists occupy their leisure hours.

This vantage point enables Sartre to escape from the dilemma posed by critics of "historicism." The problem is usually seen to reside in the need for the "historicist" to abandon the search for objective truth and agree to relativize his own judgment, if he wants to be consistent within the terms of his own approach. The contradiction into which it is held he is bound to slide, if he refuses to be thus consistent, may be put as follows: philosophy is thinking about Man and his position in the world, but Man is an historical being, and his situation is constantly changing. Hence the only kind of thinking which can interpret his role is historical thinking. This, however, is itself subject to change and cannot rise above the horizon of its particular epoch. Yet truth must be timeless. Thus in order to overcome skepticism, the historicist has to exempt historical thought from its own verdict and render its discoveries absolute. But this is inconsistent and leads to an obvious contradiction, for if thought can attain something that manifests itself unaltered through all historical changes, then clearly the Being of the world does not articulate itself completely into transitory events and ideologies.

[28] Leo Strauss, *Natural Right and History* (Chicago, 1953), pp. 22 ff. But the Whole need not be "unchangeable" in order to be intelligible, nor does the historical approach necessarily do away with the category of totality.

Thus the attainment of timeless truth through philosophy is shown to be possible, but only by relinquishing the historical approach from which the whole train of thought began. Therefore historicism is either absurd or self-contradictory. Now for Sartre this is precisely where Existentialism comes into its own, yet he would reject the assertion that ontology and historicism are incompatible. On the contrary, it is the very essence of his position that the permanent element is not something transhistorical (and therefore timeless and metaphysical), but the historical process itself, that is, the process of Man's self-creation. What Man experiences in history (and at a remove in thinking about it) is simply his own being as it comes back to him mediated by the time-sequence. The thinking that reveals the logic of history at the same time makes transparent the ontological structure of human existence. The two come together in the act whereby Man creates himself and his world. History is *causa sui*. There is nothing "behind it," neither God nor Nature. Sartre expressly refuses to ground historical materialism in dialectical materialisms. There is no dialectic of nature to render plausible the human story as a special case within the universal process. The *pour-soi* has no need of a metaphysic to sustain itself in its flight from the frozen past of the *en-soi*. All it needs is the awareness that it has made the world of history and can never cease to project itself forward in an endless quest for a union that cannot be attained.

This position appears to be unassailable in logic, but I think it must be added that Sartre skates on ice that cannot sustain anyone who stays in the same place for very long. The whole dizzying operation ultimately depends on the notion that consciousness is "choice of being," and that the entire diversity of existence springs in the last resort from the act of awareness itself, understood as the primary separation of thought from being. Compared with *L'Être et le néant* the principal difference appears to be that while in that work Sartre presented human existence as a foredoomed attempt to realize the union of being and consciousness (*en-soi-pour-soi*), he has now adopted the Marxist position that the project is executed in and through history. Unattainable in philosophy (because the world of the individual is ultimately contingent and "absurd," that is, not required by reason), the overcoming of the split is realized in practice through the activity of Man who strives to bring existence into conformity with his own essence. Possibly Sartre would add that even in the life of the species the discrepancy can never be wholly bridged. However that may be, he has at any rate closed the gap in his own thinking about history by incorporating man's *praxis* in the dialectic of being and consciousness. If human nature can be shown to be of such a kind that it *necessarily* sets the historical process in motion, the dichotomy of philosophy and science has been overcome, and the world has ceased to be mysterious.

Is this the answer to the question how history can be conceived as a whole without entailing either skepticism or dogmatism about timeless values? At any rate it is the most breathtaking attempt yet made to escape from the dilemma. But at this point a consideration of Sartre's work must resign itself to the limitations of an essay and yield the ghost. I merely note in conclusion an argument brought forward years ago by critics of *L'Être et le néant:* the principle which furnishes the ontological description from within—pure consciousness and awareness of consciousness—could never have produced the reflective report on the process from without. From the opposite standpoint, Sartre's Marxist critics have denounced the attempt to subordinate human *praxis* to ontology. Conceivably Sartre has overreached himself and fallen between the positions he seeks to transcend. It is nonetheless apparent that his *tour de force* has created a new situation for the philosophy of history: things are never going to be quite the same again. For whatever he may have failed to do, Sartre has demonstrated that if "historicism" is pushed to its furthest limit, it becomes a self-consistent position and thus has to be taken seriously.

Index

ABOUT THE AUTHOR

GEORGE LICHTHEIM was born in Berlin in 1912 and was educated at Berlin and Heidelberg. Now a British subject, Mr. Lichtheim has been involved in the major political and intellectual currents of the time, and has contributed to scholarly journals in America and Britain; his work has appeared frequently in the pages of *Partisan Review, Commentary,* and the *New York Review of Books,* and he has lectured at numerous American universities.